D0860204

DELTA TIME

Also by Tony Dunbar

Our Land Too

*Against the Grain: Southern Radicals and
Prophets, 1929–1959*

*Hard Traveling: Migrant Farm Workers in
America
(co-authored by Linda Kravitz)*

DELTA TIME

A Journey
Through Mississippi

▲▲▲

Tony Dunbar

Photographs by Patty Still

Pantheon Books / New York

330.977
D89d

Copyright © 1990 by Anthony Dunbar

All rights reserved under International and Pan-American
Copyright Conventions. Published in the United States by
Pantheon Books, a division of Random House, Inc., New
York, and simultaneously in Canada by Random House of
Canada Limited, Toronto.

Grateful acknowledgment is made to Heather Spahr for her
contribution to the preparation of the map.

Library of Congress Cataloging-in-Publication Data
Dunbar, Anthony P.
Delta time / Tony Dunbar.
p.   cm.
ISBN 0–394–57163–0
1. Mississippi River Region—Economic conditions.
2. Mississippi River Region—Social conditions.   3. Mississippi
River—Delta.
I. Title.
HC 107.A15D86   1990   89–43244
330.977—dc20

Book Design by Chris Welch
Map by Anne Scatto
Manufactured in the United States of America
First Edition

*To Patsy
and all my girls*

UNIVERSITY LIBRARIES
CARNEGIE MELLON UNIVERSITY
PITTSBURGH, PA   15213-3890

CONTENTS

Contents

Contents

eighteen

ACKNOWLEDGMENTS

I am deeply indebted to the small-town press of the Delta for keeping me informed about goings-on far too numerous for any one person to observe. My special thanks go to Carolyn DeCell at the *Deer Creek Pilot* and Mac Gordon at the *Leland Progress,* in whose columns and editorials I have found, and appropriated as my own, many insights into the attitudes and lifestyles of their regular readers. Both journalists would no doubt disagree with much of what I have written and cannot in any sense be blamed for the final product.

Along the way I have been aided in important ways by dozens of people. I can do nothing but hope that they know how appreciative I will always be for their assistance. In particular I must thank Max Nathan, Jr., who helped me balance this enterprise with other demands on my time; Rims Barber, a storehouse of Mississippi lore; Steve Suitts, for statistical ammunition; Janice McManus and Amy Baskin, for technical assistance; and Michael Blackmon, for friendly advice. They also should not be criticized for the result.

This book grew out of an exchange of letters between me and Wendy Wolf, my editor, and it would never have been completed without her encouragement and attention. At last she is free for other duties.

PREFACE

I began this book twenty years ago. On my first trip to the Mississippi Delta in 1968 I traveled with a big man in a Cadillac, accompanied by two hefty snow-white Russian Samoyeds. The man, Ken Dean, headed a little civil rights organization for people of "good will" called the Mississippi Council on Human Relations. He made quite a sight when, at every opportunity, he brought his shining car to a halt and, trailed by dogs happy to be out in the sunshine, lumbered up to the front porches of sharecropper cabins, scattering children and chickens, to ask directions. The impression he made was intentional; Dean's whole purpose was to shake things up.

At that time the civil rights movement had passed its peak nationally, but mighty shock waves were still being felt in Mississippi. "Freedom Summer," with its infamous killings, was four years past;

however, James Meredith had been shot on a Delta highway just two years before, and Dr. Martin Luther King had been slain in Memphis five months earlier. Robert Kennedy was killed that fall, while I was interviewing tenant farmers about health and nutrition. Then there was the violence surrounding the Democratic National Convention in Chicago, which registered in Mississippi as an affirmation of its own war against radicals and long-haired young people in general.

Mississippi was undergoing a dramatic political revolution in 1968, though the effects of it had not yet materialized. With few exceptions—a chancery clerk in Port Gibson, a supervisor in Bolton—officeholders and politicians all were white. This was about to change. Mississippi's national image in 1968 was personified by the balding politician or sheriff in short sleeves, wearing a skinny black tie and backed up by dogs and joking deputies. Its other image was poverty, and nobody could doubt that there was plenty of that in the Delta. A team of doctors organized by the Field Foundation had toured the Delta in 1966. A report with vivid pictures of little black children, their stomachs and navels distended from malnutrition, had fueled congressional hearings and a major expansion of President Johnson's War on Poverty. The problems caused by the breakup of the old plantation system and the displacement of unskilled farm workers by mechanization, however, were far more terrible than could be rectified by adjustments in the "commodities" or food stamp programs. My assignment on that first trip to the Delta was to try to write a report that would bring the doctors' picture back to life, reactivate the issue of "hunger," and bring some attention to the condition of these people. I had a three-page list of questions like, "Are any children in the family listless and sleepy all day?" "Do any women in the family eat clay?" "Are there holes in the floor?" "Do snakes enter the house?"

The result was a book called *Our Land Too,* which related the sad facts of the lives of tenant farmers in the Delta (and coal miners in Kentucky). While its publication had less impact on the national strategy for dealing with poverty than the author had hoped, the writing of it was an experience never forgotten. The first trip north from Jackson on U.S. 49, descending the hills into Yazoo City and out onto the flat pancake beyond, left a visual image that time has not dimmed. The fertile terrain of the Mississippi Delta, like an open sea, appearing so suddenly at the foot of kudzu-covered hills, was a tremendous surprise. Once on the plain, and looking off into the fields and down the gravel roads we sped by, I saw people everywhere. There were children in great number playing around clusters of wooden shacks. There were long lines of workers bent over in the fields. The roads were busy with mechanical pickers grinding slowly and noisily along. The Delta, Paul Simon says, "shines like a National guitar," or, from Eudora Welty, "shimmers like the wing of a lighted dragonfly." It is wide open and bright with sunshine.

On that first trip in 1968 we were exploring—looking for a community to write about and one that would take in a nineteen-year-old white boy, too. A little research had already narrowed the possibilities. Every one of the fourteen or so counties that make up the Delta met the basic criteria of poverty. All were dominated by cotton plantations and all had made the list of the one hundred poorest counties in the United States. I knew that the state government was then embroiled in a war over the federal Head Start programs, and that three competing agencies had divided up the state. The smallest, least well funded, and most "radical" of these (all were radical to those who did not think that government dollars ought to be spent giving black preschoolers a head start or a free breakfast) was Friends of the Children of Mississippi, and FCM ran the centers in Humphreys County. These centers employed and trained black housewives to manage the program; the kids, of course, were all black. Since the jobs paid exceedingly well by the standards of chopping cotton, their creation challenged the power of the plantation owner considerably. We thought that from among the boards of directors of these Head Start centers, mainly groups of farmers, mechanics, and preachers, we might find people willing to help me document conditions, and that was correct.

One of the first places we stopped was Louise, Mississippi. There in a black Mason's lodge, a truly decrepit building which served as a Head Start center for forty or more napping youngsters, bathed by sunlight streaming in through cracked wallboards, I met Collie Brown, its director, and several board members. Two of these, her husband Tiny and Noah Guider, both owners of small farms, were enthusiastic about my "studying" Louise, and we quickly made arrangements for me to return the next week, tape recorder in hand. The visits that followed were remarkable to me in many ways.

I first of all reacted to the land itself. It was and is totally flat to the eye, but rich and flush with growing crops, all baking or steaming under a vast sweep of sky. It was a fascination for me, mostly city-raised, to see the farmers go about their work, the huge combines creeping across the fields, the small groups of men gathered about pickup trucks by the dirt roads, like officers discussing battle plans, and the long lines of workers with white and red kerchiefs on their heads slowly hacking weeds two rows at a time as they moved across the endless fields. As one who loves the painful and passionate history of the South, this place evoked nostalgia: the real life of the plantations in the 1960s was so reminiscent of the lovely and terrible and glorified heritage of old Dixie that I could not get enough of it.

My ability to experience and enjoy the Delta in 1968 was limited by circumstances peculiar to those days. To interview tenant farmers and sharecroppers in their homes required that I stay out of sight during the day and venture out only after nightfall. My whereabouts had to be kept secret. We thought that if the landowners got wind of my presence they would simply order their tenants not to talk to me, and they would generally be obeyed. The plantations where most of the people lived were private property. And then, too, we wanted to minimize the danger to my hosts. I watched most of the 1968 harvest through the windows and cracks in the walls of the houses where I spent my days. At night, Tiny or Noah would gather me up, and we would drive the gravel back roads onto the plantations and interview families at their homes, everyone tired out after a day's work. We all smoked cigarettes and talked. In this fashion we tape-recorded interviews with one hundred or more tenant families and documented a large slice of life as it was then, in this one south Delta county.

There are great differences between then and now, by which I mean 1988 and early 1989 when, often accompanied by my wife, I traveled back and forth across the Delta to speak with all manner of "authorities" about the transformation. What has changed? For one thing, so many of the people are gone from the countryside, departed for the North, for Texas and Tennessee, and for the towns and cities of Mississippi. Economically, catfish, and to some extent

Cotton field in Bolivar County

factories, have taken the lead from cotton, and Wal-Marts have taken the business from the plantation store. One is as likely to see blacks as whites behind the office doors in courthouses these days. There are four-lane highways now and, as a consequence, the region seems to have shrunk. Powerful forces from outside the Delta are reshaping the life there daily, yet there is a deep cultural bedrock that refuses to give way. The forces from within, a vivid history and an impregnable race consciousness, are also strong. This extraordinary place strikes me as the American face of Zimbabwe, a country sorting out the debris left by the eradication of legal segregation. Mississippi Deltans abandoned the ramparts, the ones assailed daily in South Africa; they avoided the all-out war and underwent an essentially peaceful revolution to reach something that is today quite exceptional.

After the revolution comes the difficult part. It is the reconciliation of people who in the past have disliked even the way the other smelled. In a sideshow of the last years of the twentieth century, there is being achieved in the Delta what may be the final armistice of the Civil War. What is special to my eyes, at least now that I can see the Delta in the daytime, is that people who care enough about a certain piece of land to refuse to leave it, and who are constrained by law and grace from killing each other off to possess it, can forge community in America. The images of the past are not forgotten in the Delta. They pop up everywhere, but they are now talked about with some embarrassment and detachment: the Klan, the Citizens Council, poverty, segregation, hunger, Jim Eastland. People in the Delta have been through all that, and they survived. Not everybody who lives there is optimistic that the future promises any great improvements, but people in the Delta deserve more credit for imagination and tolerance than they think they do, and this book seeks to explain why.

DELTA TIME

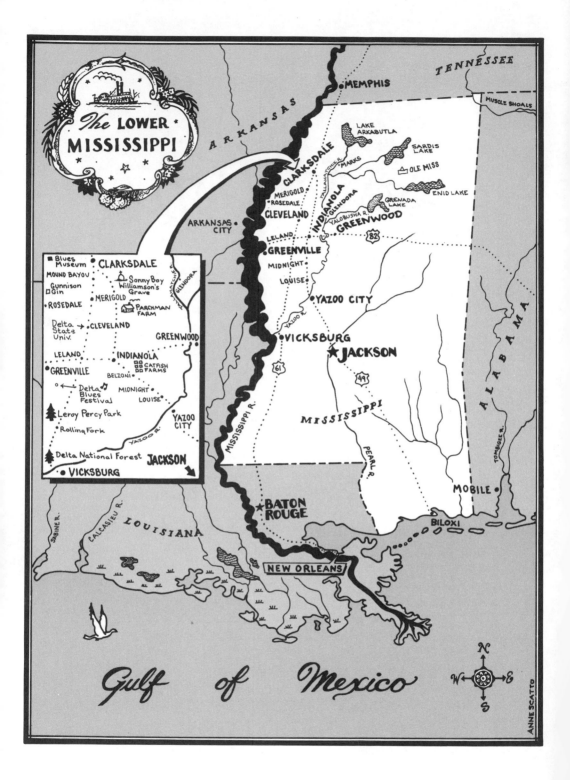

The LOWER MISSISSIPPI

TENNESSEE

MUSCLE SHOALS

MEMPHIS

ARKANSAS

CLARKSDALE

LAKE ARKABUTLA

SARDIS LAKE

MARKS

OLE MISS

MERIGOLD
ROSEDALE

INDIANOLA
GLENDORA

ENID LAKE

GRENADA LAKE

CLEVELAND

YALOBUSHA R.

GREENWOOD

ARKANSAS CITY

82

LELAND

GREENVILLE

MIDNIGHT

LOUISE

YAZOO CITY

VICKSBURG

JACKSON

61

49

MISSISSIPPI

MISSISSIPPI R.

ALABAMA

PEARL R.

TOMBIGBEE R.

MOBILE

BATON ROUGE

BILOXI

LOUISIANA

SABINE R.

CALCASIEU R.

NEW ORLEANS

Gulf of Mexico

N
W E
S

ANNE SCATTO

Inset map

Blues Museum — CLARKSDALE

MOUND BAYOU

Gunnison Gin

Sonny Boy Williamson's Grave

ROSEDALE

MERIGOLD

Parchman Farm

Delta State Univ. → CLEVELAND

GREENWOOD

LELAND

INDIANOLA

BELZONI

Catfish Farms

GREENVILLE

MIDNIGHT

Delta Blues Festival

LOUISE

Leroy Percy Park

YAZOO CITY

Rolling Fork

YAZOO R.

Delta National Forest

JACKSON

VICKSBURG

GLENDORA

TALLAHATCHIE R.

DELTA RISING

▲▲▲

If De Soto or any of his men sensed that there was any
unusual significance to this juncture with the
Mississippi it was not recorded. The surviving
Franciscan chanted no Te Deums in honor of its
discovery. The Mississippi, which they called the Rio
Grande, was just another river to cross, distinguished
only because it was wider, swifter, muddier than the
others. Here is no encouraging vision of an empire
whose wealth the great river would bear to the sea.
Here is only the reality of a difficult passage and the
foreboding sight of waiting Indians on the
opposite shore.

—Hodding Carter, *Lower Mississippi*

I t is an odd piece of land, shaped like the elliptic leaf of, say, a
▽▽▽ pecan tree, with the stem in Memphis and the tip in Vicksburg.
On the west is the Mississippi River. The eastern boundary is made
by a convex formation of hills where the Coldwater, the Tallahatchie, and the Yocona rivers begin and flow down into the Delta
to join the Yazoo and then finally the Mississippi. This is not the true
"delta" of the Mississippi (which is at the river's mouth in Louisiana). It is properly the flood plain of the Yazoo, and regularly over
the centuries, of the muddy Mississippi itself.

Some 340,000 people live on this flat land, which measures about
220 miles from north to south and 70 miles wide in the middle. Most
of them are engaged in agriculture, not small personal farms but
agribusiness, big-time stuff. Black people make up about 60 percent

Ellendale plantation, Tallahatchie County

of the population and whites make up almost all of the rest. There have been several waves of black out-migration since the Civil War, but the total population and the black share have not changed much since the Depression.

The pace of life here is slow, though you can go plenty fast down the long straight highways if you have a good car. Cotton pickers and big tractors claim the right of way, even on the four-lanes through the small cities of Greenwood, Cleveland, Greenville, Clarksdale, and Belzoni. The wealth here is in the earth. The topsoil of the Delta is reputed to be forty feet deep. It is so incredibly productive, and therefore desirable, that it has taken Americans less than 150 years to strip away all the hardwood forests and drain most of the swamps that might impede a plow. Almost all the land was originally wooded, but now there is hardly a tree on the place. It would not be much of an exaggeration to say that if you had the fuel you could run a tractor in a straight line the whole length of the Delta, from Tunica to Onward, without lifting the plow blade more than ten or eleven times to get over roads and creeks.

Since it was first settled in the 1840s the Delta has been off the beaten path, even by Mississippi standards, because it is not on the way to anything. Also, until recently, its roads were very uncertain. Malaria was a familiar disease and yellow fever an occasional terrifying reaper until the turn of this century. Even today the Delta is off the main road. Look at a Mississippi highway map and by locating I-55 you can see where the Delta is not. The federal highway keeps to the high ground; the precipitous drop-off to the Delta occurs a few miles to the west. The result of this isolation is that the Delta has not shared in the educational and social development of the rest of the country, and it has never kept pace with the cultural shifts and fads of the mainstream.

Because it was remote, because up through the 1940s the Delta was home to more black people than all the New England states combined, and because society was just a little changed from slave days, the Delta became known as a hot and mean place to live. It was the "home of the blues," the real blues, and birthplace to just about every great bluesman there ever was. It is still a primary taproot of black culture and history in America, and it is still hot and often mean. The white population, always a minority, has made its own obscure but important contribution to the nation. These people are now called farmers, but they used to be known as plantation owners, and their lives were molded by the exigencies of managing vast sections of land and a brooding black labor force, along with an impulse born in Charleston, Natchez, or New Orleans to maintain some grace and intellect in the midst of isolated, steaming, unending cotton fields. To America they contributed a myth, and a lifestyle that sometimes lives up to that myth. These planters were never as rich as their pre–Civil War counterparts back East were reputed to be, but they lasted longer. Even today most still try to live up to the image a little bit and to preserve certain Southern traditions, amenities, and prejudices.

There are no tourist attractions to speak of in the Delta. It is farmland. Travelers from afar will have no comforting points of reference other than the basic Hardees and a Ramada in the big towns. And watch out, because even these gracious accommodations fill up with crop-chemical salesmen during the week and you may have to beat it back to that interstate. There are few historical monuments and as yet no Disneyworld. The real attractions are the little pulse points, the juke joints, the comfortable eateries like the nameless crossroads beerstop in Darlove where deacons and their wives take Sunday chicken, or Ralph's Drive-In on 61 South in Cleveland where peppery batter-fried potato slices called Jojos go for about fifteen cents apiece, or Etta's on the old highway in Leland where you can buy hot tamales day or night from her porch, the wide-open spaces, crop dusters in flight, the free feeling of exploring along the Mississippi River, friendly and unexpectedly wise people, Lurline Screws's grocery in Holly Bluff, and many other little indicators that in this place lies a soul.

Without a doubt the Delta is economically one of the poorest spots in America. The tough life of the majority clashes with the apparent richness of the soil and the great amounts of capital that are invested in farming it. By all measures, for example, family income, unemployment, infant mortality, school drop-out rates, teen pregnancy rates, illiteracy, the Mississippi Delta is at or near the bottom of the list. Even planters do not seem to do that well. Many have fallen into bankruptcy since the Carter grain embargo put an end

to the good times. Yet there is considerable pride among whites and
blacks alike in their community and enthusiasm for improving
things—though not necessarily through joint endeavor.

The Delta dream for all races is to acquire money and leisure, and
of the two leisure is more highly valued. It may be a difficult place
for a young man or woman to break out and earn a big living, but
it is an easy place to spend Saturday night drinking to the sounds
of a steel guitar or Sunday morning hunting doves.

As a society it is armed to the teeth. You can count on there being
a rifle in the gun rack or a pistol in the glove box of almost every car
or pickup truck that passes you at seventy-five miles an hour on the
straight concrete roads. But a more polite, generous, and friendly
people would be hard to find anywhere. Shopkeepers, laundry-
women, and the person on the stool next to you in the drugstore seem
to be truly interested in meeting you and hearing your story. Take
the time to listen and you will see that they also know tales that,
while intensely local, touch on big themes like wealth and poverty,
black folks and white, dogs that hunt and dogs that won't. It becomes
quickly apparent that the Delta is more than a big cotton field. It is
a colorful place where some of the major currents of the American
heritage are still easily discerned, still churning, still flowing out-
ward.

Almost forgotten at the bottom of that sea is the earlier civilization of the Indians whom white and black society displaced, who
built temples and churches from dirt. Their experience illustrates
much about transience and the impermanence of life by the river.
Their relics, and the remains of the mastodons and great bears who
roamed the forests, wash out onto sand bars in the Mississippi and
its tributaries when the waters are low. The tangled jungle and
low-lying swampland bathed annually by floods, which was all that
the Delta used to be, encouraged the development of their isolated
tribes. The Indians clustered on the high ground made of sediment
deposited naturally on the banks of rivers and streams by the annual
floods. Gradually, over the centuries, they laid out networks of villages which looked toward larger principalities where they constructed ceremonial mounds. Priests and chiefs may have lived on
these mounds. The original inhabitants of the Delta preceded our

recorded history, but from what they left—the mounds, clues to the whereabouts of houses, and their daily garbage—we believe that they were peaceful fishermen and hunters.

The mound-builders' simple architecture for living quarters was to root a ring of poles upright in a shallow circular ditch, bend them over, and tie them at the top. For their civic or religious architecture, they erected squared-off mounds of earth sometimes measuring hundreds of feet on each side and standing from eight to fifty feet tall. These mounds once numbered in the thousands in the Delta, and no one can quite imagine how they were built. Despite the depredations of generations of boyhood explorers, who have pockmarked the extant mounds with foxholes and tunnels, their purpose is not well understood. Most do not have anyone or anything buried in them. The people who built them seem to have washed away, like their villages, in a flood.

The mounds occupy sites also found desirable by later white settlers. They are features in the yards of several homes, such as the Colonel Fields house in Anguilla and the expensive Cedar Grove, a bed-and-breakfast mansion in Vicksburg. The planters held weddings, musicals, and revivals atop them. South of Greenville, near the river, is a house built on top of a mound. On a grander scale, Yazoo City ("Yazoo" is said to mean "death") is reputed to be built on two Indian mounds, each about four hundred feet square and fifty feet tall. These must have been quite a sight on the flat landscape.

In the 1960s and 1970s the great aim of virtually every Delta agriculturalist was to clear away whatever forest still occupied arable land, drain the swamps, and use draglines to grade every rise and water-collecting depression until each field was perfectly, measurably flat. One inevitable sacrifice was virtually all of the Indian mounds. Aware that all evidence of the ancient settlers and their civilization would be destroyed in a flash, but without any apparent power to prevent the destruction, the state of Mississippi created a field office of its Department of Archives and History in Clarksdale in 1968. The archaeologists assigned to the office, including Samuel O. McGahey and John M. Connaway, were delegated to practice "salvage archaeology." They were to catalogue the whereabouts of the various Indian sites in fields about to be leveled and, if possible, excavate them in a hurry. The niceties of delicately peeling away the blanket of soil above grave sites and dwellings and then preserving their treasures were, by and large, thrown out the window. The state archaeologists' job was to dig fast, if permission to go onto the land could be obtained at all, and take a picture of what was there before the bulldozers arrived. They published several scientific books and articles on their researches, and, if one cares about the loss of unique and priceless, albeit abstract, things, these scholarly treatises read like lamentations about a lost Jerusalem.

For example, in *Archaeological Investigations in Mississippi, 1969–1977,* John M. Connaway, the author, first details his unearthing of an entire village surrounding a large mound, which measured about 300 by 150 feet in size, near Opossum Bayou in Quitman County. He then dispassionately records that "unfortunately when the Department was attempting to secure funds for extensive excavation of the site, it was destroyed by land-levelers." How interesting that, just as "mound-builders" now denominates an entire prehistoric civilization, so to the archaeologist does "land-levelers" describe the modern Americans.

Elsewhere Connaway writes: "The Bobo site, located near Clarksdale . . . consisted of a village area and a small mound on the west bank of the Sunflower River and was approximately six to eight acres in size. . . . In May 1973, archaeologists with the Department of Archives and History were notified by amateurs in the Clarksdale area that the site was being destroyed. The owner had sold several feet of top soil, including the mound, for use in construction of a nearby shopping center. The mound was being graded down and large earth-moving machines were hauling the soil away when archaeologists arrived on the scene. Under present state law, there was no way to stop the destruction other than to simply ask the owner. This was done to no avail. With this in mind, and with the cooperation of the construction workers on the scene, Department archaeologists spent three days at the site attempting to record as many features as possible. A number of local amateurs . . . joined in the efforts. A large number of house patterns and refuse pits could be seen after machines had removed the top soil. . . . Using certain time-saving techniques, the archaeologists began hastily recording house patterns until the owner suddenly decided not to allow anyone on the site. This was very unfortunate since only five house patterns were recorded out of a possible eighty or more uncovered in the field. As a result, the remaining features were destroyed forever, along with an excellent opportunity to record an entire village pattern for the first time in the Delta. Without the help of interested local citizens, most, if not all, of this work could not have been accomplished."

In a postscript to the excellent and no doubt scientifically useful work, the author issues an understated call for a "stronger approach to public education," and notes by way of argument that "Longstreet, Boyd, Acree, Maddox # 2, and Flowers # 3 sites, as well as the small mound at Shady Grove, have all been leveled for farming purposes; much of the Hester site has become a gravel pit; the Grand Gulf Mound was leveled to make way for a nuclear power plant; part of the Barner site was graded and paved for a country road; and the entire Bobo site was hauled off for land fill at a shopping center. Such is modern man's tribute to our prehistoric heritage in the name of progress and profit."

Connaway, who is a native of the Delta on the Arkansas side of the river, still works in Clarksdale, where he has achieved local celebrity as the professional quarterback of a sizable team of amateur archaeologists from throughout the area. While we talked in his bone-and-fossil-packed office across the street from the courthouse, a maintenance man from the Town Housing Authority dropped in bearing a stone adz he had found and which Connaway dated, after turning it over in his palm for a minute or so, at A.D. 1200 to 1400. The phone rang frequently, bringing inquiries about whether the day's rainfall would force cancellation of a scouting expedition to a distant creek bank. Connaway speaks matter-of-factly about ancient history and the significance of his finds. He thinks that the earliest Delta dwellers fished the river 12,000 years ago, when the woods were full of frightening mammals and reptiles. The first permanent culture, evidenced by villages and mounds, developed around 2000 B.C. He shows off a mastodon tusk he found on the Mississippi a year ago, which is now ring-clamped on his worktable to minimize the cracks that develop as it dries. Of his discovery he remarks, "I got pretty excited, I guess. As excited as I get." He is not much of an entertainer. He describes himself as a student of the "north Delta cosmos" who likes to get his hands dirty, and he is a Delta type who lets the evidence, in this case pottery shards, do his talking for him.

Mostly what he finds is the "middens," the trash piles of the first arrivals. He likens these caches to the washing-machine parts, broken bottles, and lost tools that might accumulate behind a tenant shack today. The mounds, in his imagination, were like country Baptist churches with a main "big-steeple" church in town. Historically, there are few data about the Indians; their culture went into decline about the time of the first European contact. Was that a mere coincidence? De Soto recorded that he found natives using the mounds, but, he said, the people could not remember who built them or when. Many were used as cemeteries, and one that Connaway excavated in 1965 had thirty people buried inside, though they were not necessarily of the generation who built the mound. In the center of Clarksdale, at the foot of Sunflower Street, there was once a mound on which the town's largest church was constructed. Now the church and mound have both disappeared. A little ways out of town, in the vicinity of Stovall, are the Carsun Mounds, which some historians think are the famous Quiz Quiz, the large village described by De Soto when his weary explorers "discovered" the Mississippi. (A more generally accepted site is also close by, in what is now the town of Rena Lara.) There is a contemporary house built on one of the Carsun Mounds now.

The frustrating thing is how little the diggers find, even when they have some time. Tiny bits and pieces of charcoal from an ancient hearth, a few arrowheads, or a piece of a pot are the keys to conjectures that provide most of our understanding of this people. To be a Delta archaeologist is to get satisfaction from such tiny scattered treasures and insignificant remnants from the past. Other than these the book is closed on the mound-builders. They have been "vanished" as thoroughly as Custer at the Little Big Horn. The Delta now belongs to the land-levelers, and it is they who must account for its present condition.

OLD RHYTHMS

▲ ▲ ▲

This, briefly, is the Mississippi Delta. Under these
conditions, against this background, and in this
environment nearly one hundred thousand white and
three hundred thousand Negroes live and have their
being. It is a strange and detached fragment thrown off
by the whirling comet that is America.
—David L. Cohn, *Where I Was Born and Raised*

T he mound-builders were displaced by European men, the
▽▽▽ progenitors of the aristocracy. First came Spanish, French, and
English traders, then the cotton planters. The "pioneers" of the
Delta were, often as not, sons and daughters of North Carolina
tobacco farmers or Mexican War veterans searching for new land
and possessed of enough grit and credit to wrest something arable
out of a malarial swamp full of water moccasins, panthers, and
bears. In time, with the help of slaves, these settlers could retire to
the shade, and thus was born the Delta planter.

One of the most enduring images of the Mississippi Delta is the
plantation owner with his white linen suit under the hot sun, wearing a Panama hat. Unlike most legends, this one is as much fact as
fancy. Until very recently, being a Delta planter had been an aspira-

tion of most Mississippi farmers, for it is a way of life that connotes leisure, influence, rectitude, and refinement. The planter was the pinnacle of an economic and social organization that flourished in the Delta long after the War Between the States burned it out in the rest of the South. It has lasted in the Delta, though in a more and more elusive form, up until the present day.

Greenville newsman Hodding Carter described something of the Mississippi planter's view of himself, in antiquity, in his excellent and often overlooked 1942 book, *Lower Mississippi:* "From the hedonistic enterprise of the river planters of the thirties grew a pleasant culture which in turn created a pleasant legend. Of the culture, there remains principally a scattering of wide-porched, stately homes. The planter legend has out-built the grandest of these; and the latter-day destruction of this myth would have been a pity had not the reality itself been a prideful thing. The men who built these homes were not cavaliers and but rarely of cavalier stock. They developed their own kindly, sturdy aristocracy. Most of them were not cultured in the erudite definition of contemporaneous Boston or even Virginia; for colic and yellow fever remedies, a sure eye and a green thumb were more important than philosophy, literature, and art on this new frontier. Primarily, they were simply farmers on a large scale. As a class they were autocratic by virtue of their sovereignty over men and broad acres, headstrong, mostly provincial in outlook, extravagant, violent, careless. But not even the most painstaking demolisher of the river planter myth can successfully dispute that as a class they were also amazingly hospitable and tenacious and clannishly loyal and generous; good livers who admired and sought to own beautiful homes, fast horses, and not infrequently a comely slave woman or two. Earthy longings, but not without merit."

New Orleans, a "town of beguiling sin" to Carter, and Natchez and Charleston were the wellsprings of the Delta's plantation culture at the turn of the nineteenth century when the northern outpost of Memphis was hardly more than a country town. In those early years the ladies, planters, and belles of the Delta traveled by steamboat to New Orleans for the Mardi Gras and opera and for other cosmopolitan delights. My own workplace today, from whose thirty-sixth floor I can gaze over the river's crescent and watch storms sweep in over

The Colonel Fields house, built beside an Indian mound, Anguilla

Lake Pontchartrain, was built on the site of the St. Charles, New Orleans's grandest hotel. It was a mecca for Mississippi planters for generations before and after the Civil War. The city is still beguilingly sinful and still smells of salt air, coffee, garlic, crusty bread, gardenias, sweet olive, and the river. Delta planters still come here to relax, but without the fanfare of a steamboat arrival, and more likely to applaud Tulane football games than to attend the opera.

Then as now, the Delta planters saw beyond local politics, crops, and the weather to the larger world of trade and finance. While Mississippi has always been poor, the Delta since its development as a major agricultural center has been an enclave of prosperity for some. The first farms were laid out by the Mississippi River and along the Yazoo to take advantage of steamboat transportation. They were few and far between, worked by slaves, and very profitable. At the time of the Civil War most of the interior was still swampland and virgin cypress and hardwood forest. In the years of Reconstruction and peace, however, outlanders in numbers migrated from the burned-out and played-out cotton land of the Deep South and pioneered this new country with its inexhaustible soil. The plantation builders, while they admired the leisurely lifestyle and the perquisites of lordship, were perfectly satisfied with the theories and practices of the New South, and they set out to grow cotton scientifically and efficiently. Their ambition was to dominate the international cotton market, and they fully supported railroad building and faster ships to move their crops to buyers here and in Europe. In the twentieth century, the Delta planters became regional and national leaders through the Delta Cotton Council and other powerful political associations dealing with levees, navigation, and agriculture. They and their kind brought the region into the modern era and defined much of the South's national agenda.

In the days of the last century when the "leading men" of the Delta numbered, by their own estimate, roughly half a dozen, the leader of these was Colonel William Alexander Percy, known as the Gray Eagle. The elder W. A. Percy, to distinguish him from his grandson who wrote *Lanterns on the Levee,* was master of plantations with thousands of acres and hundreds of sharecroppers on both sides of the river. In addition to serving with General Bowen during the siege of Vicksburg and then in the Army of Northern Virginia, he and the other landowners who survived the war directed the public life of Washington County during the successful battle to overthrow the Reconstruction administration of Adelbert Ames and for years thereafter. The colonel's son LeRoy carried on the tradition, and put the weight of his family behind the opposition to the post-Reconstruction Ku Klux Klan, in part because of the Klan's increasing anti-Catholicism, since LeRoy's wife Camille was the daughter of a French cotton factor and Delta planter, but in the main because he feared that the Klan would run off the Negroes.

In 1910 LeRoy Percy was appointed to the United States Senate to fill the unexpired term of Anselm McLaurin. He championed levee building, the cause that preoccupied him and his generation. In the election of 1911, he was opposed by former governor James K. Vardaman, whom the voters called the "Great White Chief." Vardaman was a master showman who cut a striking figure in his white suit, black hat, and black hair combed down to his shoulders, and he simply "out-niggered" Percy (to use the expression attributed to George Wallace, who vowed, when he lost the 1958 governor's race to John Patterson, never to be "out-nigguhed" again, and he wasn't). The Vardaman campaign set the tone for Mississippi elections for the next sixty years. Though he was from Greenwood, the cotton-market capital on the eastern edge of the Delta, Vardaman's support came from the hills, and he engendered in the Percy family, and those influenced by Delta leadership, an abiding disdain for the white peckerwood voter. So much did the Delta dislike his type that Theodore Bilbo, the Democratic candidate for lieutenant governor in that same election, lost to the Socialist candidate in the Delta counties of Washington and Sunflower, and bettered him in Issaquena by only four votes. LeRoy's glory occurred in 1922 when he went heads up against a Klan organization in Greenville whose kleagles, klugs, and cyclopses he likened to a "Negro fraternal order." A narrow victory for the anti-Klan sheriff in the city election that year sent a cheering crowd to the Percy home. He provided four kegs of whiskey and set off the biggest celebration in the little town's memory. Two years later Greenville elected a Catholic mayor, and the contest was over.

The family chronicles were ultimately written by the senator's son, William Alexander Percy the younger. Though he took up the family acres and law practice, he was also a poet. If anything, that raised him even higher in the estimation of the region's aspiring aristocrats. He was considered a progressive because of his attitude that Negroes should be treated respectfully, since Delta prosperity rested on their shoulders, but today's reader of *Lanterns on the Levee* might find him an unreconstructed reactionary, though with a fine sense of the ironic.

Upon surveying his neighbors and constituents, Percy found the lower class of whites wanting, and it was those he most feared. The original stock of the Delta, by which he meant the slave owners and their slaves, were the ones he preferred. "The Southern Negro," he wrote in 1941, "has the most beautiful manners in the world, and the Southern white, learning from him I suspect, is a close second." He thought they were the only classes in the South of which God must be proud. Poor whites in general, he felt, were "intellectually and spiritually . . . inferior to the Negro." He dismissed the small population of Chinese entirely by saying, "In so far as I can judge, they serve no useful purpose in community life." The bonds holding these disparate groups together in the region were disease, natural disaster, and moderate poverty. The wonder of the Delta, as he saw it, was "how all these folks, aristocrats gone to seed, poor whites on the make, Negroes convinced mere living is good, aliens of all sorts that blend or curdle—can dwell together in peace if not in brotherhood and live where, first and last, the soil is the only means of livelihood." In a more pessimistic vein, his friend Hodding Carter wrote the following year that "laughter is the only common denominator of the two dissimilar races that people the river. I wish I could say otherwise." Neither of them could imagine any ultimate peaceful resolution of the race question. Segregation could not be defended under American principles, but they felt that whites would go to war rather than submit to social equality with the Negro. It was a puzzle-box without a key.

Percy imagined, as he looked over the community on the eve of World War II, that poor whites would ultimately displace both the old planters and the Negroes. From his vantage, recalling the electoral defeat his father had suffered, the analysis made sense, and subsequent history details the rise to political power at the state government level of the class of whites Percy liked the least. "Poor whites," however, have had a notable lack of success in displacing the blacks of the Delta, even supposing they wanted to. Nor has the limited industrial development since the Second World War lured the whites from the hills. The Delta's few assembly lines are staffed mainly by blacks; the skilled white workers are brought in from out of state.

Until his death in 1942 Percy resisted industrial development in his hometown of Greenville, fearing an influx of those types he disfavored, and he found far more comfort in his lyrical view of the past than in anything he could imagine happening in the future. He was "out of tune with tuneless times," Hodding Carter observed. In public and private ways he helped to defeat the Klan's ambitions in his own town, but he could not divine a solution to the imbalance of his segregated environment. He had no formula to put forth save grace and gracefulness. "It is a very nice world—that is, if you remember that while good morals are all-important between the Lord and His creatures, what counts between one creature and another is good manners," he wrote. He was, in his own life, as perfect an example of a Delta planter as there ever will be, and for the record, here is Will Percy's recipe for the best mint juleps in the world. They were the ones made by his mother:

Certainly her juleps had nothing in common with those hybrid concoctions one buys in bars the world over under that name. It would have been sacrilege to add lemon, or a slice of orange or of pineapple, or one of those wretched maraschino cherries. First you needed excellent bourbon whiskey; rye or Scotch would not do at all. Then you put half an inch of sugar in the bottom of the glass and merely dampened it with water. Next, very quickly—and here was the trick in the procedure—you crushed your ice, actually powdered it, preferably in a towel with a wooden mallet, so quickly that it remained dry, and, slipping two sprigs of fresh mint against the inside of the glass, you crammed the ice in right to the brim, packing it with your hand. Last you filled the glass, which apparently had no room left for anything else, with bourbon, the older the better, and grated a bit of nutmeg on the top. The glass immediately frosted and you settled back in your chair for half an hour of sedate cumulative bliss. Although you stirred the sugar at the bottom, it never all melted, therefore at the end of the half hour there was left a delicious mess of ice and mint and whiskey which a small boy was allowed to consume with calm rapture.

I wondered what today's gentry thought about the changing times. We visited Mrs. Evelyn S. Pearson of Rosedale, a lady of the old tradition, who exemplifies the mannered gentility upon which Percy placed his hopes. She is a Sillers, a prominent name among planters and in Mississippi political history. Born in 1898, and nearly Will Percy's contemporary, she has seen the half-century that Percy did not. Her forebears, too, are original stock. Bolivar County was organized in 1836, and her grandfather, Joseph Sillers, moved there in 1854, having seen the area on his way to the Mexican War. This was before Rosedale existed, and Joseph cleared the land from forest that had been hunting ground to Indians. "Our family grew up with the country," Mrs. Pearson says, smiling. "It was quite new then." Joseph died a prisoner of war in Vicksburg and was buried in an unmarked grave by the Federals.

Her brother, Walter Sillers, Jr., was in the state legislature for fifty years and speaker of the house for twenty-three years. He was known as "Mr. Mississippi." She was educated by her mother's mother, who read the Bible daily in French, and for two years at Ward Belmont, the venerable Nashville finishing academy.

Mrs. Pearson lives where she was born, in a fine old home which her father built in 1889, facing the Mississippi River levee. Back then the levee would not have been so high and the river would have seemed closer. The house and lawns are draped in great magnolias that were planted "back then." "This has always been a happy house," she states with conviction. "There's always been laughter and joy in this house." And though she was alone during both of our visits, the house does have that feeling.

From her father, a lawyer, levee commissioner, and farmer, and her husband, John L. Pearson, Sr., who died in 1928, she inherited what she discreetly describes as "planting interests." With these interests, cotton farms totaling thousands of acres, she inherited also the responsibility of management as a widow in an isolated rural world connected to the outside by rivers and long dirt roads and surrounded by a black population that exceeded the white ten

Mrs. John L. Pearson, Sr., at her home in Rosedale

times over. With the help of overseers and black straw bosses and later her son (who left farming for the law and is now the state circuit court judge), she ran the land and kept the books for almost forty years. "If I had known as a young girl how much math I would have to do and how much farming would be required, I would have jumped into the Mississippi River," she says in the comfort of her dim parlor.

In 1967, the year before I first came to the Delta, she retired and leased the family acreage to younger neighbors. Now the years of tedium seem to have faded, and her recollections of how the old plantation sounded make her eyes light up. "I still miss it," she says, speaking very softly. "In late afternoon when the men were bringing in the mules the trace chains would be clinking and the children were laughing and singing and people were moving about making supper. There was so much life and so many sounds. They seemed so happy. Now when you go out to the farm there is absolute silence. When I read now how horrible the hours were and how they hated the people they were working for, I can't believe it. But I suppose that it is true. We thought they were happy, though, and I was never the least bit afraid.

"People had lots of frolicking and pleasure on the *Kate Adams*. It was a steamboat that brought the mail and carried freight from Memphis and to Arkansas City and let on passengers for excursions. In 1927 it burned at its moorings in Memphis." Indeed, I learned that Mrs. Pearson had contributed a piece on the *Kate Adams* to a history of Bolivar County published forty years before. In it she described the excursions in the early 1900s between Rosedale and Arkansas City for baseball games. The trip across the river was gay: "a colored orchestra from Memphis is aboard" and "the young folks begin to dance to the tunes of 'Clover Blossoms,' 'Eva,' and 'In the Shade of the Old Apple Tree.' " The front cabin, usually reserved for gentlemen, is converted into a ballroom; men slip into the alcove for drinks and bring "refreshing claret lemonades" to the ladies in the lounge. After the hot and dusty game, the townsfolk reboard and dress for dinner in their staterooms, "the women in dainty lawns and organdies, the men in white trousers and blue coats. Ah, those beautiful, moonlight nights on the *Kate*—and yes, those nights when the clouds obscure the moon, and we arrive after midnight to find the landing knee-deep in mud, and we lose our slippers in the bog as we endeavor to reach the waiting vehicles—hay wagons, surreys, hacks, and rubber-tired buggies." To her the *Kate* was more than a boat, "she was a personality. . . . She was truly Our Gracious Lady Kate, always hospitable, always ready for service, and as most gracious ladies are, always late!"

She continues: "In those days we had dances in the courthouse. We did not have a clubhouse. After the Civil War everybody was poor and the courthouse was the only building big enough to dance or socialize in. Our courthouse here was built in the fall of 1923, and I remember we had a big married people's cotillion club and we had our first dance there in 1923. Once we had a big bridge party to raise money for the DAR. They kept on dancing in that courthouse until 1954." She pauses and changes the subject. That year means something. Before that year, or at least when the Delta was younger, there was room for frolic and style, but after that it was a little duller.

"My society now is not the people in Rosedale, except for a few. We can't confine our life to Rosedale now. It used to be a very aristocratic town. A few are left, but most have moved away. The death knell to this town was when the schools integrated, and they were so overcrowded. I wouldn't leave it if I had a chance to go, though. I am not talking of a world made out of sugar candy, but the moral atmosphere of our town and our neighboring country was better then than it is now, though it may have been old-fashioned. We had a sprinkling of Old South and a sprinkling of New South and a sprinkling of 'go West, young man.' "

The year 1954 is an elastic concept in the Delta. Though school integration was not implemented until the late 1960s or even the 1970s, 1954 was the beginning of the end of plantation and small-town "society." A line was drawn then that whites could not erase and the façades dropped. The cheerful sounds on the plantation started to fade away. Without realizing how much the health and vigor of their own community depended on participation in the public institutions, the schools and the courthouse, a great many whites gave these things up and retreated into resentful seclusion from community life. White parents who were not prepared for the adjustment, the majority, sent their children to private academies. In a not necessarily related phenomenon, just as many blacks were being forced off the farm by mechanization, so, too, many of the white young people moved away, to larger towns or distant cities, in search of careers. In the 1970s the blacks who stayed began to campaign for and win electoral office. Today, the mayor of Mrs. Pearson's town of Rosedale is J. Y. Trice, the retired principal of the formerly all-black high school. This was a change of great magnitude, but in a remarkably short time the shock wave has passed. Like that of most white citizens of the Delta I spoke with, Mrs. Pearson's sense of the new reality is quite firm.

"Civil rights revolutionized everybody's thinking," she states. "I began to call the mayor Mr. Trice. I don't think that my tongue would have twisted into saying that before the change. That goes back to the past. We didn't walk up and willingly accept what was happening, but we didn't go kicking and screaming either. People of wisdom realize that when you are living together you have got to get along, so we do. We are so close to each other you can't get away from things as you can in the city. We have always, in the Delta, had a mixed society and have never been as intolerant as people in other parts of the country. We get along, I think, awfully well. I'm not being unrealistic, but compared to other areas of the country the Delta gets along well with blacks. We don't have much of the white-supremacy talk as you do in other areas." It is very possible that she is right. The Delta has been home to Italian rice farmers, Lebanese lawyers, Jewish grocers, Chinese gamblers, Greek river-boaters, and recently Indian motel keepers. But Mrs. Pearson has a racial identity, something she is proud of and afraid her descendants might lose. She has no problem integrating that idea with democracy.

"I think whites and blacks will work together more and more," she says. "That is, if the rest of the country is wise they will. It is not just the South. Frankly, I wonder if I would like it at all if I could see into the future. If all the lines came down I might not like the people. Racial feelings seem to be inside of everybody, to prefer our own race. The early segregationist said the bluebird doesn't mate with the robin. But it's this way. We are here. We are all together. We've got to get along. People with good intentions can make a go of it." This is the commonsense blending of ideas that Percy, Carter, and other reporters in the thirties and forties thought was impossible.

They could not imagine how whites could ever be compelled to relinquish control over the Negro.

Important thinkers like David L. Cohn and even the sociologist John Dollard saw the conflict between the Delta's race relations and democracy but then drew back from proposing a solution because they could not divine one. Nothing would ever change white attitudes, they thought, and without that the segregated caste system would never end. Now we can say they were wrong. Segregation died first and now, witness this elegant, lovely, soft-spoken lady of the plantations, traditions intact but attitudes miraculously changed. And, as I discovered, she is not unique in the Delta community.

Mrs. Pearson's daughter, who shares the great old house, teaches in a public school in a predominantly black classroom. Rosedale has the distinction of having quietly built a relatively integrated school system, in marked contrast, for example, to the nearby city of Greenville. Mrs. Pearson has visions of economic development for her little town, and talks about attracting a bridge to Rosedale: a Mississippi River crossing that would have the outstanding attribute of providing a straight route from the Redstone arsenal in Huntsville, Alabama, to the government arsenal in Hot Springs, Arkansas. The men of her family, her son the judge and her granddaughter's husband, Jack Coleman, a Republican politician, all favor the project. It would bring people and jobs to Rosedale, just the sort of change that Will Percy feared. "It wouldn't bring back the people that were here before," Mrs. Pearson says. "It would be different. But all of America is getting different, isn't it?"

three

DO DAH

▲ ▲ ▲

Let us look well at this MAN. As Captive, Hunter,
Explorer, Surveyor, Civil Engineer, Traveler, Sailor,
Navigator, Soldier. Is that not material enough,
for a thrilling romance?
—Lamar Fontaine, C.E. and Ph.D., *A Plea for Peace,*
Preparedness and Good Roads Everywhere

T he Civil War has not been entirely forgotten anywhere in the
▽▽▽ South, though the memory is fainter in some places, such as my
hometown of Atlanta, than others. A million men fought to preserve
the old way of life, and Confederate ghosts still thrive in the Delta.
We began a day in Clarksdale strolling through the old "Grange
Cemetery" at Fifth and Sunflower by the river. We learned its name
later from one of the town's Carnegie librarians. The graveyard
itself is unmarked and apparently no longer much used by the living.
It is in a black neighborhood, and on one side is the Hicks Laun-
dromat, shaded in live-oak trees. Even early in the day a few teenagers are hanging around outside it, drinking from cans and playing
the radio and doing their laundry. On another side are four tiny
shotgun houses in a row. They are a nice shade of green; their dirt

yards are carefully swept. The Heavenly Rest Church of God, a tall
brick edifice, dominates one end, and on the south side is the Sunflower River. In the next block is the famed barbershop of Wade
Walton, a renowned blues artist, and past that the drugstore of
Aaron Henry, the pugnacious civil rights leader, one of the real
grandfathers of the movement. We entered the cemetery through a
hole in the fence and made a peaceful survey.

Patty quietly busied herself taking pictures of a fallen oak, and I
walked in a different direction to see who was there. I found the
Broadhus, Butts, Ellis, and Cutrer families, names that, with the
exception of Ellis, have just about disappeared from Coahoma
County (there is a Cutrer Hill in Clarksdale, but the locals say
"Q-Try"). On the north side of the cemetery is a little group of
Chinese graves with hieroglyphs rather than biblical verse chiseled
in the stones. One of the few still legible is that of Bho Chie Pang,
whose descendants live yet in the Delta. I was looking for Confederate markers, a habit of mine since I realized that all of those stones
in the national cemeteries in Vicksburg and at St. Francisville are
only for the Union dead. Most of the Confederate gravestones were
placed over mass graves when your great-grandmother was young
by the Daughters of the Confederacy, or other patriotic groups, or
even state governments. After the Civil War the only expenses some
states like Mississippi could bear were pensions for Confederate
veterans and burials beneath iron cross markers. I found just one of
these. In the very northeast corner, near the Chinese graves and
beneath a dogwood and a magnolia that seem to be growing from the
same trunk, is the marker of Lamar Fontaine, 4 La. Cav. C.S.A., Oct.
10, 1829–Oct. 1, 1921. I scanned the faded inscription and then read
it more closely. It seems to say:

*He was the bearer of caps
and dispatches between
Pemberton and Johnston
During the siege of
Vicksburg, May, June, and
July, 1863. Author of the
Poem "All quiet along the
Potomac," and the*

Deadliest sharpshooter
In the Army of Northern Virginia.
Duty done, Honor won,
Resuraam.

My interest thus piqued, I inquired at the Carnegie Public Library
in Clarksdale (not now but once the largest in the state), and sure
enough, they had several writings and pamphlets of Fontaine's, all
original editions in a locked room containing their Mississippi collection. There I found Fontaine's Civil War memoirs, *Prison Life of the
Immortal Six Hundred.* In it he tells of being wounded at Spotsyl-
vania Courthouse on May 12, 1864, one of the very bloodiest battles
of the war, and then of his capture by the Yankees. He recounts that
he was imprisoned, along with six hundred other "immortals," by
the "Brutal Long Armed Ape," as he described Abraham Lincoln, on
Morris Island, South Carolina. He was chained below decks in a ship
bound for Hilton Head in a mass of vomit and excrement. The prisoners were supplied with salt water by their captors. Fontaine es-
caped before the war ended.

On the same shelf I found Fontaine's *The Cause and the Effect of the
Ku Klux Klan in the South,* published in 1910, which described in
romantic terms what the Reconstruction Klan meant to its members.
There is in Southern folklore and history a distinction between
today's Ku Klux Klan, the Klan of the 1920s, and the original Klan,
organized by Confederate veterans and reputedly led by General
Nathan Bedford Forrest. Forrest's plantation, Greengrove, was on
the river west of Clarksdale, and his house was burned down by Union
marauders. Forrest was a romantic, ruthless, brilliant cavalry general in the Confederacy's western armies. His military reputation
was unimpeachable (except for Fort Pillow) at war's end. When after
Reconstruction was imposed in 1867 some defeated Confederates
found life under Yankee military rule intolerable, they invented the
Invisible Empire, and Forrest likely played a large part in leading it.
With others he made it a scary and dangerous force across the South.

It made war on the carpetbagger, the black militia, and ultimately
the black vote. After the "restoration of Democracy," as the restoration of the white Democratic Party was called (Mississippi was one
of the first states restored, in 1875, through the intimidation of black

voters), the Klan faded away. It came back in the 1920s as anti-
Catholic, anti-immigrant, and generally anti-intellectual, as well as
being antiblack, and in one form or another its factions have remained in operation until today. It was against this later Klan that
LeRoy Percy fought in Greenville, and it was the earlier one that
Fontaine defended when he wrote of his enemies the Republicans:
"They were not satisfied with the murder of 250,000 of our bravest
men, the maiming for life of 100,000 more, the incarceration and
starving of 30,000 in their dungeons, and rendering 10,000 imbeciles
forever. The destruction of over two billion dollars worth of property,
and the freeing of over four million slaves, that the South had paid
the New Englanders for." In addition the Ape had disenfranchised
the whites and given the blacks the vote. Faced with that, the old
Confederate had no choice but "to free his land, protect the virtue
of his womanhood and crush the power of the black government, and
throw off the chains that were welded firmly, and remove the bayo-
nets of the Federal Army from his breast.

"The Ku Klux Klan broke the chains that were riven upon the
South, and lifted the galling yoke that had so long oppressed her
people. . . . [It] restored the ark of true American civilization." Actually, it helped to vent a lot of veterans' venom, it got the black
majority out of politics, and it lastly created business opportunities
for "White Only/Colored Only" signmakers. Fontaine revered that
"remnant of that mighty, invisible army, who have not crossed the
mystic Stix and entered the Bivouac beyond the stars." The role he
may have played in the invisible army is not recorded.

Fontaine redeemed himself in my eyes with the title of what seems
to be his last published work, *A Plea for Peace, Preparedness and
Good Roads Everywhere.* In this booklet, published on the eve of
World War I, he counted the blessings that his eighty-eight years
had brought to him. "After all Lamar Fontaine sits dreaming today,
this warm, bright July day, 1917, upon his shaded porch, in his great
arm chair, smoking his old dark colored merschaum pipe, filled with
fragrant Perique; and the soft sea borne zephyrs, fresh from the sun
kissed waves of the semi-tropic Mexic Sea, fanning his time wrinkled
brow, and heavily ladened with perfume of orange, the rose, and the
Magnolia; he seems to be dreaming." But then, quite alert, he turned
his fires on the Republican Party, whom he then referred to as "the

The Grange Cemetery, Clarksdale

Aristocrats of Soulless Wealth," and on Woodrow Wilson, who had betrayed his promise and led America into a European war. There can be little doubt that since Fontaine disliked both Republicans and Progressive Democrats then he must have been a Populist, or at least a William Jennings Bryan Democrat. That can't be so bad; my own grandfather said he voted for Bryan three times, and he may have meant that he did it in one year.

In any case, like most Southerners, Fontaine opposed intervention in a war between thankless Europeans. Spend the money instead on ROADS, he said. "Let our PEOPLE SAY," he demanded, "By POPU-LAR VOTE, whether they would have the Soldiers of America, sent into the Whirlpool of War . . . or take our Army, NOW IN CAMP, GIVE THEM SPADES, AND PICKS, and put them to making a great, magnificent, and beautiful PARK of our whole COUNTRY? Is there a sane man, woman, or child," he asked, "that does not love to travel over a good road?" And I would ask whether anyone doubts, if the proposition were put just that way to a vote today, which path our people would choose. Roads would win over war every time.

In his various autobiographical sketches, Fontaine claimed to have been born in a tent on the Laverde Prairie in Texas in 1829, to have been adopted and schooled by a Polish baron in exile, and to have been captured at age ten by the Comanches to live with the Indians for nearly five years. He related that upon his escape he drank dew in the desert and then took to sea on a ship to the Arctic. Before the Civil War he traveled to China, India, Persia, Egypt, and Syria. While in the Holy Land he studied the Koran and the "junctu-lations and intimations" of the priests, "as well as their attitudes," while muttering their prayers and rituals, until he was perfect in every detail. He was with Bolingbroke when he made his treaty with China and with Perry on his expedition to Japan. He took the oath of the Brahman priest, became one, and served as such for two years in India, China, and Tibet. He joined the Russian army and fought in the Cyrenaican war, and he was with the Herndon expedition that explored the Amazon River. He returned from South America upon learning that Civil War had broken out, swam ashore, and aided in the capture of the Pensacola forts.

I suspect that a man who could present such an autobiography may also have composed the epitaph for his tombstone. With so much to choose from, it was his army service and one poem that Fontaine wanted remembered. Never mind that the true author of the poem is generally accepted as being Ethel Lynn Eliot Beers. Because the vivid world of Lamar Fontaine is in the process of vanishing from the Delta landscape today, as haunted mansions fall before bulldozers and cotton gins give way to Wal-Marts, to be relegated to part of the heritage, I give you the once popular poem "All Quiet Along the Potomac."

"All quiet along the Potomac," they say,
    Except here and there a stray picket
Is shot, as he walks on his beat to and fro,
    By a rifleman hid in a thicket.

It's nothing; a private or two now and then
    Will not count in the news of the battle,
Not an officer lost; only one of the men
    Moaning out all alone the death rattle.

All quiet along the Potomac to-night,
    Where the soldiers lie peacefully dreaming;
Their tents in the rays of the clear autumn moon
    Or in the light of their camp-fires gleaming.

A tremulous sigh, as a gentle night wind
    Through the forest leaves softly is creeping,
While the stars up above, with their glittering eyes,
    Keep guard o'er the army while sleeping.

There's only the sound of the lone sentry's tread
    As he tramps from the rock to the fountain,
And thinks of the two on the low trundlebed
    Far away in the cot on the mountain.

His musket falls slack and his face dark and grim
    Grows gentle with memories tender,
As he mutters a prayer for the children asleep—
    For their mother, may heaven defend her.

The moon seems to shine as brightly as then,
    That night when the love yet unspoken
Leaped up to his lips and when low murmured vows
    Were pledged to be ever unbroken.

Then drawing his sleeve roughly over his eyes
    He dashes off tears that are welling,
And gathers his gun close up to its place
    As for to keep down the heart's swelling.

He passes the fountain, the blasted pine tree,
    The footsteps are lagging and weary,
Yet onward he goes through the broad belt of light,
    Toward the shades of the forest so dreary.

Hark! Was it the night wind rustled the leaves?
    Was it moonlight so wondrously flashing?
It looked like a rifle; Ah, Mary, good-bye,
    And the life blood is ebbing and splashing.

All quiet along the Potomac to-night;
    No sound save the rush of the river;
While soft falls the dew on the face of the dead,
    That picket's "off duty" forever.

four

STOPS ALONG THE WAY

▲▲▲

If one considers the generality of human meanness, one can hardly see how many landlords could fail to take advantage of the opportunities for cheating Negroes.
—John Dollard, *Caste and Class in a Southern Town*

T he great mass of those who have lived in the beautiful and ▽▽▽ troubled land of the Mississippi Delta were the slaves, who became sharecroppers, who became tenant farmers, who became day laborers, and who all along provided the muscle. I first encountered this region somewhere near the end of that progression. In 1968, only a few people still farmed on shares; the vast majority were tenant farmers who got a house to live in and a small wage and who worked on the place pretty much as needed throughout the year. Only at chopping and picking time were large numbers of people hired by the day to clean up the fields. The firmament of the old system, a worker's confidence that he and his family had a place to live, however humble, and a boss to look after his medical and legal needs, was shifting fast in 1968, and the overwhelming sense was one of great insecurity. There was universal underemployment, and except for jobs driving tractors, the work that did exist did not seem to pay a living wage.

The freedom movement was everywhere in the air in 1968, but on the surface the old ways prevailed. Blacks said "sir" and stepped aside for whites. When a black man was in trouble, he went to his white boss. Everywhere one looked one was struck by the contrast between great poverty and great wealth. The whites weren't so ostentatiously rich, but their lands were great. And on those lands there were far more black people than were actually required for farming. Consequently, there was great want, which for many approached starvation. The impressions made by that poverty on almost everybody who traveled onto the plantations in those years, the sick and the dazed-looking children especially, were too vivid ever to be forgotten.

The first place I stopped when I journeyed back in January of 1988 was where I used to live just beyond Louise, at Tiny Man Brown's house. Actually, that house was gone, now just a tangle of vines and a chimney. But next door his mother's simple Jim Walter home still stood. Before I got to the door a large black woman came out on the porch. She introduced herself as Bessie Prentiss and went on to summarize the past twenty years. She explained that the Browns did not live there anymore and that Mrs. Brown, known as Chil' (as in child), had died. Tiny Man had gotten a divorce from Colleen and was married to a woman named Christine now. They lived in Belzoni. Tiny now worked at the high school doing "anything that needs doing." Noah Guider across the way had sold his farm and died. All this was communicated in about five minutes, so it should not be said that Delta people are reticent.

With her directions I found Tiny at the school warehouse in Belzoni. He is a big solid man with shaggy hair, and though he had added a beard since I last saw him, we recognized each other immediately and had a loud reunion while other employees watched us, puzzled at why some middle-aged honky with Louisiana tags should have anything going with Brown. After he got off work we got together at the Browns' brick ranch-style home in a small suburban development in Belzoni where all the streets are named for presidents. The Browns live in Harding, just off Nixon. Actually, the

Tiny Brown, Louise, 1968

black subdivision is outside the city limits, and getting it annexed is part of the local black agenda. Tiny's wife, Christine, works at the Jockey plant, stitching men's cotton underwear. She has two children, now nineteen and thirteen, by a prior marriage. Together, she and Tiny Man, whom she calls by his real name, Thomas, have a first-grader and a little baby. Christine is from Belzoni, but typical of the Delta, she is one of the few in her family to remain. Her brother drives an eighteen-wheeler "fish truck" for the local catfish plants. One of her sisters is a lawyer; another teaches special education; and both live out-of-state.

Tiny has a curious way of popping up with big ideas in the middle of casual conversation and repeating them several times. One idea he circles back to several times that day and later is that the change in Belzoni since he and I "rode around" together is unbelievable. To make the point, he emphasizes how bad it used to be. "Belzoni, right here where we are now, this is the heart of the Delta," he says. "The cold hard fact of the matter is there was more ignorant colored people here, more scareder, more got whupped, more necks got broken, more men got run away from their families if they said anything to the white people. Wasn't nothing here but cotton fields. This is the worst place. This is the heart of the Delta. This is the worst place for racial problems than anywhere else in the Delta, right here." That pretty much sums up Tiny Man's view of Belzoni.

The young people today, he thinks, do not know much about the way it was. "They ought to go out to the creek side and cut firewood for one o' them one-room schoolhouses. One room with about six classes divided off. When one would have a class and the other gets to reading loud, you couldn't hear what your teacher was saying. Children got it so easy now. When I was going to school I didn't know what a lunchroom looked like. The only lunch I had was the lunch I carried. Some of those fatback meat sandwiches in a jelly bucket. Now these children got a cafeteria putting out a Type A lunch." He develops the theme further.

"You looked at a white woman thirty years ago you could get killed. You say something to her, they're sure going to hang you up on a rope. They wasn't going to miss you 'cause two dozen were going to come after you. Even when you were here it seemed like it would be impossible for there to be a black highway patrol like stopped you

Tiny Brown, Louise, 1988

today." I had been ticketed that day for enjoying U.S. 61 as it was meant to be enjoyed. "Not all white people believed in doing things against black people, or it wouldn't have been over now. But you couldn't ride in this car with me and Christine. If you got out of the car twenty-five years ago, you couldn't still be white. That's just how it was. Ya'll would no longer be in the white race, and they would whup us for even having nerve enough to get in the car with ya'll."

He and I take a drive out into the country to see some of the old places I had been before, usually at night. We pass Little Wimp, a barbecue joint I remembered. Its clientele is still essentially all black. Out on the highway, at the Pig Shack barbecue, the clientele is essentially all white—pig segregation! We go down to Midnight, headquarters of the Seward and Harris plantations and the C. B. Box plantation. Midnight is a little hamlet built beside Silver Creek, where seventy-five years ago steamboats picked up cotton and carried it to the Mississippi River. Now you can almost jump across the creek. Tiny points out that there is still a stand of cypress alongside the creek. "It belongs to the federal government, the Wildlife Federation," he says. "If it wasn't for that everybody around here would have a cypress house."

Legend has it that before the turn of the century, when the area around what became Midnight was mostly swamp, the town founder won a deed to the territory in a late-night card game with a group of hunters. When the hand was done the victor looked at his watch, saw it was midnight, and said, "That's what I'm going to call this place." He built the first house on the spot of the card game. Now Midnight is pretty much empty, a victim of progress. The little gin and cotton press was put out of business by a more modern and efficient facility miles away. The plantation store and related businesses closed when the plantation's need for labor diminished, and when the remaining laborers found they could shop more cheaply in Belzoni. The train station closed when the train stopped running. Now they have even torn up the tracks. There are only two nice houses: one is occupied by the overseer for the Box plantation, the other by the agent for the Robert Harris plantation. What was once the town's fanciest residence now stands derelict and abandoned, its porch falling in. The little row of stores by the railroad track that was actually the "town" is shut down. Where the plantation store used to be, now only a small plantation office remains open. So what is the interesting part? That the town was won in a poker game, made fortunes for a half a dozen, and was all of life for generations of hard-working people.

"All the big plantations in the state of Mississippi is owned by somebody in the North," Tiny opines, looking over the empty storefronts. "All the big plants are, too. Most of them originally are from the North. The older generation came down and stayed years and years, but the younger generation went back North."

He carries us to a little row of "old-fashioned" cypress-plank houses out past Midnight. "They ain't got no rooms on the side. They just go straight through. That's the old shotgun house. A lot of these big farmers have moved these old cypress farmhouses into their backyards, you know." This little line of old houses, and a few others like it, were all that remained of the type of plantation living that I remembered so well from 1968, the clusters of listing structures full of children and animals that used to give life to the farms, and at the end a look of horrible poverty. This small community had the lived-in appearance I was familiar with: the ash pile, the clothes hanging on the lines, the beat-up tractor in the back yard. Some little children came out to be sure they would get into Patty's photographs. Their parents are day workers, Tiny says. They earn the minimum wage and free rent, but even these people, says Tiny, are not so dependent on the farmer anymore. "People here have learned better than to go up there and pay two dollars a pound for baloney when you can go up to Belzoni to one of those chain stores and get it for ninety-nine cents a pound. When people got transportation and cars they put those little stores like in Midnight out of business." It is a fair guess that the price of that independence is that the landowner no longer pays his workers' medical bills.

The planters' lives have changed, too. "Money is tight for whites," says Tiny. "It's not like it used to be. Farming hasn't been too good. They've lost for the last four or five years. They're hard workers, most of them. They stay on it, out in the sun. They take a beating, too. It got to the place where a farmer couldn't no longer lay up in the bed all day and have the work go on and he could make money

Tenant farmer homes, C. B. Box plantation, Midnight

at the end of the year. He's paying $85,000 for a naked tractor, maybe $100,000 for a tractor, with nothing to go to it, it takes a lot of money. Now you take one of those cotton pickers costs $95,000, and it just works two months out of the year. It's setting up the rest of the time. Some of 'em own four and five of 'em and more. It takes a lot of money. When they could work a person for two dollars and a half a day from sunup to sundown, they didn't have to pay for nothing but the fertilizer. Labor wasn't nothing. Labor made the change. You can't hardly work these folks for the minimum wage anymore. They want more."

We drive past a couple of young men out hunting for rabbits, walking down the road with rifles on their shoulders, and Tiny ruminates about his own move to town. "As the years go by, the further we get away from the country. When I first lived in Belzoni I'd be down here every two days, then every three days. As the years go by it got to be weeks and then months and then every couple of months. Now it's once or twice a year." We get to Louise, passing combines working miles of soybeans, and I observe that the town has a new water tower. Tiny informs me that it was purchased with a block grant from the federal government. In this area you can see a great many federal programs at work, and I am amazed at how much Tiny knows about them—certainly far more than I do.

We pause in the deserted downtown section of Louise. The planting company store is closed, though the plantation office is still open. The commercial enterprises consist of Lee Hong's grocery and a movie video store. The one-room jailhouse built of granite blocks still stands next to the old cotton gin, a monument to some very hard times in the rugged past. Tiny says, "There'd be hollering in there when I was a small boy."

Tiny points out the spot in the street where Rainey Poole was killed. I had interviewed Rainey in 1968, and I remembered him as a particularly angry and self-reliant sort of man. He had gotten his arm cut off in a "truck side-swipe," but he was still valued as a tractor driver. It was obvious that he relished his ability to survive and support a family despite this handicap. There is so little traffic today that I was able to stop the car on the street and let Patty get out. While she photographed the scene, Tiny and I watched a white and a black girl walking together down the street. Tiny remarked that the white woman has a black husband. "In the old days," he commented, "they'd have run her off and they'd have hung him in that tree there."

"All right, that first post on the end down there." He points at the very spot. "That's where they beat Rainey's brains out against that post. His cap they throwed on top of the liquor store, that little building right over there. The FBI, I don't know who told 'em, got a ladder and climbed on top of that liquor store. They got his cap and put it in a plastic bag. That's the joint he went into right there. It's closed now. There were seventeen of 'em in that joint. All seventeen of 'em came out and had a party. The man who owned the liquor store he was sitting on the porch looking at it . . . He said they beat Rainey because he went in that white joint. And then they said different things. There was more to it. He was probably acting the fool. But they didn't know him. The man he worked for, if they had sent for him, he would have come got him. Whiskey . . . They throwed him in the Sunflower River. They killed him here and wrapped him up in a plastic paper and carried him right up to the Sunflower River.

"The man he worked for got the FBI out of Georgia. Wouldn't even use the Mississippi state FBI. He paid for 'em to come in here. He hired 'em. He said that body's going to be found, and they found it. They carried all seventeen of 'em to jail. They got a bond, but there was a mistrial."

We stopped down the street at the one establishment that seems to be thriving in Louise, a convenience market and gas station run by Arvell Bullock. He is the newly elected beat supervisor from Louise, and he is black. Before his election he drove a school bus. He wears a camouflage hunting cap and jacket, the working man's uniform across Mississippi, and moderates over a steady flow of talk while ringing up Pepsis and chewing tobacco and cigarettes behind his counter. He is pleased to let us take his picture but he will not sign a release for its publication. Tiny introduces me around as the "civil rights worker" who used to live here. Some remember and reintroduce themselves. They also remember that the "Catholics" began sending lots of old clothes to Louise after I left, and someone remarked that the Catholics had quit doing that when "abortion heated up" and how they now give all their money to that cause.

Down the road is the old Negro lodge hall that served as the Friends of the Children Head Start Center when I first came to Louise. Amazingly it is still in use, now as a church. Across the street, in the fork of the road created by the old highway and the new bypass, is a grassy park which, according to its sign, was built by the National Park Service of the Department of the Interior. I wonder how on earth the government decided to landscape this particular spot in Louise. It appeared to be named for the grocery store proprietor and supervisor, Mr. Bullock, indicating who snagged the bucks.

Tiny is thoroughly enjoying playing tour conductor. He says it is a relief from the confines of his job. "The job I got now keeps me indoors too much. I always like to get out and fight for a lot of people. I reckon I started out that way and that's what I love." I am starting to get tired, but he wants to show me what the plantation homes look like today. We drive out onto the Bill Dillard plantation, where there is a row of brick homes for the farm workers, and then onto the H. M. Love plantation. On this place is the Love Feast M. B. Baptist Church where I first spoke in Louise and was introduced to the community twenty years ago. We pause here for a while and walk around looking at the headstones. The cemetery is very well kept. Noah Guider is buried here, as is Rainey Poole. I look for the grave of Jenny Poole, the elderly widow with whom I had boarded. We find the stones of her husband, Peter Poole, and her neighbor Precious Poole, but I cannot find Mrs. Poole.

The church is still in use. Tiny says, "They preach according to how they feel. When I came to church out here it was according to how the old folks feel and what hit them. We would stay here all day, preaching and singing all day." I told him I remembered them also dancing on the Sunday morning I had spoken there, and he said, "They do like James Brown," a reference to a Blues Brothers' video he has at home. By one grave Tiny says, "I knew that boy well. He went to Chicago and started living in the fast lane."

I mention that Tiny's first wife, Collie, had told me the story of her own conversion. When she was a young girl of about twelve she went out in the woods with the idea of staying until she got the sign. After two or three days without food or company, she did in fact get it. She came back to the house and joined the church. Tiny says, "I never could get no religion like that. I never felt like I had religion till I got to be a grown man. Because I never did see those signs. I just couldn't picture it. Then I just made up my mind that I wanted to live according to the Bible. I don't call myself an upright man. But I've never been a whiskey drinker or much on going out. I've always been dedicated to my family." He and Christine admire Jimmy Swaggart, because they believe he helped starving kids in Africa. They send him ten dollars several times a year. They tried to like Jim and Tammy, but with all that make-up it was evident that they were not "sanctified." Christine is sanctified and goes to a church that is big on tambourines and singing, but strict on dress. She was recently put on probation for three months for having long fingernails.

Thinking back on his first marriage he says, "I'm older now. A lot of things I went through with Collie my heart wouldn't be able to take now. I learned to evaluate a lot of things. You come to know what means something to you and what don't mean nothing to you." Between marriages he had lived by himself in Belzoni for almost ten years. Of that period he says that "it was miserable. I wouldn't lie to you. A lot of people say they enjoy it, but it was miserable. You meet all these pretty girls and date 'em and after the show's over with, or after the dance is over with, you go home and she goes home and nobody but you in the room. Television. You get up and meet a strange girl tomorrow and she goes back to Winona or she goes back to Chicago or wherever. You get a letter from her. You don't see her no more. It wasn't no future in it for me. I had to have me another family."

We drive onto another plantation, and Tiny points out a big cultivator parked near the gravel road. "See that thing there, it's eight rows. That's eight-row equipment there. That thing will do what four men used to do. Just one tractor. They used to have two-row, then four-row equipment. They moved from that to six-row, then up to eight-row. So it don't take but a few men. They don't hoe no more. They use chemicals. The ladies don't hoe, don't nobody hoe no more. Now that tractor can do a hundred and twenty to a hundred and forty acres a day, plant, disk, or whatever you want, in one pass."

We go by a little house off to the side of the gravel road, and Tiny suddenly remembers that this is where Rainey Poole lived when he got killed. "See, I been away so long it takes a little while to bring this back to me," he says. It was at that house that I had interviewed Rainey Poole one night in the autumn of 1968, though we had then reached it by an old trail that ran between the house and the creek. The "state aid" road on which we are now riding was not even in existence at the time. The farmer has planted over the old road, and there are now large bean bins by Poole's house. Tiny points across the road to a white house and says, "That's the man they say really done the killing. He was the one done the beating. That's who actually beat him and shot him. He stayed right in that white house there. He was a plantation mechanic." I remind Tiny that he had told me that the killers had not known Rainey, and the version of the story he now told was a little different.

"They say what really the cause was, the reason him and Rainey had the run-in, I think I told you before, they said he was courting Rainey's daughter—this white dude was. They say Rainey went up in there to get his daughter out from up there where they was. And that's what all that was started about. That's where he stayed. They was just about neighbors. He's still alive, but he can't stay in this county. All seventeen of 'em was in this. And they either got in financial trouble, they're sick, or dead, the whole seventeen. Looks like it just brought some kind of curse upon them."

We take a trip back to where Mrs. Jenny Poole lived, the first place I had stayed in Louise. I remember her as a kind, tidy woman, a good cook, and a stern disciplinarian to her twelve-year-old grandson. Together they tended the garden, chickens, and hogs out in back of their neat white cottage. The most out-and-out fun I had had that trip was a completely uncoordinated attempt by Mrs. Poole, her grandson, and me to capture a pig in her fenced-in back yard. The object was to get the pig, which must have weighed eighty pounds, and tie it to a tree, but it raced at top speed from one side of the little yard to the other while the boy and I chased and dove for it and Mrs. Poole yelled directions at us all the time swinging at the pig with her broom. Finally I think it was she who pinned it against the fence with her knee and broom and the two of us, far dirtier and more exhausted than the pig, who wrestled it to the ground. "This is where you used to slip in and slip out," said Tiny. "Back then, we thought we could hide you back here better than anywhere else. Then we went back and reconsidered at the Head Start center. They say,

'That's a shame, all you men here and that widow lady has got more nerve than you have, taking in that boy.' "

But much has changed since then, says Tiny, again. "You used to call the Ku Klux Klan's name twenty-five years ago and it would make my heart skip a beat. Now it seems like you would say, 'We're gonna chew some bubble gum.' Because I realize now that they got to get to you, and there ain't many of 'em no more. They really don't exist. The Ku Klux Klan hasn't got no power anymore. A thirteen-cent shotgun shell will kill him just like anybody else. About twenty years ago all of 'em here then was Klan members. All the rich ones, they didn't want nobody knowing what they were doing. They was Klan members, but they didn't do no dirty work. They had it done. The rich people were more concerned about black people not voting and having Head Start to learn something than the poor was. The poor ones was doing the dirty work for the rich ones.

"Now people don't want trouble out of one another. They don't want conflict with one another. It ain't like it used to be. You say something, the man didn't like it, say if he was white, he'd go get two or three more and they'd come and publicly beat you up or run you away from your family. That don't exist no more. So I'd have to say the nature of people has changed here in the Delta. You can see that. You don't see any restaurant doors say white only. You don't see no restrooms at service stations now say white only.

"But now, it's bad to say, but this is the bottom line. Everything that was done for black people in the state of Mississippi that was worthwhile was done through a federal court order. It was a federal court order that built houses that came up to the qualifications of the standard of living. Things is a hundred percent better than it was, but it was a federal court order that did it."

Passing through the Box plantation, Tiny points out two of the old-style tenant houses left standing where once there was a row of eight or ten. These are elderly folks, he explains, who are allowed to stay on as long as they want so long as they keep up the house and pay for their own gas and electricity. Both structures are what Tiny calls the "bungalow" style: a high-peaked tin roof over a square of two rooms in front, two rooms in the rear, and a porch. These were a step up from a shotgun house, he says, and, with a builder's eye, he says that the high roof design was a waste of lumber, most of it

Plantation homes in Humphreys County

cypress. The bean fields crowd the houses closely, but both still have a little garden plot. "They lucky to have that," he remarks. A lot of people still work on this plantation; the farm is about six thousand acres in size. Most of the people live on the place in brick homes of various sizes "according to the size of the family." These newer houses have indoor toilets and running water. Tiny again shows that he is on top of the federal programs. This water system, he says was put in with a loan from the Farmers Home Administration. Every homeowner paid something down and now pays a monthly bill for his water line. The water tower for the system was erected at Midnight.

Back on U.S. 49 driving toward Belzoni we stop for a minute to look at a red-brick school building, circa 1960. Now that the public schools are consolidated in the county seat, it is the site of the Riven Oaks Head Start Center, part of the Friends of the Children of Mississippi system, now in fifteen counties. FCM was founded in 1966 when the federal Office of Economic Opportunity capitulated to pressure from Mississippi politicians and terminated the "radical" Head Start program administered by the Child Development Group of Mississippi (CDGM). CDGM was replaced in Humphreys County by a program controlled by local whites called Mississippi Action for Progress. The former CDGM Head Start women refused to go along with the restructuring, however, and organized Friends of the Children of Mississippi. For eighteen months, a time of trial still remembered by the oldsters in the county, the FCM centers operated without federal funds, supported at subsistence level largely by the Field Foundation. The centers functioned in ramshackle churches, abandoned school buildings, and, as in Louise, converted lodge halls. Finally in 1968 FCM picked up federal OEO backing for centers in four counties. Over the past twenty years what was called "radical" has become institutional, and FCM has been given old county school buildings like this one.

So many of the generation of twenty years ago came to Head Start with swollen bellies, distended navels, and dull eyes. Overcoming malnutrition and parasites were the program's immediate tasks. That first generation is now leaving college or the service and making its way into the mainstream of life. Some of them are working in catfish plants. It cannot be said that they have made it yet, but by and large any of their children who are now entering Head Start at least have a nutritional foundation and a weather-tight home that makes growing and learning possible. Kids are now brought in by yellow school buses rather than by pickup truck. There are, however, fewer children to serve today, and the tenor of the program has shifted away from gut-level survival to the three Rs. The true impact of this one lasting Great Society program will be measured in the progress of the children now beginning.

We take pictures of the Riven Oaks School, but without the children around—it's Saturday—you would have to know something about the place to find it interesting. The same is true of the dirt trail that branches off into the surrounding bean field and stops at three distant trees. "They were here when you were here," says Tiny, meaning the three houses and the three families that once went with the trees.

Approaching Belzoni he comments, "I still don't like Belzoni. I'm a country boy. But I can't get Christine to go back to the country. She don't want to go where she'll get her car muddy and dust come in her house." We drive up on the immense new bridge that rises in a perfect half-orb above the Yazoo River and provides a nice view of the courthouse in downtown Belzoni. "This is something big for this county," says Tiny. "They say they just put this bridge here because this is the catfish capital of the world. I reckon it's the only thing attractive they could put here." The bridge is high enough to afford passage to an Exxon oil tanker, but the Yazoo River is only deep and wide enough to handle a grain barge. It is difficult to comprehend the bridge's purpose, but there is no danger of its ever washing away in a flood. A tornado might get it, but if the Delta is ever inundated by the one-hundred-year flood predicted by the Army Corps of Engineers, it is to this bridge that I would flee.

As this odd and enjoyable day comes to a close, Tiny talks about his own metamorphosis from a farmer and a mechanic to a warehouseman. Credit goes to Christine, he says, who got him to quit his fourteen-hour-a-day job as a farm equipment mechanic and get a job with the school system. For a year and a half, when she got home from the Jockey plant, she would drive him to school every night where he was taught the fundamentals of "management" and how to operate a computer. He was guaranteed the warehouse job when he graduated, and he did graduate. This is, in a small way, what equal opportunity has meant in the Delta. The benefits of working for the school system are good, and a stable family life is possible, but there is a price to progress. "Staying in the office, that's what gets me. It feels so good to get out. Being cooped up in that office sometimes five hours at a time, I'm back behind that desk, ooh, it just gets boring. You know that's week in and week out. Taking the inventory, it isn't hard to do. It's just counting them little ol' items. Then you have to go back and make a check. Sometimes you have to go back and make another check to be sure it's accurate. It's aggravating. All them items like teaspoons and forks, plastic forks, and all that. All those little ol' items like pepper and salt, plus the meat, just all those little items. It gets to be a headache." I can sympathize.

five

SANCTIFIED

▲▲▲

Things didn't seem to be coming along too well in the
Delta. On Saturdays we would spend all day canvassing
and often at night we would have mass rallies. But
these were usually poorly attended. Many Negroes
were afraid to come. In the beginning some were even
afraid to talk to us. Most of these old plantation
Negroes had been brainwashed so by the whites, they
really thought that only whites were supposed to vote.
There were even a few who had never heard of voting.
The only thing most of them knew was how to handle a
hoe. For years they had demonstrated how well they
could do that. Some of them had calluses on their
hands so thick they would hide them if they noticed
you looking at them.
—Anne Moody, *Coming of Age in Mississippi*

T hough its embers still glow and some say burn, the civil rights
movement in Mississippi is now venerable enough to be historic, complete with reunions, banquets, and awards. A town like
Greenwood has as much history to celebrate, though recent, as any
site of a Civil War campaign. Greenwood calls itself the Cotton
Capital of the world, and its still-thriving cotton exchange has traditionally been rivaled only by Memphis as the largest cotton market
in America. It is the seat of Leflore County; both town and county
are named for Greenwood Le Flore, the half-Acadian, half-Indian
negotiator for the Choctaws at the treaty of Dancing Rabbit Creek.
He presided over the cession of Choctaw lands to the whites and
removal of the tribe to Oklahoma, but he stayed behind to acquire

15,000 acres and hundreds of slaves. He served in the state senate between 1840 and 1844.

Leflore County has always had, since it was created, a majority black population. The fourteen-year-old Emmett Till was kidnapped here in 1955, beaten up, shot, tied to a gin gear, and dropped into the Tallahatchie River. The men who confessed to his abduction denied the murder and were acquitted in about an hour. Seven years later, in the summer of 1962, Sam Block, Willie Peacock, Lawrence Guyot, and Luvaughn Brown, young activists with the Student Nonviolent Coordinating Committee (SNCC), began a voter registration campaign in Greenwood. Shortly thereafter the county board of supervisors stopped distributing surplus commodities to 22,000 county residents. As winter progressed SNCC launched a nationwide campaign to obtain donated food, and its arrival brought hundreds of people to the Freedom House in Greenwood to get food and to try to register to vote. In the midst of this, a civil rights worker named Jimmy Travis was seriously wounded by automatic weapon fire outside of town. Byron de la Beckwith, the man accused of killing Medgar Evers, made his home in Greenwood, and it was here he returned to live after his acquittal. Stokely Carmichael spent time in the Greenwood campaign. Now the Greenwood Voters League, instrument of black power even before SNCC workers focused on that city in 1962, has an annual banquet. There you can see that the civil rights struggle has progressed, or at least that it has dramatically changed.

The festivities were held last year at the Leflore County Civic Center, and about six hundred people came to meet Toni Seawright, Mississippi's first black Miss Mississippi. Seawright was introduced by Alice Harden of Jackson, the state's first female state senator. The sign of the times was that about half a dozen white candidates for statewide office and just about every local white politician also attended. White and black flesh was pressed together.

There are similar events dotting the Delta calendar. Howard Taft Bailey was given a banquet at the Holmes County College cafeteria to honor his retirement from the county board of supervisors in 1987. Holmes County was the birthplace of the White Citizens Council in Mississippi. Mr. Bailey was a field worker for the Federation of Southern Cooperatives, and he was elected to the Holmes County

Cypress Park Elementary singers perform "This Land Is Your Land" at the October Fest in Cleveland

Board of Election Commissioners in 1968 when such a position was a lightning rod for violent opposition. He was chairman of the Holmes County Freedom Democratic Party from 1966 to 1972, and was ultimately elected to the county board of supervisors. In 1980 he was elevated to president of the board, highest ranking job in the county, and he kept that office until he retired. His generation is now passing.

The University of Mississippi now presents a Distinguished Black Mississippian Award. In 1988 those recognized were Robert Clark, the state's first black congressman; the Most Reverend Joseph Howze of Mobile, the first black bishop to head a Catholic diocese in the United States; country music great Charlie Pride, who is from Sledge, Mississippi, in Quitman County; and state Deputy Attorney General Robert Gibbs. The posthumous award was given to Fannie Lou Hamer, the lady famed for saying that she was, "sick and tired of being sick and tired." Mrs. Hamer, a sharecropper from Sunflower County, had run against arch-segregationist congressman Jamie Whitten despite the fact that almost no blacks could then vote. She was an active SNCC worker in Ruleville and a chief organizer of the Freedom Democratic Party in Mississippi. Now she, too, is in the history books, and for several years the Mississippi NAACP has given an award in her honor. Another sign that the emphasis of black struggle has changed is that in 1987 the Fannie Lou Hamer award went to Dr. McKinley Martin, president of Coahoma Junior College, who is noted less for his activism than for his contributions to education and to business development. His credentials include activity on behalf of the county industrial foundation, his presidency of Delta Wire (a supplier for Goodyear Tire and Rubber Company), and his efforts to create new jobs and attract new industry to the area.

While they may be history now, the images of race hatred that Mississippi presented in the 1960s are still remembered around the world. Arun Gandhi, the grandson of Mahatma Gandhi, and his wife Sunanda spent much of 1988 at Ole Miss working on a study comparing prejudice in Mississippi to that in South Africa. Mr. Gandhi said that he hoped his work might spur what he called the stalled American civil rights movement into motion. In frequent speeches around the state he pointed out that while whites and blacks now vote, go to school, and work together in Mississippi, they still do not socialize much. True enough, but it was perhaps an overstatement to tell a _Los Angeles Times_ reporter: "There is no real integration. Whites have taken a hard position; blacks are taking a hard position. There is no dialogue between them. Tensions are building and confrontations are inevitable. . . . The Mississippi Delta is a very sorry situation. You see these white plantation owners in their big mansions and right next to them are black people who work for them living in shacks that are ready to fall apart." That is a little irritating. The Delta has never had that many white mansions, and few of those still standing are occupied anymore. There are shacks, to be sure, but nothing to compare to the sixties. If Mr. Gandhi wants to see mansions where the white paint is fresh, he might better look in the suburbs of Memphis where people with real money live.

Something else he might see in Memphis is the Lorraine Motel, where Dr. King was shot. It is now undergoing an $8.8 million conversion into a civil rights museum. King, too, is history now, and he is widely honored in Mississippi. Highways have been named for him in Jackson, Tupelo, and many other towns. His birthday is celebrated with gospel singings, church services, school closings, in plays, and in commemorative advertisements for McDonald's hamburgers and Jitney Jungle supermarkets carried in newspapers throughout the state. Congressman Mike Espy raises King's memory when he admonishes young listeners to take the stairs to success, "study and cut off that television." Mr. Gandhi is simply wrong if he believes that the images and the reality of race relations have not changed in the past twenty years.

One day in the summertime I drove with Tiny Brown to downtown Belzoni so that I could renew an old acquaintance with Ernest White, who runs the Humphreys County Union for Progress and had just, at age seventy-seven, been elected city alderman, and Pearl Carpenter, one of the women who came out of the plantations to set up Friends of the Children of Mississippi. Tiny again commented as we went through town that "when you was up here working, I couldn't drive with you in the daytime. They expect it now."

Mr. White is what Tiny refers to as one of the "godfathers" of the community. He was one of the first to try to register to vote in the 1950s. When NAACP leader Gus Courts was shot in Belzoni in November 1955, Ernest White picked him off the sidewalk and drove him to Indianola to get medical attention. Court's predecessor as NAACP president, the Reverend George Lee, had been shot and killed while driving his car outside of town in May 1955. Alderman White recalls, "That was when they still had the power and could do like they wanted to. They killed Reverend Lee. When Courts was shot he had a little store here on Church Street. Somebody passed with a shotgun at night and blasted him through the store window. Because he was active in civil rights. He was a threat to them. Reverend Lee was the president of the NAACP. He was shot right here in Belzoni. After he was killed, Mr. Courts became president of the NAACP. So they just figured he was the leader. Get the leader, scatter the bunch.

"T. V. Johnson, he had the funeral home down here. We was all in the truck together. We organized the NAACP and started together. T. V. called me that night and told me to go down to Gus's store because something had happened. He was a leader, too. He thought it was a trap set up for him. So I went out to the store there, and when I got there people were all out in the streets, white and black. So I went up there and saw what happened to Gus and put him in the car. Myself, Red Baker, and my son. We got a shotgun and we got a rifle. We took him to Indianola. They had called from city hall and told us to prepare to bring him there, but we felt like they would finish him off. So we went and took him on in to Indianola to Dr. Battle's office, a black physician. He's still living as far as I know. He looked him over and advised us to rush him to Mound Bayou. That's where we took him that night. He survived that attack and went to Chicago. He never did fully recover from it. That kind of stopped the NAACP here for a spell."

I asked Mr. White what difference the election of black officials would make in a city like Belzoni, and he said, "Economically you won't see any change. Politically you will have some clout there. You'll be looking out for the good of the community. You'll be looking out for equal opportunity for people who have been denied equal opportunity. That'll help some." He is, in other words, cautious about what black officials can accomplish, but he expects them to look out for black interests.

I asked whether or not the young people appreciate the struggles of the old, and he says, "I don't know. Sometimes I don't think they know what's happened. They haven't had the experience. They have the educational ability, but they just haven't had the experience."

Mrs. Carpenter recalls her own early battles. Three civil rights workers lived in Belzoni, she says, Willie Ware, a boy named Johnny, and one whose name she has forgotten. Willie Ware got her to register to vote. She was a maid at city hall then, and she was fired. "I wasn't getting but twenty dollars a month. But they fired me 'cause I was a civil rights worker. They got all our names on the record. All the civil rights workers. They know all about you, your name's on the record, you can believe that."

Still? Maybe so, says Tiny. He points out that the names of all the black people who registered in the 1960s are kept on the "federal book" down at the courthouse. These are the people who registered right after the Voting Rights Act passed. Those who come to register today sign a separate book. Mrs. Carpenter's story is not finished. "I was with the Friends of the Children of Mississippi. CDGM didn't have enough money for the county, so they closed Humphreys County out. But we kept our children together. We never did let them go. We worked eighteen months for nothing. What little money we got was from the Field Foundation. We was getting thirty dollars every two or three weeks. We begged money. We all donated what we could, whatever we could do."

This story is interrupted by the arrival of the school superintendent, Lonnie Haynes, and his wife, who have come by out of politeness to meet me on their way to a superintendents' conference in Jackson. The election of Haynes, a former band teacher, six years ago was one of the first accomplishments of the black electorate of the county. After his departure, Tiny remarks, "It makes me feel like my putting my life on the line wasn't in vain when I see these black elected officials."

I ask him whether during the days of the civil right struggle the schoolteachers contributed much, and he says, "Most of the schoolteachers were afraid to participate. They were afraid of losing their jobs. If they done anything for us they done it under the table. Their job was on the line and everything they had was pinned on the job. A lot of the people was poor, like Pearl, and didn't have much to lose, or people who were independent like my folks who was already established. By me working it wasn't going to hurt my folks. Folks like teachers, you didn't get no assistance from. They came forward after the gun wouldn't fire."

Mrs. Carpenter adds, "They came forward after the door was open. When you was fighting even to get to the door it was kind of hard to get people out. They was afraid of losing their job. If they lived on a plantation they was afraid of moving. Then they wouldn't have anywhere to live."

"Our people, they forgets too quick," interjects Mr. White. His project is affiliated with the Greenville-based Mississippi Action for Community Education (MACE), and he describes the MACE program that began in the seventies. "They came in and tried to start some economic development among blacks. One time we had a co-op back here. Sold fertilizer, cottonseed, chemicals, and things to the black farmers. Ain't no black farmers farming here now. The object was to build up our economic base for black people in the community where they could help themselves. Under MACE we got a grant from—let me think—Cummings Engine, to put this building up. We built the building and everything." Now they have bought two nearby houses which they are in the process of renovating, and they have plans to build twenty-two units for the elderly in a year or so. The Humphreys County Union for Progress is a membership organization, charging five dollars annual dues. Once a month a lawyer from Greenwood Rural Legal Services comes to advise any members who drop in. "They mostly bring it here and we try to help 'em thrash it out," says Mr. White. I asked if the people of Belzoni are still as interested as they once were in this type of program. "I would say no," he says. "They'll come here for assistance, but having a firm commitment to it like they had when it first started, when the civil rights first started, I don't think they're as dedicated to it now as they once were.

"I guess we forget. You get out and get a chance at the job opportunities and that has a tendency to make you a little bit more independent. People have better jobs now. We've got people in the banks and whatnot, different agencies now, that they weren't working on then. So they can get more independent. And naturally they won't be quite as enthusiastic about it as when they first started. It kind of grew old and kind of went away. You've got people working here now, you know, as supervisors. You got people working in the welfare department who didn't used to get it. You got people working in the bank."

Tiny adds, "It's like the NAACP. People in Mississippi don't feel like they need the NAACP like they once did. They ain't got a strong membership in the state of Mississippi like there used to be. Folks don't know."

And Pearl Carpenter says, "Before, we was afraid to even walk out the door. And coming to a program, a building like this to educate and let us know we could go out there and could get out and vote, well, people were afraid. We learned we could elect anybody we wanted. We could go in any store we wanted to. It gave us strength. And now we are independent. So I still feel proud of it. You know if they don't come in like they should and participate in the meetings and things, you still know you've done a good job."

Mr. White believes that some old problems still persist. "We've got some good candidates. If you could get the people to give them proper support, then we could win. You know a lot of blacks are still kind of reluctant. You take out on some of these plantations, they wouldn't stop doing what they're doing today if it was the day of the election, even if the man might let 'em get off. He probably would let them off, but a lot of 'em just won't go. They won't insist on going down there. So you got a lot to overcome yet. Then some got that 'don't care' feeling. 'I don't care what happens.' They can't see nothing has changed."

"We come a long ways, and we got a long ways to go," says Carpenter.

POND LIFE

▲▲▲

Mississippi Catfish Time

Have you ever been catfish cooking on a sunny day?
Everybody is sitting and looking, looking over this way.
Bring on the cornmeal, boys, and roll it good and
then . . .
We're gonna tell ya'll where that good eatings at.
Just smell that catfish cooking in the frying pan.
Get a load of ole' Willie. He's a real catfish man.
Hushpuppies and french fries. We get can't get enough.
When all the ladies are cooking that sure 'nuff good
stuff.
(Chorus) Oh it's Mississippi catfish.
Honey don't you just wish you had a plate right now.
Going down south, it will melt in your mouth.
Mr. Catfish take a bow.

—David Hall, songwriter (famous for "The Ballad of
Buford Pusser")

I was introduced firsthand to the catfish business by Ernest ▽▽▽ White. As we sat in his Humphreys County Union for Progress office discussing changes he had seen, the talk shifted to the new catfish plants. I mentioned that I had never been in one. "Do you want to go?" he asked brightly. He had not been inside one himself and plainly enjoyed the thought of escorting me to the Delta Pride plant located just outside the town limits. He was sure they would let us in, since he is now a person of some importance, but it was a sort of test run. As we approached the gate, we discussed con-

spiratorially how I was to be introduced and decided it would be best
to say frankly that I was writing a book about the South. It worked.
After the guard at the gate announced that Mr. White, a writer, and
Tiny Brown were there requesting a tour, the manager himself came
out and made us welcome.

I had seen classy ads for Mississippi farm-raised catfish in airline
magazines ("Think of it as a chicken that doesn't cluck"), but it
certainly surprised me to learn that in 1988, in Sunflower County,
Mississippi, the very heart of the Delta, catfish was the biggest crop
and that old King Cotton came in second. I had no clear idea how
you raised a catfish on a farm, but I have since found out. I have also
learned that the catfish industry has managed what the cotton industry never could—to get the processor into the Delta. Whereas for
a century the textile industry steadfastly resisted all enticements to
build plants near the cotton patch, catfish processing plants have
sprung up all over the Delta, making it not just the largest producer
of fish but also the largest packer of filets.

To date, the industry is essentially a local enterprise, distinguished from most Mississippi businesses in that it is not entirely
dependent on capital from outside of the state. Nearly 50 percent of
the catfish raised in the country is produced by Delta Catfish Processors under the name "Delta Pride," and this is only one of several
major catfish processors in the Delta. Stock in Delta Pride is entirely
owned, or so I was told, by some 166 farmers in proportion to the
number of acres of catfish ponds each operates. Delta Pride's farmers
own about 56,000 acres of ponds, which is about 87 square miles of
inland sea. How is that sea created? It is not hard to divide flat,
square cotton fields into shallow, square fishponds that look for all
the world like multipaned windows from the air, using land-leveling
equipment, big "Ukes" left over from the flat-earth movement of the
1960s.

A lot of the Delta has been put back under water to raise the 280
million or so pounds of catfish now sold each year. This is a big
business, but it has its pitfalls. Feeding so many fish at the rate of
150 pounds of food per acre per day is a bigger chore than slopping
the hogs, and it calls for mechanical food blowers to saturate the
water surface with what catfish like to eat. Basically they enjoy
soybean meal, and producing that from the local harvest has given

another important boost to the Delta economy. To get something to eat, these catfish swim to the top, reversing a millennium of genetic coding that tells catfish to feed off the bottom of the creek.

Then there is stress. Living in a square acre pond with five thousand other fish is stressful enough, but any major prolonged temperature shift, which is not that uncommon in the wide Delta plain, can send whole populations of fish belly-up, a prospect that causes more than enough stress to the farmer as well.

Another problem is water loss, but no one seems to have successfully tackled this one. The average catfish pond requires 60 million gallons of water to fill and 40 million gallons a year to operate. With new ponds being built at a rate of three hundred per year, ground-water levels have dropped as much as nine feet in some areas because of pumping. It seems odd, in an area where so much money is invested in draining water off the land and pumping it into the Mississippi River, that there should be a ground-water shortage. Obviously, there is a problem of coordinating technologies (and in fact, some scientists have suggested trying to pump water from the four reservoirs on the Delta rim into the ground to replenish the aquifer, rather than flush it out toward the sea). One partial solution is to use Mississippi's own claylike mud zeolites to filter out the ammonium buildup in pond water and thereby reduce the amount of water used to clean and replenish the ponds. If only there were a way to keep acres of water from evaporating in the July sunshine, then the entire problem would be solved.

Since raising catfish requires land, few blacks participate in this profitable end of the business. As far as black processors, I know of only one, Edward Scott of Minter City who runs Pond Fresh Catfish. It is a medium-size operation with a 50,000 pounds per day filet capability that employs about seventy-five workers. By contrast, the plant I visited in Belzoni, which is not the largest in the Delta by any means, is designed to process up to 225,000 pounds per day. Blacks do, however, make up most of the work force in the processing plants. These plants, which are now big employers at Indianola, Isola, Belzoni, Inverness, Greenwood, Hollandale, and Tippo, are sparkling clean, freezer-cooled, fast-paced operations where squads of hairnetted workers wearing yellow slickers face fish by the ton.

The fish themselves go from flopping in a pool to fileted and frozen in a matter of minutes.

Much of the work on the lines is monotonous and obviously governed by the stopwatch, since each stage of the operation, the beheading, skinning, slicing, and freezing of the *poisson du chat,* is carefully regulated to keep the line moving on schedule. Time-and-motion experts design these plants. For instance, fish are eviscerated at the rate of fifteen per minute before being sorted into one of fourteen size categories and whacked into filets and nuggets (the "belly flaps"). There is, however, no fish smell in the air; the entire atmosphere is cool and efficient. In these respects it strikes the visitor as very dissimilar from the Delta world outside, where heat promotes lassitude and leisure, and farmwork promotes irregularity of lifestyle.

There is perpetual activity in these plants; they are also quite colorful. Bright orange bins and hampers of fish and ice are pushed across glistening white floors by black men covered in sky-blue aprons and white hairnets with bright yellow plugs in their ears. Stainless steel and ice are everywhere, as are computer-driven weighers and sorters and strange devices, like a machine that jabs 241 needles full of "shelf-life extender" (sodium tripolyphosphate and lemon juice) into passing fish. It looks like nothing so much as an immense operating theater in a hospital where the patients are quite small and plentiful and are not expected to survive the attention.

That scientific sense is present in a variety of aspects. Before a farmer may bring his product to Delta Pride, for example, he must present samples for testing one and three days beforehand. The main tester is Stanley Marshall, whose style is simply to microwave the whole fish for a minute or two and then fork out a bite. Methylisoborneol and geosmin are all a whiff of off-flavor to him, and he routinely rejects 50 to 70 percent of the hundreds of samples he evaluates weekly. Those farmers either lose a sale or they must fiddle with their pond water until the fish can pass the test.

The pay for plant workers is not that great. At the new Mississippi Farm Raised Catfish plant in Itta Bena, for example, employees make $3.35 to $3.65 per hour in 1988, though the company says they can make up to $2.00 per hour more based on their performance.

Sorting catfish nuggets, Delta Pride catfish plant, Indianola

This base is about what farmworkers and supermarket cashiers make, and there is really very little industrial competition. The federal minimum wage sets the prevailing wage rate in the Delta. There has been a moderately successful organizing campaign among catfish workers by the United Food and Commercial Workers Union based locally in Memphis. Its lead organizer in the Delta is Bobby Moses, not the same as Robert Moses, organizer in the early days of SNCC. The first plant to be organized was Farm Fresh Catfish in Hollandale in 1985. Since then the union has won representation elections at the Pride of the Pond in Tunica, Delta Pride in Indianola, and ConAgra ("Country Skillet") in Isola. Moses says that the union's initial contracts with the processors raised wages 50 to 60 cents an hour above the prevailing average of $4.00. Other benefits won at the Indianola plant included a pension plan, an extra week's vacation, two extra holidays (including Martin Luther King's birthday), and an extra coffee break. It is the nature of the business that when loads of fish come in, they must be processed immediately. In peak times, a worker may be kept on the job until ten P.M. or midnight. The contract goal for the 1990s, says Moses, is to win overtime pay for anything more than eight hours a day.

For his part, the farmer got about 75 or 80 cents a pound for catfish in 1988. The supermarket price ranged from $2.47 per pound for whole fish to $5.11 per pound for filets in Los Angeles. Obviously, the money is in the middle.

Around this $750 million industry has grown a marketing superstructure. There is now a Catfish Institute funded by fish feed mills and processors which spends about $1.5 million annually promoting catfish through sophisticated ads seeking to make the consumer associate "Mississippi Prime" with catfish, just as they do "Florida citrus" with oranges. A congressman from Alabama, which ranks a distant second to Mississippi in catfish ponds, has proposed organizing a catfish caucus since "there are certain parts of the country that don't even know about catfish." There is a Catfish Farmers of America, heavily dominated by Delta producers and landowners. Delta Pride's executive chef is John Folse, who runs Lafitte's Landing restaurant in Donaldsonville, Louisiana. His contribution to glasnost was to spend eight days at the Sovereign Center Hotel in Moscow in 1988 during the Reagan-Gorbachev summit serving up pan-sautéed fish, with crawfish, in a Cajun butter sauce; stuffed Delta Pride catfish Baton Rouge, with shrimp, crab, and crawfish stuffing; and Delta Pride catfish beignets, in mustard batter with sauce creole.

Many of the Delta plants do what is called "further processing" and pack breaded filets, "Cajun spiced" fish, and items of that sort. An oven-ready frozen catfish entree produced in Inverness coated with a "Cajun sauce" won the top prize given by the leading national grocery and food industry publisher as the best new product in 1987. The Delta Catfish stockholders met to celebrate their award at the private Humphreys Academy in Belzoni, which reveals their race and social status. A future winner might be the fish 'n' stick—a wiener-shaped boneless catfish convenience food cooked with a hush-puppy batter being tested at the Mississippi State University—but we hope not.

The Greenville Lions Club has an annual Catfish Grand Prix in which anyone who wants to can enter his or her own fish. Contestants are put into troughs and raced for trophies in heats of six. These fish have clever names according to their sponsor, like "Hobby-Long Cat-Sidy" for S&L Hobbies, and "Running Bare" for Essentials Lingerie. This attraction, like most in the Delta, has something for everyone in the family, including three-legged races, watermelon-eating contests, and seed-spitting competitions, which are very popular with children.

The dimensions of the catfish bonanza have attracted the notice of out-of-state financiers. One good-ol'-boy-made-good, Greenwood native Kerry Hamilton, recently sold his Aqua Culture Products, Inc., to Aqua Group Inc. of Tampa, Florida. This group of investors run by Floyd Smiley, former president of Borden Foods, also took a stab at buying out Delta Pride. From his new office in Tampa, Kerry Hamilton wrote his hometown newspaper that "going up Valley Hill, I stopped my car and looked back over the Delta. That summer haze was beginning to lift and I could see a crop duster in the distance artfully weaving its way through the sky. I thought to myself 'thank you, I will never forget where I came from and I will try never to let you down.' "

At the end of my first visit to a catfish plant, Ernest White pointed out to me—just to record the fact—that about 95 percent of the

Jim Ewan, Director of Quality Control at Delta Pride catfish plant, Indianola

workers in there were females. He also voiced the opinion that "you can't count on them places to last."

That view is disputed by most of those with whom I spoke. One Washington County planter told me that the success and profitability of catfish farming is inevitable. Why? Catfish, he says, are the most efficient converters of meal to meat yet discovered. While it takes two and one-half pounds of meal to produce a pound of beef, barely a pound and a half of feed is required to produce a pound of catfish. "Its conversion ratio is so much better than a cow's or a hog's or a chicken's that in the long run there isn't any way for it not to work economically." Simple arithmetic.

My personal verdict on Delta farm-raised catfish is that they have great texture and will take on whatever delightful flavor you add to them, bread them in, blacken them with, or fry into them. They are almost perfect for the American palate, and they are exceedingly nutritious and free of any unpopular fats or cholesterol. But for a fish that can carry its own weight on the plate, I'll take one that raised itself in the Mississippi River.

seven

OUR LITTLE TOWN

▲▲▲

Tall cotton and smiling people are waiting for your
arrival . . . a trip back in time . . . you will find a
combination of the unlikely and the unmatchable,
cradled in unequalled Southern Hospitality.
—*Mississippi Travel Guide, Fall–Winter 1988*

Driving through the Delta it would be easy to miss seeing one of
▽▽▽ the truly profound changes that has occurred here over the
past twenty years, unless you are caught speeding, as we were twice
in Washington County—pulled over by black troopers wearing
Mountie hats with gold peanuts on them. Such misfortune does offer
at least a chance to meet government face to face; without that it
might entirely escape your attention that a democratic revolution
has put blacks in charge of police stations, sheriffs' departments,
town councils, and school boards in a good part of the Delta. The
towns might look just the same as before, but a real struggle toward
an accommodation is going on daily among its citizens.

In 1976, Unita Blackwell made history when she was elected
mayor of tiny Mayersville in Issaquena County, the first black

woman to be elected mayor in Mississippi. Today, the political scene in the Delta is full of such firsts. In Coahoma County, Andrew Thompson, Jr., was elected sheriff in 1988 and became the first black to be elected countywide since Reconstruction. He said upon winning that his sons were quite enthusiastic about having their father become a sheriff, and "I think they are quite proud of me." Seeing Thompson, who is a very large man, I was reminded of one friend's comments about these pioneers: "I always said that it was unfortunate that the first black sheriffs all were kind of black images of the white sheriffs that have preceded them. They had to be six feet tall. They didn't play for Ole Miss, but they had to play for Jackson State or Alcorn. They had to be a football player, big, burly, growing a paunch, tote a gun, and walk around in cowboy boots and a hat. The fact is that they could have elected a five-foot-two-inch-tall black woman who didn't carry a gun and could still be a good sheriff, but the folks wouldn't have elected her because they had this image of what a sheriff is. The blacks wanted to do something new and different when they got the vote, but they had to keep some of the symbols that people could identify with to win the office." What difference does one sheriff make? The sheriff's staff in Coahoma County numbers twenty-five.

In Bolivar County in 1987, when Rosie Simmons was elected circuit clerk, the papers reported that she was the first black ever elected to countywide office. That is technically right, but Blanche K. Bruce, born a slave in Virginia, bought a plantation in Bolivar County after the Civil War and was appointed sheriff of the county. In 1875 he became United States senator from Mississippi. By the time his term ended in 1881, Mississippi was back under white control and Bruce left the state.

Mississippi, in fact, has more black elected officials than any other state in the union. All in all there were in 1988 in the Delta eighteen elected black county supervisors, nineteen election commissioners, forty-one school board members, eighteen mayors, two sheriffs, three school superintendents, and about ninety-eight aldermen or other municipal governing officials. True, many of these officials run little towns that are not much more than crossroads, like Renova and Falcon, but it is still substantial black political power.

The change is due not only to the heft of black voting strength, which has steadily built up since the Voting Rights Act passed in 1965, but also to the pressure of federal lawsuits that have forced counties and municipalities to draw new district lines to create voting areas where black candidates will almost certainly win. The basic thrust of these suits has been to give meaning to the concept of one man, one vote by ending at-large municipal and county voting districts, which favored whites, and replacing them with a ward system, which, depending on where the lines are drawn, assures some seats to blacks. Drawing those lines is the stuff of sophisticated lawyering, judging, and demographics. With help from national groups like the NAACP Legal Defense and Educational Fund and the ACLU, local attorneys have brought class-action suits that have successfully challenged at-large systems in a number of key Mississippi communities. Demographic data, which means information about past voting trends sufficient to establish racial bias, and the computer ability to draw new lines that satisfy the courts, have come from organizations like the Southern Regional Council in Atlanta. The overall strategy of the plaintiffs in these suits is to create districts that have a great enough black majority, say 65 percent, so that blacks will likely win a seat, but not so great a majority that too many black votes are siphoned off from neighboring districts. Many of these suits are just now resulting in judgment or political compromise.

Rolling Fork, for example, had its first town elections in seven years in 1988; the delay was caused by a pending voters' suit filed by black residents. The court established three black-majority wards, one white-majority ward, and one at-large ward. As a result, the first three blacks ever to hold municipal office in the history of that town were elected in October. In Indianola, under the new ward system, there was a special election in June of 1987 that elected four black aldermen and gave the town its first majority black board. In its first election since 1981, Cleveland elected three blacks to its seven-member board of aldermen under a ward realignment plan approved by the United States Justice Department. Mississippi is, of course, still subject to the Voting Rights Act, which mandates that all jurisdictions in the state must receive clearance from the Justice Department before modifying any laws that affect voting.

By and large the transfer of political power is being accepted by some whites as a positive occurrence and resisted by others with no more than griping. For example, one Bolivar County planter complained to me: "When the African-American brethren get elected mayor, the first thing they do is get a police chief and two new police cars, and I'm talking about a town with six hundred people. What's Winstonville got? About three hundred people. They built a big new brick city hall with an office. Then they got the finest police cars to ride around in, with the uniforms to wear, paid for by the property owners." That's politics; the days of armed resistance are over.

Belzoni, a town established in 1895, elected its first black officials in March of 1988 as a result of a court-ordered ward system. Three of the five-member board of aldermen elected were black. One was the seventy-seven-year-old Ernest White; the other two blacks sworn in, Sarita Randall McGee and Lawrence Browder, were barely thirty. I dropped in on Mrs. McGee at her home and got a very surprising idea of how younger black officials view politics. "I don't hold vendettas against people," she said. "I cannot punish somebody in Belzoni who is white for something that happened fifty years ago. That's where we make our mistake. This is 1988. Forget the past, join hand in hand, and work for improvement. If we don't, all of us will sit right in this little town and go down." My first reaction to her statement was that the activity she was willing to forgive and forget occurred more like twenty years ago than fifty; my second was that this woman is extraordinarily generous to forgive, put the past, no matter how recent, behind her and move ahead. She is not blind to Belzoni's current problems, but she is surely one of the city's and one of the Delta's biggest boosters. The foremost problem she sees is that some whites are still trying to hang on to an unreal world. "Some whites," she says, "still think that black means ignorant. The whites around here spend all of their efforts to send their children to the academy. Then they struggle to send their kids to college so that they can come back and live right next door to me. It's just a waste of money and a waste of time. In the real world it is not all white. It is black and white. And we're just going to have to get used to that."

McGee has a master's degree in library sciences, and she is a librarian at the Belzoni Middle School. She is a product of Humphreys County public schools. But most of the people who graduated with her, she says, went far away from the Delta to start a career, and they have no plans to come back to Belzoni. Why? "Number one, there's nothing for them to do here. A friend of mine teaches in Baton Rouge. Another is an accountant in Nashville. Another friend of mine is down in Pascagoula. There is nothing here. The people who stay are not trained. We provide them with a living. But what Belzoni needs is jobs, not handout programs. The children younger than I who are finishing high school and going on to college are not coming back, period. I mean, who is going to stay here to work at ConAgra for the rest of their life fileting fish every day?"

"It's not all in controlling this or that board," she says. "That's what most people seem to think, but the idea that we must get people in Belzoni to believe in is that we have got to work hand in hand, blacks and whites together. Not whites doing this and blacks doing that. Economic development initiatives have failed in the past because whites have not communicated with blacks. For example, we had a 'clean up' day in Belzoni. Nobody made an effort to go into the black community and try to get it cleaned up. But any way you come into Belzoni you have got to come through a black neighborhood first. To make a difference you have got to get everybody involved. The whites have got to make the black community aware that economic development is going to help us as well as them."

As you see, every Delta political discussion centers on race. Nobody ever mentions the Chinese, the Lebanese, the Italians, the Greeks, or the Indians (Asian) in his or her analysis, though the Delta is famous for having substantial populations of each of these, and more. The Lebanese came to peddle, the Chinese and Italians to pick cotton, the Greeks to run restaurants, and the Indians to run motels, spreading the fragrance of curry to motel offices throughout the region. Perhaps there are not enough of them to matter politically, or perhaps they have been successful in not getting involved in the greater race war. The state senator from Mrs. McGee's district, however, is Ollie Mohamed, whose family on his father's side goes back to Lebanon. He runs the supermarket across from her house.

Yet these various groups, though everywhere apparent, never

figure into the basic analysis. The Chinese, for example, have been in the Delta as long as anybody can remember. They are the third largest population group in Mississippi but are so numerically over-whelmed by whites and blacks that coming in to "show" does not mean very much. In the 1870s, when they were imported to the Delta as farm labor, the Chinese assumed a position somewhat remote from either dominant race, though they were generally sliced on the sour side of the melon. By the turn of the century they mostly ran grocery stores catering to blacks. In some towns today, like Merigold, just about the only store still open is the Chinese grocery. They were sent to schools of their own, since they were clearly not "whites." They owed part of their survival to the fact that as a community they tried hard to stay neutral in the larger community affairs and racial matters. As a real estate broker put it to me, "The Chinese did not come out of the backs of their stores until World War II." And were rarely active in politics. An exception was John L. Wing, mayor of Jonestown from 1965 till 1973, who may have been the first Chinese mayor in the United States; another was Luck Wing, mayor of Sledge. Still, the Chinese have gradually bridged that gap. A great many joined the Baptist Church, and their dead are buried in the white cemeteries. Long before final desegregation, Chinese were ad-mitted to white schools. Today, the children of the Chinese often attend the private academies. Many have become pharmacists. Now in their third generation in the Delta, the Chinese have "made it" here. Yet there are fewer of them here than in the past.

The younger generation has of late begun seeking opportunities outside of the Delta just like everybody else. In an effort to bring them back, at least for a party, several mid-Deltans put on what was styled the "Big Event" in Greenville in 1987. For two years invita-tions went out to "Southern Chinese-Americans" all over the coun-try. The logo for the Big Event was a panda bear, representing the Chinese heritage, coming out of a bamboo triangle, representing the Delta. About six hundred people "came home" for a once-in-a-life-time reunion, to dance at the city convention center. There is also a business aspect to this sort of celebration. In 1988 the Clarksdale Chamber of Commerce and the Clarksdale Chinese Association hosted the first of what they expect will be an annual Chinese New Year festival. Following that a group of area businessmen went to

Gravestone of Bho Chie Pang, Grange Cemetery, Clarksdale

Taiwan to generate investment prospects, and a return delegation from the Republic of China was expected soon afterwards.

Finding the gravestone of Bho Chie Pang near that of Lamar Fontaine in Clarksdale's Grange Cemetery prompted me to look in the city telephone book to see if any Pangs remained in the area. There was one listed, Linn K. Pang, and I called on him, expecting to meet a tiny, timid shopkeeper, my stereotype. Instead I found a seventy-five-year-old retired farmer with a full-bore Mississippi accent and a booming explosive laugh that punctuated almost every carefully worded sentence. He looked at our photograph of Bho Chie Pang's grave and exclaimed, "Well, I'll be goddamned. You know my daddy made that stone." But he couldn't decide who Bho Chie was, only that he might have been the relative of a Pang who now runs a restaurant in Greenville. The Pangs, he said, "is a big durn family."

His father was a merchant in the town of Dublin, a few miles south of Clarksdale. "I used to hear him talk about walking from Dublin to Marks, and I recall hearing him talk about camping overnight at the crossing at Tutwiler. Walking was the only transportation you got then."

Linn was one of nine children. His mother died young, and he says of his father and sister, "They was the backbone of the family." When he was fifteen his father hired a tutor to teach him Chinese. "Until then I spoke just as much Chinese as you do," he told me. He joined the navy, fought in the war, came back to the Delta, and with his sister's help bought a 600-acre farm near Dublin. "It was a small place according to who my neighbors were": planters with 1,500 to 15,000 acres. "I was the small boy around there, and they've tried their level best to get it, too." He lets out a whoop, because he did not part with his land, but has acquired more. With a relative he owns one of Clarksdale's shopping centers. He quit farming "when I found out I didn't know how. I was a slow learner. For thirty-one years I couldn't learn, and then I thought I'd let somebody else have it." He recalls when "we'd work the whole family, from grandpa down. If the baby couldn't work, it'd tote water." He is speaking of black tenants, not his own family.

Now he lives with his sister's daughter and her husband, Gilroy

Chow, who is an engineer. "He's got nearly as many degrees as you've got," boasted the elder Pang. Actually, he has more. Their family is quite extensive. Linn's niece has thirty first cousins and most live in the Delta. And they have prospered. Two of Linn's nephews are pharmacists and one is a dentist. Big gatherings around births, deaths, and weddings demonstrate the strength of the community. Nearly one thousand people came to Gilroy's wedding, including the judge and the lieutenant governor. An average wedding may draw four hundred, "and that's not just passing the table, that's a ten-course dinner," says Linn.

I ask about past discrimination, and the elder Pang tightens up. After staring at me for a moment he says, "There's always been some discrimination. Even now I expect there are some white people you don't like." He does tell me that "my daddy, when he moved his store to Marks, always went along with what the white people said. Donations came, he gave. He wasn't big enough to take a big part, but he'd take a small part. And right here in Clarksdale, I couldn't say that anybody would be better liked than our family. There's three brothers and a sister in my niece's family and there's four deacons. Now that's not just a small church. I'm talking about the biggest church in Clarksdale. It takes in the whole two blocks out there in West Clarksdale. That in itself speaks pretty good about how they are standing in the community."

He laughs about his brothers who will travel hundreds of miles just to play in a golf tournament. "Back then in my days if you had two hundred dollars you'd stay home and try to raise a family with it. There's more money now, and a lot of improvement in the style of living. But I just can't conceive in my mind how the economy of this country is going." He trails off.

Then his eyes light up and he shows us a treasured possession—an ornate tea set he brought back from a recent trip to China—and he begins to tell about the things he saw on his visit. He mentions, too, that distant relatives are still immigrating to the Delta from mainland China. My eyes wander as he speaks to a shelf full of jogging and tennis trophies, won in Mississippi by nephews and grandnephews. Strange that in this remote rural spot a Chinese beachhead has been won and a community has flourished.

A word also about Delta Jews in the Diaspora. Like the Chinese they never fit neatly into the region's caste structure, though among the original founders of even the smallest Delta towns, it seems, was a Jewish merchant. They came to Mississippi as peddlers and traders during the two decades before the Civil War, mainly disembarking in New Orleans off ships straight from Europe, and they made their way north along the river from plantation to plantation, selling wares wholesaled from Baltimore. Generally they had been prohibited from owning land in Europe, but there was no such impediment in Mississippi, and many settled in.

During the War Between the States, most Mississippi Jews followed the example of Judah P. Benjamin, Jeff Davis's secretary of state and war, and served the Confederacy. Jews were never segregated, but were educated in white schools. Several were prominent in the Masonic order, such as Sol Summerfield of Yazoo City and Charles Blum who served a term as master of the state lodge. Blum came to the Delta as a peddler and opened the Blum Company in Nitta Yuma in 1885. The town of Marks was named after Leopold Marks, a merchant and cotton farmer, who was Quitman County's first state legislator. Henry Kline came from Lithuania near the turn of the century to farm in Anguilla, founded Kline's Department Store, and was chairman of the Sharkey County Democratic Party. The Roslyn Hotel in Greenville, owned by Leon Fletcher, was once reputed to be the finest accommodation between Memphis and New Orleans. Some of these businesses thrived, like Morris Lewis's Lewis Grocery Company in Lexington and the Stein Mart chain organized by Jacob Stein in Greenville. At various times since World War II, Alligator, Louise, Rolling Fork, Rosedale, and Yazoo City have all had Jewish mayors. Greenville had the largest Jewish congregation in the state until the 1960s, when it was superseded by Jackson's. Its Congregation B'nai Israel was founded in 1869 and one hundred years later had nearly two hundred families in membership. But the ambiguous position of Jews in Delta society was illustrated, historically, by the yellow fever epidemic of 1878. When the fever killed about a third of Greenville's two thousand citizens in that year, a burying ground was provided on the Blantonia Plantation, divided into sections for whites and blacks. A third section was set aside in the middle for Jews. A few Chinese also died in that epidemic, and they were buried with the Jews.

The Jews' position on race relations in the 1960s ranged from moderate to reactionary. An example of the latter was the statement by Clarksdale's Rabbi Benjamin Schultz, quoted in James Silver's famous book about the Ole Miss riot: "If Mississippi had prevailed, pro-Communists would be off American college faculties. Corruption of our youth would stop. If Mississippi with its States' Rights philosophy had its way, big government, provocative dictatorship and eventual national bankruptcy would be thrown out the window. If Mississippi had its way, 'red-baiter' would not be a dirty word."

Yet, as a group, the Delta Jews have had a beneficial impact on the cultural climate of the area out of proportion to their numbers. But today those numbers are shrinking. Membership in the Greenville congregation is down to 121, and Clarksdale, with only fifty Jewish families now, can no longer support a resident rabbi. Its youngest couple, one member told me, is thirty-seven years of age. The decline is due to the same factors that are gradually driving all of the educated folk out of the Delta: not enough opportunity to make money. "It's big news around here," the Clarksvillian reported, "if we locate a company that will have five employees." One must ask, however, whether it is opportunity or imagination that is limited.

Belzoni's Sarita McGee exemplifies the positive spirit in the Delta. Her view of the future is more than upbeat. It is a call to arms. "I think that it is going to be tough, but we've got some women here who are really go-getters, and there are women in town who have decided that they're going to get out and make it on their own and create jobs for people. I think that we are going to survive. I really do. We are going to have to create for ourselves. We are going to have to make ourselves attractive. I think the money we are spending through the economic development group is going to work. I am optimistic about the future, and I am not dismal at all." She acknowledges that Belzoni's low educational level is a drawback, but she scoffs at the idea that the work force is untrainable. She points out that probably fifty people every day drive north to Indianola or

Greenwood to work in factories, and if there were jobs in Belzoni, they would prefer to stay home.

Her ideas are echoed by Joyce McNair, a math teacher at the public high school, who joined us in the McGee parlor midway through our conversation. Mrs. McNair says flatly that "the schools will provide whatever training is necessary to meet the demands of any industry that wants to come here." Both of these women are very excited about their (black-run) school system. "Right now," McNair says, "the students do well on their achievement tests in general, and all they need to do well is an opportunity." The public school systems, she thinks, can much more readily adapt to the demands of industrial training than can the private academies, which, she believes, lack the support programs or the financing to prepare children adequately. Furthermore, they lack the "public relations" that you get in a school that is community-based. In other words, the children schooled in the academies do not get training on how to live in the real world. Mrs. McGee's own daughter goes to an integrated Girl Scout camp every summer, and "all the children mingle together, but then they are separated in school. They'll pass on the street and the little girls will say 'Hi, Serena,' and their parents will pull them off. You see, it's just not real."

"We know each other in Belzoni, and in time we will learn to walk hand in hand," says Mrs. McGee. "I'm real optimistic. I just think that things have got to be good here. You know you have to take where you live and deal with it. I like Belzoni. I am here to stay."

The highest ranking political figure in the Delta is its United States congressman, Mike Espy, the first black congressman from Mississippi since Reconstruction. He represents Mississippi's Second, the district that speaks for cotton and farm programs in Congress. Espy, age thirty-four, is the rising black star of Mississippi politics. He came not from a civil rights background but from a series of middle-management-level jobs in state government. His family owns several funeral homes. In 1986 he won his first term against a Republican white incumbent from Greenwood. In doing so, Espy succeeded where Robert Clark, Mississippi's first black state legislator and foremost black politician, had twice failed. The 1986 victory,

most analysts thought, was achieved because whites voted with their
feet and stayed home, so uninspired were they with Espy's opponent.

Since going to Congress, however, Espy has done just about everything right by the reckoning of his constituents. He was appointed
to the seat on the Agriculture Committee traditionally reserved for
the representative from the Second District; he was the only freshman appointed to the Budget Committee; and he has served farm
interests faithfully. He has stood solidly behind Delta farmers on
every issue related to their loan and subsidy payments. He got the
U.S. Army to buy vast quantities of catfish. Billy Percy organized a
reelection fund-raiser for Espy in Greenville and praised the congressman for "amazingly catching on to the intricacies of the Farm
Bill in defending our position in this area." Those present, including
some of the biggest farmers in the Delta, plunked down $32,000 into
Espy's campaign chest.

Espy, whom colleagues describe as mild-mannered and hard-working, is no rabble-rouser. He is the Harvard-educated son of a Yazoo
City funeral-home director, and on the stump he has just a little
more pizazz than an undertaker. Much of the excitement he gener-
ates is because he is black, but he avoids the word "racism" and
speaks of "distinctions in treatment." It is clear that he has a vision,
however, of a brighter, more prosperous Delta and believes that it
can be attained. He cosponsored a bill that would create a "heritage
corridor" running fourteen miles wide along each side of the Mississippi River from Wisconsin to Louisiana to help identify and preserve the folklore, culture, and history of the area. Along with Jamie
Whitten, the seventy-seven-year-old dean of Mississippi's congressional delegation and once a leading segregationist, Espy cosponsored a bill to create a Lower Mississippi Development Council. The
bill passed in 1988, and $3 million was appropriated for a study of
the region that includes the entire riverbanks area south of Illinois.
Once the study is complete, more federal money will presumably be
forthcoming for improvements. The Delta is expected to be the ultimate beneficiary of most of this attention because of its 43 percent
poverty rate, overall unemployment rate of about 17 percent, and
black unemployment rates as high as 36 percent in some spots like
Sharkey County. America is a great chain of states, Espy argues in
a standard speech, and the whole will be made stronger by focusing

on the weakest link. That, he believes, is the Mississippi Delta. Espy also got a bill passed establishing a National Catfish Day.

Back home, Espy has helped to form a Mississippi Forward Foundation, a nonprofit organization funded mainly by corporations in the state, which is designed to provide scholarships and to promote development projects. And he has worked the chamber of commerce banquets. He was well received at the Greenwood–Leflore County chamber's breakfast in 1987, for example, because of his success in getting $3.5 million appropriated to extend the runway at the local airport. This is constituent service. He helped Curtis Smith of Ruleville obtain the medals he earned for fighting in the Mediterranean in World War II. People remember these things.

Espy keeps an office in the Greenville City Hall and another in Yazoo City. The congressman is also hard to track down. When I tried to arrange an interview with him I was told by his Mississippi staff that that was the exclusive province of his Washington press secretary. After several letters and telephone calls to that department, and confirmations and reconfirmations, I arrived at the Greenville office at the appointed time only to learn that communication between Washington and the Delta had failed. The congressman had just finished a tour of the Boeing plant in Greenville and was somewhere on the road to Yazoo City. This, however, gave me the opportunity to chat with an embarrassed Owen Brooks, who is Espy's Greenville field secretary. Brooks is a Boston native who came to Mississippi with the movement. Before joining the congressman's staff, he was an organizer and community worker for many years with the Delta ministry and with MACE. Now he keeps two phone lines busy doing just about the same thing he did then—counseling people who are having problems with public housing programs, with the police, or with Social Security—but now he does it for "the congressman" and obtains better results.

Espy was opposed for reelection in 1988 by Jack Coleman, a white Republican, and Dorothy Benford, a black independent. The campaign was typically nasty for Mississippi. Coleman is a Madison businessman with close ties to Delta farmers. He is originally from Rosedale and is married to Mrs. Pearson's granddaughter Sara. He accused Espy of being antibusiness, of having accepted more money from the "National Gay Rights Political Committee" than any other

congressman, and in general of being a scoundrel. Benford, a one-
time campaign worker for Espy, charged that Espy's reelection committee was infiltrated by Marxists. A month before the election
someone carved the word "Nigger" and various other racial slurs on
the doors of the Espy home in Madison.

A procession of prominent Democrats, including Sam Nunn of
Georgia, Bennett Johnston of Louisiana, and Bill Bradley of New
Jersey, came to the Delta to campaign for Espy. Nunn said that the
neat, serious candidate had been so aggressive that "I'm afraid we're
going to have everyone in the U.S. Army eating catfish three times
a day." Bradley's visit was hosted by Hiram and Gail Eastland at the
family's Adair Plantation in Sunflower County. The remark a gray-
haired tenant farmer made to me that "I ain't never seen a white
person campaign for a black person, but I've seen plenty of black
people campaign for white folks" is no longer universally true.

With that sort of help and with solid black turnout, the Democrat
Espy won 40 percent of the white vote and virtually all of the black
vote in the same year that George Bush swept the state for the
Republicans. One planter in the district told me, "Espy has been
very intelligent, I think, in how he handles himself, especially since
he won the first election. He's done everything he can to enamor
himself to the agricultural segment of the economy. He has been
very responsive as far as farmers go. He obviously didn't know anything about agriculture. He's a lawyer by trade, by education, but
he's a quick study. He knows a lot more now than he did two years
ago. In a word, he's responsive. All those 40 percent of the whites
that voted for him weren't farmers. There were plenty of other
people who perceived that he's not a Jesse Jackson type." While
Dukakis won approximately 50 percent of the vote in the district,
Espy won 65 percent.

The definition of a "Republican" from Professor Ray Marshall's
childhood (someone who lives amongst us Democrats and if the
Republicans get the White House he'd get the post office) is no longer
true in the South. To the contrary, Republicans are now the conservative majority in much of the region. A national look at the 1988
election returns might lead you to suppose that the candidate with
the black support automatically loses, and that candidate is generally a Democrat. The Delta, naturally, is an exception to that rule

because a majority of the voters are black. Espy's victory depended on something more, however, because his district is substantially bigger than the Delta. In 1988 he bucked the national trend by showing that a black Democrat could carry a district that was almost half white.

The coalition that elected Espy is reminiscent of the power bloc that controlled the Delta following Reconstruction and before disenfranchisement in 1890: the few white planters and the many black voters. Back then the arrangement worked for the planters because undeniably they controlled the black vote, through the use of both sticks and carrots. The black vote is free today, and the system now works because both sides see mutual advantage in it.

Some of Espy's successes in 1986 and 1988 might have been due to Jesse Jackson's runs for the presidency, which fired up a lot of black voters in the Delta and got them involved in grass-roots Democratic Party activity. Jackson was unquestionably the Delta's candidate. He was the overwhelming victor in the area's primary, and on the night of his 1988 speech to the Democratic National Convention in Atlanta the streets of the black neighbors throughout the Delta were just about empty. While Jackson won most of the delegates in his party's primary in Mississippi, the reality is that Mississippi is still about two-thirds white and predominantly conservative. Not only did Bush easily defeat Dukakis in the presidential race, but Republican Trent Lott defeated Wayne Dowdy, giving Mississippi two Republicans in the United States Senate.

Delta farmers seem to like the idea of having a black congressman. They expect it improves their image, and they can lord this symbol of tolerance over all of those out-of-state liberals who do not have a black congressman. Without wishing to be more than moderately preachy, I will suggest that the process of wisely governing requires also a strengthening of the local community. Although increasing the southward flow of dollars through the pipeline from Washington may contribute to that goal, it is ultimately the willingness to fortify the essentials of local life, such as the public schools, that pulls the community and the commonwealth forward.

I sense, however, that there is a leadership vacuum in the Delta. Up through the 1960s one could say without much doubt that the plantation owners held the power. They controlled the basic features of local life—the police, the banks, the schools, the courthouse, the road money, and generally the newspaper. They were the Delta's voice in the statehouse at Jackson and influenced Mississippi politics far beyond their number. They had substantial say-so in national affairs that mattered to them, mainly farm programs and flood control. They were generally well-respected people, and their advice was often sought on matters large and small.

Much of that power is gone now, but to whom has it been transferred? Black voter power has taken over many town halls and school systems, but there is really not much to govern in most small towns anymore; the power of the schools comes from the jobs they provide. School employment, in fact, may be the major force creating a black middle class, but it is not power over whites, for their kids do not go there, and it is not even ultimate power over the school system itself because that is run according to state and federal guidelines. It could not be said that blacks "run things" in the Delta today. Farm economics have taken the blacks off the plantation, but (of those who stayed in Mississippi) many have not moved to stable employment situations. Rather they have taken jobs at fast-food franchises or gone onto public welfare. They have little economic clout, own virtually none of the land, and, as Deltans, have no major impact in state government. So who is in charge?

Perhaps Uncle Sam. The major player on the Delta stage today is unquestionably the federal government. It gave blacks the vote and gave the minimum wage to farmworkers and maids. It enforces minimum standards for farm housing and job safety. It regulates the pesticides and the herbicides, devises the labyrinthine farm program, and tells farmers what to plant. It insures, and thus essentially holds, many a mortgage. It gerrymanders electoral districts to assure black representation. It oversees the schools, the highways, the public health, the wildlife, and the river. It is first and foremost the giver of crop subsidy and welfare payments, which is the big money that comes into the Delta. As Tiny says, "Everything that was done for black people in the state of Mississippi that was worthwhile was done through a federal court order." But with all of that involvement in the common lives of people, it would be hard to say what the federal mission is today in the Delta. It had a mission during Reconstruction, and during the Depression it got planters to plow under every second row of cotton. It had a mission during the Great Society when Head Start and community programs like MACE began. It had a mission in the late 1960s and 1970s when it desegregated the schools and registered the black vote.

Today, one only sees extensive, local manifestations of an enormous, faraway bureaucracy at work. Part of that may be the Reagan-Bush retrenchment, and part of that may be the innate inability of government, because it is big and slow, ever to really manage the always-changing affairs of its citizens. Espy's Mississippi Development Council may energize the federal presence, if it is funded. Ultimately, however, it is the people of Tunica and Quitman and Sunflower counties who must take the reins. Which people those will be and where they will head remains an open question.

eight

DELTA DREAMING

▲ ▲ ▲

And in the Delta they spend money just like it's water.
If they have a good crop in the fall time, there's just no
end to the money here. If the cotton people make
money, then *everybody* has money in the Delta. They
just hand it out in bonuses to the people that live on
the plantations. They give them labor bonuses, and
Christmas money, and money on their birthdays. And if
they go into the store to buy something, they'll buy for
everyone in the store, you know. They have big hearts.
And the merchants are happy when there's a good crop,
because business is good then, you know. People in the
Delta are not conservative like the people in the
Mississippi hills. In the Delta everybody borrows to
make their crop, but everybody gives, too, everybody's
hand is open.

—Ethel Wright Mohamed, quoted in *Local Color: A Sense
of Place in Folk Art,* by William Ferris

T he idea of a town has often required some imagination in the
▽▽▽ Delta. Plantation living patterns meant that there were lots of
tenant houses in the vicinity of the big farm's commissary and cotton
gin. If there was a public road running past the gin, and especially
if there was a doctor, a gas station, or a post office in the vicinity, it
was called a town.

Midnight, in Humphreys County, is a good example of such a
town, now nothing but boarded-up stores and a closed gin. Midnight
was so small to begin with that after the commissary and Chinese
grocery store closed, all that was needed to kill it was the Arab oil

embargo, which knocked out the gas station. A lot of little crossroads stores and gin towns were hurt back then when the oil companies stopped selling gas to the little guy. A few years later the state decided to finish the job and built a bypass around Midnight. Is that a big waste of state money? Just down the road a few miles is Louise, where I used to live. It is marginally more alive. All of the dry-goods merchants, who did well up through the 1960s when the town had a little snap on Saturday nights, are now gone, but a black-run grocery and gas station is a regular hangout. There is still a "Chinaman" store. The town doctor, who used to have separate waiting rooms for whites and blacks, moved away, however, and (big surprise) no product of modern medical education has moved in to replace him. Louise also has a bypass now, so nobody has to slow down and maybe buy something. Another example is Doddsville, whose hometown-boy politician, "Big Jim" Eastland, led the United States Senate's drive against domestic communism in the 1950s and dominated Mississippi politics for decades. It is now just about out of sight. There is a bypass around Doddsville, too. The story is pretty much the same in Benoit, Nitta Yuma, Falcon, and Silver City. Those are the old towns on the line of the Yazoo and Mississippi Valley Railroad, but the train doesn't run there anymore.

Even some of the bigger towns are feeling the pressure. In Leland, Mac Gordon is publisher and editor of the *Leland Progress,* circulation 1,500 (a paper once run by Larry Speakes). Twenty years ago, says Gordon, you had to bump people off the sidewalks in downtown Leland. On Saturday night the department store had twenty clerks working. The couple who owned it would go home, throw the money on their bed, and count it. Now that store is closed. You cannot buy men's underwear or socks in Leland anymore, Gordon complains. He suggests that a good title for my book would be "Collapse of the Mississippi Delta." His words are echoed by Leland writer Robert Neill, who observed that "there are not that many little boys running around loose anymore in the country." On the fifteen-mile stretch between Leland and Indianola, on the old main road, he recalls that there were ninety-eight houses twenty years ago. Now there are nine. Leland had three lumber yards, and now there is not even a men's clothing store. With a touch of humor Neill notes that there are still four flower shops and several drugstores in Leland.

"Weddings, funerals, and staying well in between are all still good business."

Failing some miraculous industrial development, Leland will lose all sense of its separate identity in the next few years and become essentially a suburb of Greenville, nine miles away, according to Gordon. The causes he blames, from the white businessman's perspective, are repeated around the region: years of low farm prices, desegregation, and the opening of so many private schools that kids do not know each other anymore. There is another cause. Leland's streets are not exactly empty. On any afternoon there are a fair number of smartly dressed black teenagers hanging around. The girls are wearing Reeboks and primary-color sunglasses, and carrying Gucci bags. Where do they get them? Wal-Mart.

For anyone unfamiliar with a Wal-Mart, it is typically a vast budget department store, part of an 1,100-store chain created by Sam Walton in Arkansas, who many say is the richest man in America. There are about forty Wal-Marts in Mississippi, and almost every one of them has helped to knock out a small town. Leland is actually caught between two: one in Indianola and one in Greenville. It is not a plot, just good business in the short run. Even we shopped at the Indianola Wal-Mart, because we were in a hurry, as we shot through town on the bypass, to buy some gloves to help us thaw out in a January snowstorm that we had not imagined would occur in the Delta. And Wal-Mart is not the only company helping to cripple the small retailer. Though we chose not to, we could have bought Brie cheese and Bremner wafers at three o'clock in the morning at the all-night superstore in Clarksdale, Mississippi. And you cannot beat the breakfast special, scrambled eggs, bacon, biscuit, and coffee for $1.59, at the twenty-four-hour Jitney Jungle Deli in Cleveland. The café by the courthouse is dead and gone; now we have the superstore on the highway.

Mac Gordon does have a legitimate gripe if it is true that, as he says, the big chains like Wal-Mart will not advertise in the small-town papers. The Delta's little presses are hurting and gradually shutting down. The _Sunflower County News,_ for example, printed its last issue in May 1988. Marilyn Brumley would no more write the news from Parchman Prison. Her last column reported that the local doctor was visiting his parents in Baltimore: "The last time he visited them . . . his car was broken into and everything stolen. Let's hope he has better luck this time." Who will share words of comfort like that in the future? In 1988 Hal DeCell, coeditor for thirty-seven years of the *Deer Creek Pilot* in Rolling Fork, died, leaving the future of that newspaper in doubt. We had met him in the spring, and he spoke then of his concern for his little town, which had lost twenty stores in the past two years. Driving through Rolling Fork, said DeCell, "you've got to look damn fast to see it." He found grounds to be optimistic, though, in that whites were coming back to the public schools, and "there has been so much change that blacks and whites don't think about race too much anymore." His own editorial page had always toed a moderate line. In the dark days of the sixties he had seen "the hopeful signs growing day by day that no longer will it be sufficient for seekers after public places of trust to 'cry nigger,' " and he thought the paper had done something important when it was the first in the Delta to run a black bride's picture. When we were there the staff photographer was Eddie Neal, a black man.

Small-town papers like DeCell's are important for making people feel that they are a part of a place. Birth, wedding, death, and all of the watermarks of one's life in between can be commemorated over the years in the paper, and from its pages scrapbooks for every man are created. The *Belzoni Banner* even prints a list of children reported absent from school; I guess so you can keep tabs on your kids. True, many editions are heavy on preprinted messages from Congressman Espy and Senator Lott, or weekly editorials prepared by the Mississippi Economic Council, and some of these even dominate front pages. Several have a clearly conservative bent, like the *Greenwood Commonwealth,* once run by James K. Vardaman, which occasionally carries not one but two columns by James K. Kilpatrick. The *Commonwealth* also does an exceptional job of reporting controversial local issues and is well regarded by blacks for covering their meetings accurately. The local papers perform a housekeeping service that the networks and big presses are not likely to attend to. The photograph of a Sunflower County road crew illegally repairing the parking lot of the private Indianola Academy in 1987, printed in the

Hal DeCell, editor of the Deer Creek Pilot, *at his desk, Rolling Fork,*
1988

Enterprise-Tocsin, put an end to that practice, at least for a time. The twenty-six-year-old editor of the *Yazoo Herald* was shot when she photographed county employees working on a private driveway in 1987.

Despite the cracks in the infrastructure of Delta towns, there is still plenty of creativity in them. People work hard to preserve their leisurely ways. Amid floor-length mirrors and arrangements of white orchids and starburst fugi, Delta debutantes are welcomed in society at the Greenville Golf and Country Club. The Southern Debutante Assembly has its annual White and Gold Ball at the Greenwood Country Club. Similar processions of teen beauties, in white gowns smothered in carnations and gold bows, are a feature of life in every Delta county and one of the main reasons that most counties have country clubs. The "little season" of the debutante continues throughout the hot summer months, and those lucky enough to be honored as debs will attend enough dances and garden parties during that period that they will be able, blindfolded, to inflict similar tortures on their own daughters twenty years later. It goes without saying that all of these young ladies are indescribably pretty, and that their portraits fill up a significant number of column inches in the small-town newspapers during the year.

Another reason for country clubs is the food. Clarksdale Country Club chef Douglas Doty can whip up extraordinary medallions of lamb with roquefort and pasta. The Cleveland Country Club has always thought a good sauce chef is as important as a good bartender. One of the big annual events there is the cotillion and stag dance where tenth-graders, by invitation only, are initiated into the club. By the way, want something good to eat in Clarksdale but you're not a member of the country club? Try Boss Hogg's barbecue where just about any night, Thursday through Saturday, you will find Boss Hogg himself cooking forty or fifty pounds of ribs right out on the sidewalk.

It follows that beauty pageants are taken seriously in the Delta. Delta State University names not one but the "Top Ten" beauties right before Christmas. Miss Teen-USA for 1988, the fair Kristy Addis, is from Greenville. It was the unanimous opinion that a milestone was reached in 1987 when Toni Seawright became the first black to wear the crown of Miss Mississippi. For black church-goers in Greenville there is a Miss Baptist pageant, and contestants for that crown are considerably more modest in their attire than the Top Ten from DSU.

There is no shortage of women's organizations. The Greenville Junior Auxiliary holds an annual charity ball to present the new king and queen in January. The 1988 theme was the magic and mystery of Egypt. The *Delta Democrat-Times*'s account gives some idea of the scope of this pageant:

"The Egyptian theme will begin at the entrance where guests will be greeted by a large, seated pharaoh as they enter the festive Egyptian setting complete with desert and oasis. . . .

"The focal point and main attraction of the ballroom will be a 17-foot tall sphinx. This huge structure is being welded and molded and will be covered with papier-mâché by members of the decorations committee. A 20-by-30 foot oil painted canvas of a pharaoh's head will serve as a backdrop for the band in the main ballroom. This 'oasis' area will contain a pyramid-shaped stage, lush with lighted greenery. The brilliant turquoise, brown and terra-cotta colors in the painting will be repeated throughout the ballroom.

"The tables will be part of the desert area and will be decorated with printed Egyptian fabric. . . . Court members will walk through the granite color sphinx as they are presented. . . .

"The little girl representing the kindergarten court will wear a white Swiss batiste dress trimmed in white and beige eyelet.

"Third grade girls will wear white linen dresses featuring collars made with beige French val lace.

"The outfits of the kindergarten and third grade boys will depict the look of English excavators with khaki tops and shorts accented with a military belt and knee socks."

There is a serious side to the Junior Auxiliary, since its purpose is to encourage well-to-do women to do volunteer work in areas such as drug education. As an organization, it seems to be run from the Delta. It is headquartered in Greenville, and four of its past presidents have been from Leland. There are black service groups as well. Delta Sigma Beta sorority puts on an annual free "Breakfast with Santa" for the children of Clarksdale and Marks.

There are plenty of opportunities in the Delta for good works among the poor. In Sunflower County and in Greenwood, there are chapters of Habitat for Humanity, the Georgia-based program that enlists volunteer labor to construct low-cost, no-interest, financed houses for poor people willing to invest at least five hundred hours of "sweat equity" in building a residence. The program has brought in young Christians from Waco, Texas, to build a home in Doddsville, and the organization held its international board meeting in Greenwood in April of 1988. The local Greenwood-Leflore affiliate has three completed homes to show off. While three new homes make only a modest dent in the housing needs of Greenwood's poor, it is three more homes than had existed a year before, and they were built without any government help.

The arts are alive and doing tolerably well in Delta towns. If you could measure per capita interest in the arts, I suspect it is higher in Clarksdale and Greenwood than it is in New York or Atlanta. The Mississippi Delta Arts Council is based in Clarksdale and has opened some lines of communication across the cultural divide. Run by a racially balanced board, it has won a National Endowment grant to renovate the seventy-year-old, segregated Paramount Theater into a fine-arts complex. A fund-raiser for the center produced by Jon Levingston, whose family runs the local furniture store, featured Alex Haley, Donna Mills, William Shatner, and Lonnie Shorr. These people are serious about projecting the image of a community that has put racism behind it. Jon's brother, Bruce Levingston, is a concert pianist in New York, and the two brothers have founded an endowment for the humanities at Delta State University. Governor Mabus recently appointed Jon chairman of the Mississippi Arts Commission.

There are festivals throughout the area. The Delta Blues Festival in Greenville has become internationally important. The April Catfish Festival in Belzoni is a pleasant open-air event that provides the chance to see who can eat the most catfish. If you are hungry, all you have to do is volunteer. My favorite is the Cleveland October Fest, the "happiest little festival in Mississippi," mainly because the location, the tree-lined main street of town, is so pretty, and because I like watching the children from Cypress Park Elementary wave little American flags and sing "This Land Is Your Land." They also have a barbecue cook-off contest there. For the uninitiated, picture an all-night drinking party around a customized mobile cooker pulled behind a truck from Tennessee or Texas, culminating the next morning in a moment of elegance when the judges come to your linen-draped table, uncork your wine, lift the Lillian Vernon cover from your china platter, raise the sterling silver fork, and delicately sample a select portion of your roasted hog. To be such a judge is an experience for which I am available if called. The team of cooks from Texaco provides not only French wine but its signature container of Halvoline on the table.

There is a lively theater scene in the Delta. The Greenwood Little Theater puts on a full season of classics such as _Our Town_ and _A Christmas Carol_ and conducts a student summer workshop. Mississippi State University hosts touring companies, such as Atlanta's Carl Ratliff Dance Theatre and the National Shakespeare Company, and has its own university stage group. If you want to hear some good Benny Goodman music, about sixty-five unreconstructed high school band veterans play non-rock 'n' roll in the all-amateur Greenwood Community Concert Band. Greenwood suffers big-city arts woes, too. In 1988 the forty-seven-year-old concert association went on a sabbatical because it could no longer attract audiences sufficient to pay for the type of performances, like Arthur Fiedler and the Boston Pops, that its seven hundred members had come to expect.

The Delta has its share of local artists as well. Belzoni's Ethel Mohamed has become a folk artist of wide reputation. Rita Halbrook of Belzoni forms impressions of Mississippi catfish and quilts in abstract patterns from paper she makes with rice, wild flowers, weeds, and old rags, "cooked, beaten, and formed into art." Encouraged by members of the Lu-Rand Homemakers Club, Christine Holloway of Coahoma County has entered and won state poetry competitions sponsored by the Extension Home Economist Office. Yazoo County lithographer Paul Russell, known locally as Wallace Brasher, has done shows from Boston to Miami, and says he was commissioned by Pat Nixon to paint a mural on the wall of the Nixons' vacation home. Anguilla's Henrietta Farrar is well known for her paintings of cotton bolls and country scenes. In Inverness, seventy-nine-year-old J. S. "Red" Bell makes small wooden crosses, some just an inch tall, to give away to special people he meets, about five thousand so far. A truly unusual artist is blues great James "Son" Thomas of Leland, who sculpts heads with marble eyes and painted teeth so frightening that they will scare the kids.

The cultural anthropologist might find it interesting to note that in recent times Clarksdale seems to have developed a love affair with impressionist art. Clarksdale frame-shop owner Angelo Balducci told a local journalist at the end of 1987 that for the past six months he had been doing a new and brisk business in large prints from the impressionist period. " 'In my business I have seen a definite local preference to this style. In the past oriental prints have been popular in the Delta for many years,' he continued. Although he has framed a number of Audubon-style prints, he says duck scenes are not the trend this year either. . . . 'Last year customers were interested in English hunt scenes, but not this year,' he said."

Where does the money to finance art appreciation come from? You might wonder the same thing if you browse through Clemmie Collins's Fireside Shop in Cleveland, which displays one of the finest and costliest collections of early English antiques this side of the Atlantic. The Delta planter's ability to indulge in fine things may wane when the price of cotton is low, but in good years the farmer or his wife evidently knows what to buy. In this respect one must ask whether the planter, who always complains that his black tenants love to spend cash and would rather borrow than save, sets a better example.

One of the things that has always made the Delta an interesting spot on the Southern Baptist landscape is the popularity of vice. Part of it just comes from the plantation lifestyle and part is explained by the river culture—somehow the banks of the lower Mississippi have always been a place to look for card games, brothels, and strong drink. Delta towns are pretty sedate-looking today but there is a lot going on in them that passersby do not customarily see. The Tallahatchie County sheriff declared that he was "amazed" when federal agents came onto his turf and seized fifty-one slot machines in a sweep of businesses in Webb, Tutwiler, Sumner, and Glendora. The sheriff probably would have been less amazed if he had ever been inside a Delta country club—it would be unusual for such a private club not to have an electronic poker machine somewhere on the premises. A local legend in Cleveland is Hayse Moore, who, with his wife, used to run the Hayse-Marie Club on U.S. 61. A former sheriff of Bolivar County says that Moore had a reputation for running the finest nightclub and gambling establishment in the Delta. The legalization of liquid refreshment in Mississippi in 1966 eventually put Moore out of business, but many marked the club's passing with regret.

A Cleveland businessman told me, "In the days of the black market tax they had slot machines all over here. As a child growing up in the Delta there were slot machines everywhere. One-armed bandits. If the adults were talking and wanted the kids to be entertained or leave them alone, they'd give you a roll of nickels to go play the slots with. They were at the country club. We had a thing called the Benoit Outing Club over at the lake. It was a big work boat that they brought in and pulled up and turned into a club, a place to buy your bait, play your slots, and drink beer."

Sins of the flesh are farther from the surface but not forgotten. The First Christian Church led an antipornography campaign against the sale of adult magazines and videos in Clarksdale, though the not entirely sympathetic newspaper editorialized: "We might suggest that the pornography problem in Clarksdale is not as grave as is being presently represented." The Indianola public schools resolved that students with the AIDS virus would be allowed to attend public schools if the district health officer certified that they posed no threat to other students. The newspaper reported that "Indianola has no students with AIDS, but the school board adopted a policy, anyway."

I ran into an old acquaintance at a benefit for an arts federation in Jackson. I had met Mary briefly several years before in Nashville where she was studying French literature. Then she was all seriousness, intent on making A's. Now she glided around the crowd sipping sparkling water, radiating relaxation, good health, and wit. Though I had known she was from Mississippi, I had not placed her in the Delta. We chatted about my book, and she invited me to visit her home on a later trip. In that next encounter it was revealed that she had been both a debutante and head majorette in her high school. Today, she is married to a banker's son and lives discreetly on display, she says, in a south Delta town.

They dwell in his family's compound of three houses built around a swimming pool, bright with flowering oleander and shaded by tall magnolias. It is very pleasant to be there both because she is charming and because we are quietly attended at poolside by a black woman who appears, just at the moment when the ice cubes start to slip away, to offer us something cool to drink. Mary is even more relaxed than she was in Jackson.

"Was I fast in high school? Well, dear, I guess we all were. We were wild. All we ever wanted to do was get out and go to dances. We'd drive all over the county. There really wasn't anything else to do but get out and go. We were prim and proper too, of course, and didn't allow any heavy necking until the second date.

"I was deflowered on a John Deere tractor. That doesn't sound very romantic, does it, but I assure you it was. We have such beautiful moonlight here. It's a wonder I didn't get pregnant. Thank the Lord for that. We were just a little wild, I guess. We'd go skinny-dipping in the river. We weren't supposed to date the football players, but of course we did. They just swept us away, or if they didn't, we'd sweep them.

"I went to the Methodist Church every Sunday. Church was very important in our family, and I went to Sunday school every week until I got out of college. Our whole family went to Wednesday night supper, and of course Daddy was an elder. One of my earliest memories is seeing him pass the collection plate, and my mother likes to tell that I hollered out in church, 'Bring me some soup, Daddy' because I thought that's what it was. We were very traditional, I suppose, and I guess we still are.

"It's a safe and secure feeling growing up in a little town where you know everybody. We've still got some of that now, but not as much. Everybody pretty much knows me, of course, because of our position in the community, but we really don't have that many close friends. We entertain a lot. Last weekend we had about fifty people here for a party, and the next morning I came out and seven or eight of them were sound asleep right here in the pool chairs. I just brought them inside and fixed them bacon and eggs and Bloody Marys and about noon they all went home."

It was not so long ago, I remarked, that she had lived quite differently in Nashville. I had heard that she had later moved to New Orleans for a while, then to Memphis. "Basically I was searching for myself," she said. "Actually I think I kept finding myself, but I didn't like what I was finding so I would look some more. Probably I was trying to find someplace in the world that was as nice as where I grew up. I wanted a warm, sunny place with lots of boys to admire me." She laughs.

"And I suppose I wanted to be somebody but I didn't have talent for very much, so I came back here." I said something polite, but she breezed on past. "I came back here hunting for a husband and got one. You couldn't ask for a nicer man. Our life is really very comfortable here. Many of the farmers have been on bad times and of course the bank suffers along with them. And you know the black people will probably elect the mayor in the next election, which might cause a few stresses and strains. But on the whole life is pretty damn good."

I press to find out what she does with her time. "I already told you I give parties," she says. But it turns out she does more than that. A friend of hers in Florida designs women's clothing, and Mary is thinking about opening a sportswear shop in the Delta to sell it. She goes to a certain number of obligatory banking and civic functions with her husband. And she does volunteer work, which includes teaching reading in a class for adult illiterates. Can she find satisfaction in doing that? I ask, and for the first time see an angry flash in her eyes.

"Why, of course I can," she says. "I think we do a lot of good. Our life here is very meaningful. Why, we have a town to care about. Though it may not be much, we like it here just fine."

Pride, parties, politics, and generally alcohol are features of small-town life. In fact, moonshine has lost little of its popularity. State ABC agents broke up eight stills in Bolivar County in 1988 and more in Grenada and Yazoo counties. They treat matters as they have always done: smash the cooker with an ax and haul the whiskey downtown for testing. The still operators, when caught, are familiar faces and generally offer little resistance. Jail time is the hazard, but the profession can be fairly lucrative and is almost universally respected. Sometimes the agents will sniff out a marijuana patch, as they did in the summer of 1988 in Bentonia, but there is nothing new about that either. Fifty years ago Bolivar County deputy E. M. East discovered fifty pounds of marijuana on a plantation south of Shaw and arrested two men for trying to sell it.

Hard drugs are a newer and bigger problem here, as elsewhere. Black Roy's Place, what the police chief called a "crack house," was busted in Leland in 1988. The mayor of Shaw and thirty others were arrested in the summer of 1988 for allegedly dealing in cocaine. A white businessman in the county seat sent me a clipping about it with a note, "Here is an example of local corruption from black-run towns." On the other hand, when sixteen Indianolians were arrested for cocaine dealing in 1987, it was a black officer who did the fingerprinting. In any case, drugs are a big problem here as elsewhere. They have replaced "the movement," one Leland woman told me, and local government in the Delta is not well equipped to cope. The root of the problem is lack of jobs. One is tempted to say there is no solution for that, but the Delta has a tradition of trying to manage its own affairs and it is not impossible that it has a bright future if it draws on all of its talents to create one.

The area needs to do something. Mississippi's high school dropout rate in 1985–1986 was 38.2 percent, or 15,800 kids, putting the state third from the bottom in the South, but the Delta statistic was even a little worse. In most Delta counties the number of people age twenty-five and over who have an eighth-grade education or less exceeds the number who have a high school diploma or a college degree. Even by the conservative figures of the U.S. Agriculture Department, the unemployment rate was over 13 percent in most Delta counties in 1985, and soared to more than 19 percent in northernmost Tunica County (adjacent to Memphis). On an annual basis the government sends more transfer payment checks, for items such as crop subsidies, welfare, and unemployment compensation, to every Delta county than there are people in those counties. The largest single occupational group in all Delta counties is "consumer services," which takes in working at the gas station or at McDonald's. In a time of overall economic growth nationally, the total payroll in Issaquena and Quitman counties actually declined between 1977 and 1984.

The Senate Select Committee on Hunger took testimony in the summer of 1987 in Itta Bena, one of the prettiest towns in the Delta. The name means "Home in the Woods," but most of the woods are gone now. Just south of town on Route 7 there is a cotton field beside the road that runs two miles from tree to tree. That is a long row to plow and is the reason that there are tape decks in tractor cabs. There are places where there is nothing on the horizon. The fields just meet the sky. The only blemish on the town square of tidy old stores, divided by the Illinois Central Railroad, is that the train station that was once the center of town has been torn down to make way for a Piggly Wiggly supermarket. A drawing of the station by local artist Mozelle Webb has been reproduced as one of the favorite Christmas cards of the Delta.

Rims Barber, of the Children's Defense Fund, spoke to the Senate committee in Itta Bena about the facts of poverty in the five surrounding Delta counties, Tallahatchie, Sunflower, Leflore, Humphreys, and Holmes. In these five, he reported, blacks make up 62 percent of the population, 54 percent of the workforce, and 84 percent of the unemployed. The average unemployment rate was 16 percent in 1986; for blacks it was 24.9 percent. The infant mortality rate among blacks was 21.5 percent. (In an area where almost everybody was birthed by a midwife, generally at home, now the law states that even midwives must conduct deliveries in a hospital. Isn't that a little too much regulation?) And hospitals are scarce. There are no doctors to deliver a baby in Humphreys County anymore. Mothers go to Hollandale or Greenwood or farther, to Jackson. Incredibly, out of a total five-county population of 134,220 in 1986, 45,655 people received food stamps.

Breaking the cycle with economic development is a major emphasis in most communities, and the search is on for business ready to relocate to the Delta. For example, the Greenwood-Leflore Chamber of Commerce and Economic Development Foundation had eighteen economic development executives spend the day in Greenwood right before Christmas in 1987. One local employer, John Sturm of Irvin Industries, praised the low absenteeism and turnover of his plant's workers. Incredible was his reported statement that 85 percent of his workers were female heads of households. What in the world do the men do? Very possibly they work in a catfish plant.

The question is, can these local efforts make a difference? Is the problem of such proportion that only massive federal intervention in the economy can solve it, or is it so deeply rooted in racial polarity that only serious efforts to harness white and black energy on the local level would make change a possibility, no matter how many government dollars were thrown into the area?

For the present the problem is not being addressed in either fashion, and the little towns of the Delta continue their see-saw existence between charming vigor in good years and near extinction in bad. And the bad show signs of prevailing. By and large the Mississippi Delta is losing population. Every county, except Warren, where Vicksburg is located, and Grenada, which is mostly hill country and has the benefit of an interstate highway, lost population between 1960 and 1980. All of the counties entirely "Delta" are projected by the federal government to keep losing people through 2020 except for Washington on the river, where Greenville is located. It is predicted to grow from about 72,000 to about 74,000 people over the next twenty years. Its neighbor to the south, Issaquena County, is expected to drop from a 1980 population of 2,513 down to 2,369 in 2010. What can a loss of a few hundred people here or there mean? It means that more and more little towns are simply shutting down. Something must be done to prevent these predictions from coming true or else the Delta will be reforested naturally.

In Greenville I asked a prominent planter the general cause of the Delta malaise. He gave a standard reply, a dearth of business moving in, but I asked him to explain the cause of that. He did so by posing a question: "If you were a business seeking to relocate, would you prefer to go to Fayetteville, North Carolina, where the schools are half-white and half-black, or to Greenville, Mississippi, where the schools are 90 percent black? What city would seem more attractive to the managers who must relocate, and which is more likely to give the appearance of having a healthy local government?"

Every chamber of commerce in the country is, of course, courting businesses, and those engaged in that pursuit know that it is difficult to say why industry prefers one location to another. But this gentleman's comments seemed to presuppose that industry either does not

Fourth Street, Clarksdale, 1988

like blacks or that it will deduce that a school system so out of balance is evidence of a very strained social relationship. If the former is true, nothing can be done, but if the latter is correct, then it is within the power of the Delta's citizens to create conditions conducive to expanding that elusive "opportunity." They can work to improve the schools and put everybody in them. They can push their big products, land, labor, and agricultural know-how. For a century, the Delta has been one of the world's premier laboratories for growing major crops well. If it could just market that genius in the modern world. If it could just accomplish with its human resources what it has with its natural resources.

nine

TAKING THE OATH

▲▲▲

It was a summer of wisteria . . . the odor, the scent,
which five months later Mr. Compson's letter would
carry up from Mississippi and over the long iron New
England snow and into Quentin's sitting-room at
Harvard.
—William Faulkner, *Absalom, Absalom!*

My fellow Mississippians: Our day has come, and what a
glorious day it is.
This is our day of hope and destiny, and we are eager to
be about our business. My speech will be brief—for the
labor we have to do is long—and the future of this great
state requires our deeds and not our words.
—Governor Ray Mabus, Inaugural Speech

M ississippi as a whole cast a big vote for change in the election
▽▽▽ of thirty-nine-year-old Ray Mabus as governor in 1987. The
clean-cut state auditor from Ackerman, who had exposed graft and
corruption in the procurement practices of the supervisors of several
counties, Mabus campaigned as the "new broom." He was also Ole
Miss and Johns Hopkins–educated, magna cum laude from Harvard
Law School, blessed with a pretty and educated wife, and seemingly
untouched by any race prejudice. He actively courted and won the
black vote. From the vantage point of one who saw and judged his
wildly enthusiastic campaign cadre at rallies like the Neshoba
County Fair, it was evident that Mabus was also the candidate of the
bottled-water crowd.

His central campaign theme was education: increase teachers' salaries; get Mississippi off the bottom. Then he wanted a new state constitution and the imposition of a county unit system to diminish the power of the old-guard county supervisors over the purse strings.

He won the election with one-third of the white vote and 90 percent of the black, defeating a conservative Republican, and his inauguration was a triumph. The setting was the steps of the state capitol, on an intermittently raining, cold January day, on a platform festooned with red, white, and blue bunting, in front of crowds of people waving American flags and campaign hats. Four former governors sat together on the grandstand: J. P. Coleman, one of the last of the segregationist governors, during whose administration, in 1956, the State Sovereignty Commission was created to resist integration; Bill Waller, first of the moderates and first to say that the "N" word had no place in Mississippi politics; William Winter, the cerebral aristocrat who had a foot on each side of the great divide between black and white, new and old, and who retired to become chancellor at Ole Miss; and Bill Allain, Mabus's predecessor, who was elected amid crazy charges of sexual misconduct with prostitute queens in Jackson, who was almost a recluse once in office, who disliked flying and therefore forswore the trade junkets some thought necessary to "sell Mississippi," and who declined to seek a second term.

The entire atmosphere of the day was refreshing. Hundreds of well-attired supporters joined the governor-elect for a prayer breakfast at Galloway Methodist, the Mabuses' Jackson church. The inauguration itself began with a key symbolic act: Harry Bowie, a black civil rights activist from Greenville, gave the benediction, followed by various anthems, presentations, introductions, and the administration of the oath of office by Judge Roy Nobel Lee. In the inaugural address, the new governor determined to, "renew the quest for what Mississippi can become." He said, "A new day depends on our resolve to banish racism from the state of Mississippi." And he let the crowd know that, "We don't have to be patient anymore because our day has come." The message was *change*. Race as an issue was a story of the past. What Mississippi wanted now was to get off the bottom, not to be last anymore: to change.

After his speech, the governor and Julie Mabus, a professional woman with a master's in business administration from Columbia and a "brunch club" appearance that is very appealing in Mississippi, stood in a line greeting well-wishers at the governor's mansion. This itself seemed to be a history-making event as the obviously affluent and the obviously otherwise stood patiently together in a line that stretched beyond the lawns of the mansion, out the gates, and around the block. The people kept coming all afternoon for a chance to shake the governor's hand, and he stayed there ninety minutes after his scheduled departure to give everyone that experience. The inaugural ball that evening was by invitation only, but anyone wanting an invitation had only to call and request one. Almost fifteen thousand people came to the Mississippi Trade Mart to dance. Finally, at about ten o'clock, the band cut into a rock 'n' roll number and the nation's youngest governor and his first lady got on the floor and let it rip. They were hip.

Mabus also had a new legislature to work with. There were thirty-two freshman members of the State House of Representatives, and most were disposed to support the governor. The leader of the legislature's old guard, Buddie Newman, had retired, and his forces were ousted by reformers who replaced him as speaker with Tim Ford of Tupelo. Greenville's perennial power broker, Representative Sonny Merideth, on the losing side of the uprising of young Turks in the state legislature, was replaced as chairman of the House Ways and Means Committee, but in deference to the good ol' boy network, he was still given County Affairs. By contrast, Aaron Henry, who has been the rock of the civil rights movement in Mississippi for thirty years and president of the state NAACP, and who has represented part of Clarksdale in the legislature since 1980, chairs no committees. In the house chamber, Henry sits as far forward as possible, within arm's reach of the rostrum. Clipped to his nameplate is the Mississippi state flag, bearing the stars and bars of the Confederacy. (The 122-member state legislature contains about 20 blacks, not nearly in line with the state's 35 percent black population.)

The governor initially had great success. His first drive was to raise teachers' salaries by $3,700 to bring Mississippi in line with the southeastern regional average. This campaign to do something for the state's teachers has been an enduring feature of life in Mississippi. I recall that in 1968, when I first came to Mississippi, giving teachers a $1,300 raise had been the major issue then facing the legislature. In 1988, aided by a $118 million surplus left over by Governor Allain, and a windfall of $145 million in unexpected tax collections, Mabus's plans went through. He did not get everything he wanted. The teachers' raise was $2,110, not $3,700, for 1988, but the legislature decreed a $3,800 raise for 1989. At that time, three months into his term, being against Ray Mabus was deemed almost unpatriotic in Mississippi.

Then, in one of the strangest political moves in the history of the United States, or at least of Mississippi, the governor announced that he was supporting a white Tupelo woman, Billie Thompson, to replace Ed Cole, the black chairman of the state Democratic Party. It is possible he had no idea how the announcement would stun the state's blacks, who had given Mabus 90 percent of their vote, but only if he was unfamiliar with the history of the civil rights movement in Mississippi. Just such a fight for control over the party had led to the creation of the Mississippi Freedom Democratic Party in 1964, which tried unsuccessfully to be seated at the National Democratic Convention held that year in Atlantic City. That black organization returned home to Mississippi to become the "loyalist" Democrats (who were loyal to the national party platform and its ticket), and they competed with the all-white "regular" Democrats until the two groups were finally able to overcome their antagonism and merge in 1972. The terms of the merger were that there would be two co-chairmen, State Representative Aaron Henry of Clarksdale, president of the Mississippi NAACP, and Tom Riddell of Canton. In 1980 Governor William Winter led a drive to have only one chairman: white Jackson lawyer Danny Cupit was elected, and Ed Cole was made executive vice-chairman. Cole was elevated to the chairmanship in 1987 and became the only black state party chief in the United States.

Cole had gotten his start in politics in 1971 when he managed the unsuccessful gubernatorial campaign of Charles Evers, the canny mayor of Fayette, from whom Cole says he learned everything he knows. Since then Cole has been brought into the party's mainstream. He became the first black on the staff of U.S. Senator James

Eastland and then, in 1981, a staff assistant to Senator Stennis, who retired in 1988 after sixty years in public office, forty of them in the Senate.

Mrs. Thompson was a businesswoman and described herself as a "yellow-dog Democrat," meaning that she would even back a yellow dog if he were a Democrat. She had supported Mabus throughout the campaign. This in itself did not seem sufficient reason for the governor's backing. Cole had supported former governor Bill Waller in the primary, but he had switched to Mabus in the runoff. What puzzled black leaders was not only that Mabus would be so insensitive to what the party chairmanship symbolized to them, but that he continued to push Thompson, even though everybody knew she did not have the votes. The cagey thing to do as the train left the station without the governor would have been for Mabus to jump in the engine and yell full speed ahead. But he did not do it. Instead, Mabus refused to comment publicly on the fight and watched Ed Cole be elected by a vote of 56 to 41. The only conclusion that could be drawn from the embarrassment was that Mabus, his feet firmly planted in the new age, his training and experience from Harvard Law and the law firm of Sargent Shriver, did not realize the power of the old world in Mississippi. He was on an entirely different wavelength from the tough political dealers who had hammered out the racial compromise that made state government function, but he would have to learn how to tune them in.

The loss illustrated the danger of ignoring Mississippi's recent civil rights history and took the steam out of Mabus's drive. While he remained publicly popular and retained the support of the majority of blacks, he could no longer call every play, and politics as usual returned to the state legislature. Mabus wanted to rewrite the unwieldy constitution of 1890, an antiblack, anti-industry document that was originally designed to eliminate the black vote (over the opposition of Delta planters) and to commit state funds to levee building (enthusiastically supported by Delta planters) and that has had to be amended ninety-five times just to keep it in line with the United States Constitution and to permit the formation of corporations in the state. He lost on that. His effort to impose a county unit system whereby county purchasing would be centralized, and presumably better supervised, died as the deadline for passage expired in May. Instead it was put up for a county-by-county vote at the time of the presidential election.

Despite these setbacks, Governor Mabus has captured quite a bit of attention for Mississippi. On May 15, 1988, he and the governors of Arkansas and Louisiana, Bill Clinton and Buddy Roemer, boarded a barge in Rosedale, which calls itself "The Delta City of Brotherly Love," and were towed out to the middle of the river to announce a tristate effort to increase development and to fight poverty in the region. This is about the most noteworthy event in the history of Rosedale except that Davy Crockett is said to have crossed the river here on his way to the Alamo. The governors signed two accords, one promising to work together for the common good, and one promising to work together for some international trade. Significantly, the guest of honor was His Excellency Nobuo Matsunaga, ambassador of Japan.

I visited Rosedale the day before the ceremony to see what effect all of this was having on the little town. It turned out that nothing at all was happening there: whoever was planning the elaborate event was obviously able to work more efficiently from some remote location. I went to the office of the mayor, J. Y. Trice, who was scheduled to kick off the morrow's events with an invocation, but he was still at home eating lunch. I walked around the tree-shaded downtown area, which is only a brief occupation and one that allows you to be thoroughly eyeballed by the few folks hanging out around the courthouse.

Upon Mr. Trice's return to the three-room city hall, he invited me to sit on a folding chair in his small office filled with dusty stacks of paper and official reports. His own desk was occupied by an auditor going over the books, who remained there throughout our chat. Mr. Trice is a retired school principal, and he has served as Rosedale's mayor since 1984 without pay. He is not the town's first black mayor; indeed, he beat a black incumbent for the job. He is a pleasant and well-fed fellow, whose shirt pockets are full of pens and who refers to himself as "we." He arrived in Rosedale in 1969 as principal of the black West Bolivar Training School, and he presided over the ultimate integration of the local schoolhouse. About twenty-five of the

white students pulled out for the private academies, but the flight
was less than in other districts of the county. The mayor boasts that
Judge Pearson, the town's most influential white, says that Rosedale
has never had a mayor like Mayor Trice. "It was a double compli-
ment to us because a white man is saying it, and he is in the crowd
that he is saying we are better than." Near Rosedale is a state park,
the Great River Road State Park, and Trice "pins a flower" on himself by admitting he gave it that name. The town has good race
relations, says Trice. About two-thirds of its 3,000 people are black,
but there are two whites and two blacks on the city council. Trice
has hired both white and black police chiefs in his time. The town
needs jobs, and his main hope lies in the concept of a four-lane bridge
and railroad spur across the river at Rosedale. Having given me the
basic picture, the mayor excused himself for a nap.

The following morning dozens of reporters and camera crews
drove into town and loaded themselves onto a Jantran oil barge at
Rosedale harbor, and hundreds of schoolchildren came in by bus to
cheer and wave American and Japanese flags as the dignitaries
began to arrive. Finally, the barge was pushed out into the river by
the towboat _Log Loader._ This very picturesque gathering coincided
with a less ceremonial but more hard-nosed affair, the annual convo-
cation of the Delta Council, held at Delta State University in Cleveland. The Japanese ambassador was scheduled to speak there, too,
and before the governors actually got around to signing their agree-
ments on the barge, a speedboat was sent to retrieve the ambassador
so that he could get to Cleveland on time. After Governor Mabus
docked he also went to Delta State to speak. Mabus's talk was short
and left no doubt who the principal member of the intended audience was. "In 1987 the level of Japanese investment in the United
States stood at $30 billion," the governor said. "In Mississippi, Japa-
nese investment is only $20 million—one fifteen-hundredth of the
total. In Alabama, investment from Japan is twenty-two times
higher than it is in Mississippi . . . Mr. Ambassador, I want you to
know that we are not content with kudzu. We want different kinds
of plants. We want to do business, to make products, to take our
rightful place in the new world economy. We do not intend to be left
behind any longer. We want our economy to grow like kudzu."

Clearly, at that particular juncture in our nation's history, Japan was the friend to have. During his stay, Mr. Matsunaga was feted at the Indianola Country Club, selected by the host committee because it would admit black guests for the occasion. I do not know what the ambassador thinks of Mississippi, but it is clear what Mississippi thinks of him or at least what it hopes he can do for Mississippi. Before the summer ended, Mabus and the other two governors were bound for Japan in search of development prospects. If their efforts bear fruit, Japanese businessmen might find their investment in the Delta rewarded with the kind of extraordinarily loyal work force and captive body politic they are reputed to enjoy in Japan.

While Mabus is often described as an outstanding and dynamic leader, especially by young professionals, black and white, he has done little to bring other reformers into government with him. The state auditor's job, which Mabus used as a springboard to the governor's mansion, was not filled with a reformer when Mabus left. Voters rejected Michael Raff, the civil rights candidate who was alone in backing Mabus's call for a statewide county unit system, in favor of a numbers-cruncher named Pete Johnson who switched to the Republican Party once he got into office. Mabus has made a few key appointments of blacks, including Lee Roy Black as director of the Mississippi Department of Correction and George T. Watson as his public service commissioner. When he appointed a woman, Louisa Dixon, as commissioner of public safety, Bill Minor, most credible of all Mississippi journalists, said, "If forty years ago I had written a story predicting that in 1988 Mississippi would have a woman at the head of the Highway Patrol and a black man running Parchman Penitentiary, I would have been fitted for a strait jacket."

Yet Mabus has not brought those who fought the civil rights struggle in the 1960s into his inner circle. One such aging veteran made a remark about Mabus that may also be true of much of the state's younger generation. "He has no sense of history," the man, hardly an old-timer, said. "He can't tell the difference between those who fought for civil rights in the sixties and those who fought against it. If you're not a Yuppie driving a BMW, don't look to get appointed to anything. I'm lumped in the same category with Dub, Bubba, and Billy Bob. If you ain't under forty, he forgets you. We have been written off as ancient history." It may be that this drive for "change" in the abstract, not born in the fire of the 1960s, is what Mississippi needs, but it may also be true that a lack of understanding of how lively those fires still burn led the governor into the Ed Cole debacle.

I talked to the governor about his own upbringing, his education in the public schools of Ackerman and at Ole Miss, but I found the boyhood he described to be oddly untouched by any racial dilemmas. It could also be that race and civil rights as topics simply do not interest the governor much. They are the stuff of history, and the governor is a man of the present: a manager, a builder, an admirer of the arts and style. Our interview took place in his office in the capitol building. Joining us was his communications secretary, Cliff Treyens. Like many of the people around Mabus, Treyens is very young and from out of state. He explained that it was the governor's policy to have someone sit in on all meetings, "in case the governor later wants to write a letter." Cliff also taped the interview.

The governor was seated with a window to his back when I arrived, and he was talking on the telephone. The patter was tough, and I wished I knew who the subject of the conversation was: "The bottom line is don't trust anything he says, ever." As we talked, Mabus was distracted several times by some person invisible to me, who kept opening a door beside the governor's desk, trying to talk to him. Between these interruptions he answered my questions automatically, like one who has been interviewed several times too often.

The governor and I are about the same age, and I wondered where he had been twenty years ago. "Twenty years ago I had finished my junior year in college. I had grown up in a small town in north Mississippi called Ackerman. I had a typical small-town boyhood. Only child of older parents. But I played ball, fished, and played in the woods and did what little boys did in north Mississippi in the fifties and early sixties." He went to Ole Miss because his father had gone there, and was there from 1965 to 1969, years of crisis in Mississippi. Riots and killings had accompanied James Meredith's enrollment at the university in 1962. Freedom Summer of 1964 had put the state on almost a warlike footing. Meredith himself was shot in 1966 when he crossed the state line from Memphis in a march toward Jackson. These events seem not to have much marked the governor, however, or at least he did not take my bait and comment on those days. In fairness, however, it should be said that when Mabus addressed the 1988 graduates of Ole Miss, he recalled "some words spoken on this campus when I was a student by a figure who was controversial then, but whose past has left a void that has never since been filled."

Robert Kennedy cared deeply and he braved anger and he said to the students of my youth things that need to be heard anew. He journeyed to Ole Miss more than twenty years ago, and despite the prediction of trouble your predecessors here cheered him wildly. He said to them: "Your generation is the first with the chance not only to remedy the mistakes which all of us have made in the past, but to transcend them.

Those words may guide Mabus yet. It is plain that he does not intend to waste his substance on reliving civil rights struggles of the past when the book on that subject is closed in his mind.

"Mississippi never had geographical segregation," he avers. "My playmates, as a lot of people's playmates when they were little, were fully integrated. You had white playmates and black playmates. Then when you got to be six you went to different schools. Once those social barriers, like schools, restaurants, hotels, football teams, and stuff like that, started breaking down, Mississippi had a lot shorter distance to go to get to an integrated society than a lot of other places did simply because there never was the geographical-type distance. Simply because we didn't have any big cities. In a small town you are going to know everybody regardless of their color and status in life. I think that once the civil rights revolution broke down some racial barriers, it freed everybody in Mississippi. It freed whites and blacks. Now when you've got a playmate of a different race when you are five years old, you go to the same school. That's making a big difference.

"Mississippi has some serious problems, as does the rest of the South. For a century, into the sixties, the politics of race were the overriding dominant factor to everything, and in a lot of ways it kept us from dealing with a lot of our problems, like education, economic development, running government, transportation, things like that. What the civil rights revolution has done is it allows us to work with real problems. I think that one of the things that people realize is that we are in this together and that you don't make progress as a state if you leave a whole segment of society behind."

I was struck that in his mind the civil rights struggle is essentially a battle won and that the way is now cleared to address real problems. Mabus believes that public school desegregation is just about licked. He says that more than 90 percent of Mississippi's kids are now in public schools. (I checked that figure against my trusty *World Almanac* and saw that he was just about right. Only some 50,000 of Mississippi's half a million elementary and secondary school children were in private schools in 1986.) Mabus speaks of the existence of "pockets" of private academies. "We've got some serious problems in Mississippi that are to some extent magnified in the Delta. One has been the historic neglect of education. Making sure that people have tools to compete in the modern-day economy is one of the things we are trying to accomplish. The second thing is improving the workforce we have got now through adult literacy, bringing in high-skilled, high-paying jobs and not doing what we have done in the past, which is selling Mississippi cheap. Those unskilled, low-wage jobs, they're gone. They are in the Philippines and Taiwan now. Now we look to child care, welfare reform, things that taken together will make us a more competitive society. There is no quick fix. It will take us a decade or two."

Agriculture, he explained, now plays a small part in the state's economy. It employs few, he says, but surely that is an understatement. My impression, leaving the governor and his aide, is that Mabus does not much like the old Mississippi. Big farms, the academies, the domination of the Delta, are all things to be put behind us and, the governor almost says, need not really be taken seriously anymore. He points to the fact that he did not come up through the traditional political ranks but won by virtue of a heavy media campaign. He says the same is true of Mike Espy, Mississippi's first black congressman, who became known not through the civil rights movement but through television. To hear Mabus speak in the summer of 1988, the Mississippi good ol' boy network had entirely ceased to exist. But then, who defeated the governor's call for a new state constitution?

After that session I drove north on I-55 toward Greenwood. Lulled by the blur of pine trees along both sides of the highway, with nothing to distinguish the scenery from Ohio or Oregon, I might have thought the governor was right. The past is past in Mississippi. But at the Greenwood Ramada, at the Mexican buffet, a party of twelve whites dining at the table next to me did a loud round robin of Jesse Jackson jokes and filled the dining room with laughter. Outside, a little group of black children and another of white children both splashed in the pool. The parents, reclining in armchairs on opposite sides of the pool, glanced at each other occasionally, and to my mind there was a little awareness and watchfulness there; something more significant passed between them than a poolside nod between strangers. The past is not that far gone.

ten

TRICKY
CURRENTS

▲▲▲

The Mississippi folk Negro today is a genial mass of
remarkable qualities. He seems carefree and shrewd
and does not bother himself with the problems the
white man has to solve. The tariff and currency do not
interest him in the least. He has his standard, silver,
and he wants no other kind. As for the so-called Negro
Question—that, too, is just another problem he has left
for the white man to cope with. Seated in the white
man's wagon, and subtly letting the white man worry
with the reins, the Negro assures himself a share of all
things good. Once a landlord was asked if the Negro
really had a soul. "If he hasn't," the landlord replied,
"it's the first thing that a white man ever had that a
Negro didn't share if he stayed with him long enough."
—WPA, *Mississippi: A Guide to the Magnolia State*

No one could seriously dispute that there are a quite a few good
▽▽▽ ol' boys left in Mississippi public life and in lay positions as
well. One of these is Charles W. Capps, Jr., who has represented
Cleveland in the state legislature since 1972. A Mason and a Methodist, Capps is chairman of the Appropriations Committee and has
influence far beyond Bolivar County as chairman of the Democratic
Party's Southern Legislative Conference. With silvery white hair
and eyes that twinkle when he smiles, Capps personifies the Delta
politician as well as anybody, and he is definitely a very savvy good

ol' boy. My visit to Cleveland coincided with the annual meeting of
the Delta Council being held in Greenwood. Capps is a prominent
member of the council, which he describes as the "number one regional organization in the United States." The council was organized
in the 1930s to promote cotton, and it is "made up of the best we have
to offer." Through the Delta Council, and its offshoot the National
Cotton Council, agribusiness has written the national cotton program since its inception. Its annual meeting is traditionally held at
Delta State, and over the years it has been addressed by almost every
secretary of agriculture and such luminaries as William Faulkner,
David Rockefeller, and George Bush. Dean Acheson announced the
Marshall Plan at the Delta Council annual meeting in 1947. When
my interview with Representative Capps concluded, he was to go to
meet the Japanese ambassador's helicopter to escort him to the
governor's meeting on the barge in the Mississippi River, and then
to the council meeting. The Delta Council is to Southern agriculture
what the National Rifle Association is to gun owners: it projects their
views to the nation at large.

Capps and I talked at his real estate and insurance office on a side
street in Cleveland, where, beneath nicely framed popular prints of
Robert E. Lee and Stonewall Jackson, he conducts his business. The
representative's forebear, it turns out, was a private captured at
Vicksburg, who after the war was one of eight Mississippians selected to escort the body of Jefferson Davis from New Orleans to his
final place of burial in Richmond.

"I came out of the plantation system." Capps says flatly. His father
was a cotton merchant in Cleveland. "We've always owned land."
Capps has farmed that land since 1966. He served as sheriff before
that; in Bolivar County he was the last of the "plantation sheriffs."
He got paid according to the taxes and fines he collected, a system
that made some sheriffs rich men. If Capps is rich, he does not show
it off. Except for the aberration of Reconstruction, the big planters
always elected their sheriffs, and they picked men who respected
them. In Capps's time, he says, he never sent a deputy onto a "man's
place without first talking to the man, and the boss man brought the
suspect in. Now the norm is strictly trained law enforcement just
like anyplace else." Of course, there are not that many hands left on
the big farms now and not that many crimes in the country.

He thinks the black family was the major casualty of the breakup of the old plantation system, for reasons I had not heard before. "We completely destroyed the relationship between the black man and his wife," Capps says. Under the sharecropper system, the husband controlled all of the money. In the 1960s farmers went to the "day system"; each family member was paid individually, and all were paid the same amount. By that "we did a terrible thing, unintentionally, to the husband. The effect was that the husband lost control of the family."

Eventually, of course, husbands and wives alike were displaced from the plantations by bigger tractors and combines, and many people moved to towns like Cleveland. Cleveland is fortunate to have factories, including Duo-Fast, Travenol, Baxter Labs, and Douglas & Lomason, that have absorbed a fair share of black workers. Capps credits Cleveland's success to its extremely aggressive pursuit of industry in contrast with other towns (he mentions Clarksdale) controlled by large farmers.

"Historically, in the Delta we have had too many families for the farms. The sons of the planters do not stay here unless there is enough land to support them. They are not the ones that run Travenol. Those people come in from outside. There is but one way to promote this region and that is to totally educate our people, make them stay in school, stop this teenage pregnancies thing, and make sure that all of our people can do something. If they can't, the taxpayer will have to pay for them out of welfare or at Parchman. All of the cheap-labor industries have moved to Mexico."

Since he represents several of them, Capps is also concerned about the boarding up of many little towns. "Look at Shaw. None of these towns are surviving very well. In Duncan, for example, the trend is continuing, the battle is lost." And he says that he lacks the imagination to know how to save them, which is quite an admission for a politician. He thinks that taking over the governments of these small municipalities may be an illusory victory for blacks, because it will make the towns less attractive to developers. "If you were Japanese and looking all over the country, you would not want to come to an all-black locale," he opines, without explaining that conclusion. (This is the second time I have heard this theory; the first time the bias was ascribed to industry in general.) Obviously, Capps attributes certain prejudices to the Japanese. I admit I do not know. Do the Japanese not like the black race? He looks hopefully toward the second generation of black elected officials, who may perceive that to survive they will need to coalesce with whites. "Both races need each other. We're here, we're not going to leave here. And if we don't work together, we will sink together."

Like most people Capps is bothered that young people are deserting the Delta, but he knows that for the educated there is nothing to do. "I have counseled my son," he says, "that if he wants to make a living he can run this insurance business here in Cleveland, but if he wants to share in the economic prosperity of the country he must go elsewhere. But he enjoys the Delta life, the hunting, the fishing, and all that. My own life is here. When I was at the age of decision, I saw a brighter future. This was the most prosperous area of the state for people like me. Now the only ones who stay are the ones that absolutely have something to do. The blacks are not going to leave, and unless something changes we will end up with a few wealthy older people and many uneducated blacks." For that reason he professes to be totally committed to public education, and he was, in fact, one of the most potent movers behind Governor Mabus's successful initiative in the 1988 legislature to raise teachers' salaries.

Capps's own district is 60 percent black, but the only opponent he has faced in the sixteen years since his first election in 1972 was a young white county attorney whom he narrowly defeated in 1988, and who made points by attacking Capps for his "liberal" causes, such as supporting a state lottery for education. Capps may be a business-oriented pragmatist, but if he is liberal it is a latter-day conversion. He recalls a 1959 "gentlemen's agreement" among the candidates for the various county offices which provided that if any one of them won because of the support of the voters from the all-black town of Mound Bayou, that candidate would withdraw. Capps was one of those who did win, numerically, with the Mound Bayou vote, and he did not accept election. "That was my code of honor then." Thus, in the old days, were even those few blacks who managed to register excluded from politics. Capps seems to have made the mental transition. This old sheriff, for example, speaks admiringly of Mike Espy, who he says has opened doors for Mississippians that have never been open before because Espy is a black and a Democrat.

Capps speaks with a chuckle about what makes the Delta unique. It has always been, he says, "fully wide open" as far as drinking goes. As sheriff, he used to shoot up stills, but there were also two wholesale whiskey houses in Cleveland back when the state was dry. In the thirties and forties there was casino gambling in Cleveland with croupiers wearing tuxedos. Now the atmosphere is less elite, but you can still find crap games and bookie joints. Any place that touches water has that kind of environment, he thinks. Capps is a member of the Merigold Hunting Club and does enjoy the finer things of life. As a younger man he says he spent "many years" of his life in the lobby of the Peabody Hotel and wanted to be buried there. He goes to New Orleans when he can and eats "all over town."

The hope for the future, as he sees it, is an improved transportation system, a new bridge across the river at Rosedale, and more dollars for education. In answer to my question whether this was not simply looking for more help from the almighty federal government, he said, "I don't know how we can help ourselves. But remember, the rest of the country only progresses as fast as we progress." I wonder if that is true. The rest of the country seems to be doing fine, while Mississippi staggers along behind.

"Working together" is a catchphrase for leaders of both races today, but in my view, it will be a long time before the people of the Delta forget about race. It goes too deep. Lewis Baker has written that whites in the Delta have a businesslike attitude toward race, and I suppose that is true of the whites. They realize that their economic livelihood is tied in some way to the greater number of blacks who thrive in the area. Among blacks, there is generally a polite silence about race, but one senses that many blacks, and maybe whites, grew up in families that did not so much suffer in silence as hate in silence. I feel it most among blacks who did not grow up in "movement" families, who were not indoctrinated in "the Dream," and who are not now particularly forgiving toward the white community. They remember who the community's bigots were, not so much from personal experience as from what their parents have told them, and they avoid their young. Thus are prejudices passed along. Some of them expect the whites to abandon the

Delta, since after the black man quits there will be nobody left to do the white man's work.

In reality much of the work is not the white man's, but is for the benefit of the insurance companies, the elusive Arab landowners, the banks, the "system" in general. Even in simpler times targeting the oppressor was not easy. Across the Delta, after the Yankee armies passed, thousands of black people took to the roads in a march to the river, to freedom, with no other purpose than that. For weeks the eerie processional continued. They trekked along, singing, praying, some dancing, some quiet, toward freedom's star. Ultimately, most walked back home and settled for a great deal less, and for a hundred years since, whites and blacks have stared at each other across a divide that never went away.

The white counterpart, who came by his prejudices equally honestly through inheritance, is the thirty-year-old son of a north Delta politician who told me, "Daddy always said if you spread all the money out equally, the same people would end up with it." The young man had moved away from the Delta and entered the oil business in Montana, but he had come back because "where people know you, you can do a lot more things. I don't know if it is a security blanket, or just a fact." What he is doing sounds pretty sophisticated: he sets up companies to borrow low-interest money from the Farmers' Home Administration to build low-income housing. These can be tax shelters, and he tries to sell interests in them to investors in New York City. He is indirectly sipping at the federal trough and knows it. "If you took away the farmers' government subsidy payment, the welfare, and the unemployment check," he says, "this whole place would blow away."

He sees his odd little homeplace as part of a world scene. Through his church he goes to Honduras every year as a volunteer with the Honduras Baptist Dental Ministry, and for the most part pulls teeth. One year he met a Nicaraguan contra leader and was impressed. He and all of his friends, he says, are very pro-contra. In his own estimation he is a "semi-open-minded" person. "A lot of things are bred in us," he says. In high school in the Delta he was a "liberal" and thought blacks had a hard time. When he went out to the Dakotas he found that people hated the blacks, and by the time he got back to Mississippi, his stance was "down nigger." He remains friends with a high school buddy who has turned into a black man's lawyer, but he is increasingly concerned about preserving racial identity, culture, and position. He has only scorn for black politician-lawyers, who he thinks do nothing but create suits, and for several recently elected black officials, whom he sees as semiliterate and corrupt.

Indeed, a small number of area officials have been accused in the past year of taking payoffs to protect gambling or dealing in drugs. This young man's concerns go deeper than that, however: he perceives another danger. When blacks achieve full power, he asks rhetorically, what is the next stage? The obvious answer that frightens him is property taxes. Since the whites have the money, where are the blacks going to get theirs? They will either take it from the government, ethically or not, or tax it from the whites.

What is the solution? For many of his contemporaries it is to leave—to move to the white hills of Arkansas, western North Carolina, or Montana, "where the hunting's good, and there ain't no niggers." But for those who, like himself, are determined to stay in the Delta because "we love it here," he does not seem to have an answer except wait and see. He can appreciate what he calls a "miracle" of change in his own father, a politician who was raised as a racist but who is active in the state's biracial Democratic Party coalition. Yet, "Dad still thinks whites are superior. He wouldn't have a black to dinner." And the son? "I have a black friend, but I wouldn't invite him for dinner. That's the way I was raised."

What is it about dinner? The biographies of just about every Southern white man and woman who was raised in the old way, but who awakened to fight for equal rights, contains a cathartic episode when they found themselves actually eating dinner with a black person. Some passed the test; others rushed from the dining room ill, but it is almost always a major event in a white Southerner's experience. Once this baptism is done, they are dedicated race-mixers for life. It is a lock. Based on the reported history, it is clearly easier to share a pipe with, wrestle with, and have sex with a black person than it is to eat dinner with one. Do blacks have an equivalent fear of whites? If so, they have kept it better concealed. Everyone does manage to eat together in fair proximity and race-mix at outdoor events like the Catfish Festival in Belzoni. A young white who wished to bridge the gap and assert some leadership might build upon this familiar idea and host a fish fry in his own back yard. Eventually it's bound to start raining and everybody would have to move inside for shelter.

The young man's analysis, that Delta blacks can only get theirs by taking ours, typifies an observation concerning pies made by a Cleveland High graduate I know who says, "Black people can have a pie and you can still have a whole pie, too. Instead of holding your pie so nobody else can have any of it, you have to understand that you can make new pies for other people. We just make other opportunities for people to have other pies. That's not well understood in the Delta. In fact, the Delta has not understood that at all."

Local politics in the Delta might be increasingly controlled by blacks, but the complexions of the chambers of commerce remain unmistakably white. When Archie Manning, who was one of the U.S. Jaycees' ten outstanding young Americans for 1988, speaks to the annual banquet of the Indianola Chamber of Commerce, there may be a few black members in the audience, but the all-white character of its directorate is not noticeably diluted. It should be recorded that Manning, raised in Drew and a model of good manners and Christian athletics, is still a favorite son of the Delta, despite his ten losing seasons as the New Orleans Saints' quarterback. He is heard to say that he is sometimes surprised and even guilty to find that he does not live in Mississippi.

The Indianola chamber does have a biracial committee that meets monthly to keep open the lines of communication between black and white communities. But does the organization detect any irony in the celebration it holds each August to honor the faculty and administrators of the local schools? The staff of the 99 percent white Indianola Academy is honored with a luncheon at the Indianola Country Club. The staff of the public schools is honored with a luncheon at the 99 percent black Gentry High. Could any of the black students, or even the faculty, at Gentry High get through the doors of the Indianola Country Club if they wanted to? At which luncheon do you think the food tastes better? Which uses paper napkins and which uses linen?

Speaking of country clubs, they are not merely a fringe on the fabric of Delta life; they are strong threads. A longtime friend of mine and manager of a Delta club describes these institutions as "the last citadel of the white race." That may be overstating it, but the country clubs are undeniably an important element in Delta society. Just about every town of any good size, like Webb or Shelby, has one.

Not all of these clubs are magnolia-shaded white mansions. Far and away most of them are ranch-style clubhouses with a pretty nice swimming pool out back and a big square, flat golf course surrounded on all sides by flat bean and cotton fields. They are not splendid, just comfortable places to bring the kids swimming, to eat a well-cooked meal, and to play poker with the judge. If you think deals are cut here, you are right, but if you imagine a stately or solemn atmosphere, that is wide of the mark.

"They are," the manager says, "the cheapest baby-sitter you can get. You send the kids out to the pool first thing in the morning and let them stay there all day, every day." As for the parents, "They drink. That's one of the reasons they have a country club is that they can have a liquor license as a private club in a county that doesn't have liquor by the drink. It is a place to have their social functions, to play golf, to have a swimming pool and tennis courts, and it is definitely not public. Although this club is funded with Farmers' Home Administration money. I never could figure that out. The membership is all white, and as far as I know, that is true of all the country clubs in the Delta. In the winter months, in the rainy season, one of the things is gambling. I can make some money with that because if I go down and stay with them all night and bring them drinks and cook them breakfast, then I can take home $250 to $300 in sales and tips." The favored game is "Murder," a progressive card game with wild cards and highs and lows. At this particular club the pots run from $500 to $2,500.

Business is not a major topic of conversation at the clubs, but they are key stations in the good ol' boy network. As one fellow told me, "In the clubs with sophisticated bookkeeping systems, like the Cleveland Country Club, the Greenville Country Club, the Clarksdale Country Club, or the Greenwood Country Club, you can go in and eat and have drinks and have it charged to your account back home. Your credit is good. I went to a wedding in Clarksdale one time, and they would not sell me a drink for cash because that was against club rules, but they could charge it to my own country club back home."

Would the dues-payers welcome black members? The club manager thinks so, but only "if you could separate them and poll them one at a time. They would say that it would be all right if they were clean and educated and didn't cause any trouble. But as a group, 'I don't want Mrs. Jones sitting next to me to know that I'd let a black person come into our church or our country club. Don't ask *me* to be the first one to speak up.'"

As the country club symbolizes white power and community, so does the public school system symbolize black power. In most counties the school system is now the largest dispenser of jobs, and increasingly these systems are run by black county supervisors, superintendents, and principals. That fact is simply the result of black voting power and white apathy toward public education. The chambers of commerce might accomplish something far more positive if these two symbols of community polarity and power, the white's club and the black's public school system, could each be made to lay out a table for the faculty and administrators employed by the alien camp. Maybe that should be the Indianola chamber's program for next year.

eleven

IN ACCORDANCE WITH GOVERNMENT REGULATIONS

▲▲▲

Within the frame in which I picture spring are all
the flowering trees—the dogwood, red bud, red haw,
and black haw, blooming in profusion across the
Delta. And, picturesque indeed were the gnarled, old
peach and apple trees which still stood around
abandoned houses there.
In summer my world was bound in gold and
green—the gold of golden sunshine and the vibrant
green of growing plants.
—Ruby Sheppeard Hicks, *The Song of the Delta*

Fifty miles east of Rosedale lives a working farmer, Matt Dale. ▽▽▽ Along with his wife, Pie, his brother, his sister-in-law, and four tenant families, he farms 1,300 acres near Glendora in Talla-hatchie County. The Dale brothers' plantation is called Ellendale, for their mother, and they all grew up there. They remember when the farm was crowded with tenant families who lived in old pine-board cabins. Now the four who remain live in brick homes. The Dales are modern farmers with two center-pivot irrigation systems that auto-matically describe a circle within a mile-square field, raining down well water at the rate of one inch per day. They have raised children here: all of the girls are leaving for careers or marriage; Danny's

Matt Dale, Jr., Glendora, Mississippi, on his backyard deck by the Tallahatchie River

boys may stay to run the farm. Country life for the children has not been what it was for their parents. Whereas Matt and Pie sort of grew up collectively with the planters' children throughout the area, all going to the same schools, all traveling to the same dances, all involved in the same clubs and cotillions, their children's generation has been split up among several schools, public and private, and seems more driven to depart the Delta than to preserve its special amenities. "We do what we can to hang on to the Old South lifestyle, but it isn't easy," says Pie with a shrug.

The Dales have gotten involved in a major political fight over land use and levee building that has divided the once united front of farmers. The dispute is really between two ideas that once existed in perfect harmony—profitable agriculture and the "Delta way of life."

Planters now generally call themselves farmers, but all of them know the history of their land. They also know that farming today bears only a surface resemblance to the plantation agriculture of history and literature. The expanse of flat land is still there, but it seems that there is a lot more of it. Where once woods broke up fields, now the plow runs in an unbroken line from the highway to the horizon. The trees are gone, the fields and the machines that pass over them are immense, the crops are more diverse than in the days of King Cotton, and the mortgage is unmentionable. Much of this, it seems, is the result of government policy. At any rate, the government's fingers are so intimately entwined in today's agriculture that it is difficult to differentiate between what is policy and what is not.

Obvious developments in the past three decades are that the hardwood forests have shrunk and the cypress swamps have been drained for agriculture. Is this the result of drainage and flood-control programs of the Corps of Engineers and the Soil Conservation Service, which make it less risky to develop formerly flood-prone acres, or have the government plumbers merely been called in after the fact to protect expanding farms? Everyone has a theory, but it is clear that during the fifty years prior to 1985, the lower Mississippi alluvial plain lost approximately 3.6 million acres of forested wetland, much of it to agriculture and levees. According to the Environmental Defense Fund, between 20 and 25 percent of that loss was due exclusively to the construction of federal flood-control and drainage projects. In other words, these forests were eaten up by levees and dams, and if it had not been for the construction of these impediments to nature, landowners would never have cleared the land in the first place.

This conclusion essentially repeated that of the Fish and Wildlife Service of the United States Department of the Interior in 1979. That report concluded that while the connection was not certain, peak losses of bottom-land hardwoods occurred between 1957 and 1967, a period corresponding to the completion of numerous Corps of Engineers and Soil Conservation Service drainage control projects. The report projected that hardwood forest in the Delta, already reduced to about 930,000 acres, would be reduced to about 700,000 acres in 1995.

Controlling water sometimes seems to be the government's main ambition in the Delta. The two major federal water-control programs are the Soil Conservation Service, whose projects are designed to manage watersheds up to 250,000 acres, and the Army Corps of Engineers, which manages the big rivers and builds levees and floodways. About 90 percent of all these projects nationally during the past fifty years have been constructed in the Mississippi River basin of Arkansas, Louisiana, and Mississippi, of which the Delta constitutes about one-third. The beginning of this massive federal intervention in the flooding and land-building cycle of the Mississippi River was the Flood Control Act of 1928, passed in response to the great flood of 1927, which put about 12.6 million acres under water. Obtaining passage of this act was the crowning triumph of the career of LeRoy Percy, who convinced Congress that the Mississippi was not just any old river, but that controlling its channel and flow was a central national concern. Prior to 1928, levee construction had been a matter for the states and, as a practical matter, the landowners adjacent to the river. The unevenness of levee building had put not only neighboring planters but neighboring states, like Arkansas and Mississippi, in conflict with one another. Dynamiting levees downriver, or across the river, to relieve the immediate pressure in front of one's home was not unheard of.

In April 1927 the levee broke at Mound Landing, south of Scott, Mississippi, and a great brown sea ten feet deep swirled across the

Delta, covering an area about the size of Rhode Island for several months. The only spots above water were the Indian mounds and the long thread of levee that had not broken, and this is where tens of thousands of refugees made camp. The more fortunate had evacuated beforehand. Evelyn Pearson, for example, caught a train for Tennessee the day the water began coming over the levee and recalled that "a lot of people on that train left their homes never to see them again." She was lucky, and likes to say that "I can honestly tell you that I've never gotten my feet wet in the Mississippi River." The water threatened civilization throughout the lower valley, and New Orleans was saved only by blowing up the levee at Caernarvon below the city to allow the water to rush out over an area populated mainly by oystermen and river rats and into Breton Sound. The city of Greenville itself was under water for seventy days.

While national attention and concern for the refugees was at its peak, Congress took action and adopted a flood control plan conceived by Major General Edgar Jadwin, chief of the engineers. The entire grand plan was placed under the purview of the Mississippi River Commission, which had been founded by Congress in 1879, a seven-member board appointed by the president. Under its auspices came the Mississippi River and Tributaries Project, which is still the operative plan for control of the river. The original Jadwin idea resulted in the basic components of today's defensive line against the Mississippi. It provided for the construction of the five big spillways between Cairo, Illinois, and New Orleans, including the one most used, the Bonnet Carre just upriver from New Orleans; higher and better levees; and in Mississippi, a system of four reservoirs and dams on the tributaries of the Yazoo River as a means of keeping water out of the Mississippi River, and out of the Delta, in times of emergency.

Since then the levees have grown steadily higher and fatter, and river channelization, drainage structures, control structures, and dredging projects have spread far and wide across the Mississippi watershed. Scale models of the system, and even of the Mississippi River itself, are used as laboratories in the Corps's district headquarters in Vicksburg and in Memphis. It seems so elaborate and well thought out that one might assume it is impregnable. That is, until one gazes over the mile-wide Mississippi above Greenville and begins to contemplate how much muddy water is rolling relentlessly past the spot throughout the day and night, all at a level several feet above the tops of the soybean plants growing on the dry sides of the levees. What contains this flow is a grass-covered earthen embankment about 150 feet wide at the base and 40 feet tall, on which cows graze, hunters walk, and children play. Neither the cows nor their masters could abide there but for the levee, yet one wonders if the continuing cost and the eternally necessary expansion and improvement of the system to contain that inevitable catastrophic flood—the one that predictably will come every hundred years, or two hundred years, or never—is really worth it. "It is far cheaper to hold the raindrop where it falls," says Tulane's Oliver Houck, a vigilant critic of the overall Corps of Engineers strategy. "That was the original Soil and Conservation Service motto. It requires incredible plumbing to pass the drop along."

William Alexander Percy, LeRoy's son, asked the question, is it worth it? back when the project was not so grand: "The low levees of 1893, ineffectual as they were to keep the Mississippi off the cotton fields, [nevertheless] had certain real advantages. When they broke, the water trickled in gradually, stood quietly over the land two or three weeks, deposited a fine nutritious layer of sediment and withdrew without having drowned anybody or wrecked any buildings or prevented a late planting of the crop. You called that an overflow. Our great dikes of today, when once breached, hurl a roaring wall of water over the county, so swift, so deep, so long lasting, it scours the top soil from the fields, destroys everything in its path, prevents crop-planting that year, and scatters death among the humble, always unprepared, and unwary."

Questioning levees was heresy in the Delta when Percy penned those words, and it is just about as well received today by some landowners. Nevertheless, a controversy began in 1988 when the Corps dusted off its 1930s plan and began moving ahead with an "Upper Yazoo Project," which aims to provide flood control for 1.13 million acres and prevent 64 percent of the annual flood damage in the area along the major interior river system of the Delta. It is a project that Will Percy thought represented "unsound engineering" when the Delta Council first discussed it before World War II, but "Will Whittington [the Delta's perennial congressman] wants to, so it must be right. . . . We endorse the bill, gingerly, comforting ourselves it won't pass anyhow."

Actually, it did pass, and the work began in 1976. The Corps initially accomplished the complete dredging and channelization and leveeing of the Yazoo River from Yazoo City north to Belzoni, and, of course, the construction of two mighty high bridges over the rivers. These structures replace picturesque concrete bridges from which generations of little boys fished, and the major benefit they bestow is to provide vistas across miles of Delta farmland. Neither Belzoni nor Yazoo City has experienced serious flooding since 1982, but local flood control is not really the point of the waterway improvements. They are primarily designed to get the water moving out more quickly, to flush the Delta's overflow out into the Mississippi River in a hurry so that upstream plantations will dry out more quickly after heavy rains and thus permit the tractors to get back into the fields. The other purpose is to decrease the risk to suburban developments, mainly those around Greenwood, from a major storm.

At this writing the future of the Upper Yazoo Project is not yet certain, but the Delta Council has supported it and the Corps says it is moving ahead. Mississippi's Governor Mabus and the Delta's congressman, Mike Espy, have called for a study. The project in full bloom is expected to require, or eliminate, 3,743 acres of bottom-land hardwood, 1,037 acres of wetland, and 9,333 acres of cleared land. The projected benefits, depending on your point of view, are the significant reduction of annual flooding, the virtual prevention of any farmland going under water in the typical twenty-five-year flood, and the expected conversion of 7,600 wooded acres to agricultural crops owing to the project's ability to reduce flooding on these lands. Of major significance to Mississippians: unlike new flood-control projects that require substantial local financing, the $360 million Upper Yazoo Project would be paid for entirely by the federal government.

The progress of the plan has been slowed, however, by the kind of opposition the Corps must take seriously: a number of planters along the upper Yazoo tributaries who do not want new levees coming through their fields and barnyards. One such opponent is Matt Dale.

The Tallahatchie River, which every country music fan knows is the river into which Billy Joe McCalister jumped, runs about one hundred feet from the Dales's home. Their tastefully decorated "pool house," where guests can sit on wicker furniture and sip a cool drink after a swim, is built on the old river levee. This earthwork is about five feet tall, built in the forgotten days before World War II. This little levee has never been breached. Even during the 1973 flood (which some called a "seventy-five-year flood" and others called a "one-hundred-year flood") water never came within two feet of the top of the Dales's levee, though rainwater stayed on their fields for days. What the Corps wants to do now is build a levee 100 to 150 feet wide, 200 feet back from the riverbank. Not only would that eat up a lot of the Dales's real estate, including their large pecan orchard, but it would leave their house between the levee and the river.

"If I had to face what I faced in 1973 every twenty-five or forty years," says Matt Dale, "I personally would rather that than to have the levee and improved drainage from my fields. I know others have different points of view, those who have had water in their houses. But if I had to choose between facing the proposed levee every day for the rest of my life or a flood every twenty-five years, I would pick the flood."

Dale has taken a leadership role in the "Save Our Yazoo" effort, and he argues convincingly that there are feasible alternatives to the levee that might satisfy upstream farmers. Dale's great-uncle, Congressman Will Whittington, was the legislative architect designer of the four manmade lakes, Grenada, Enid, Sardis, and Arkabutla, created in the high valleys above the eastern rim of the Delta. They regulate how much water flows into the Yazoo. If the Corps did not keep these reservoirs so full year-round to accommodate recreational users, Dale argues, then in times of heavy rainfall they could better serve their original purpose of containing water. All of the subdivisions in Greenwood that flooded in 1973, he says, were outside the original ring levee built to protect the town. His solution to that is to build new ring levees around these subdivisions. He could support dredging the Tallahatchie and stabilizing the banks with rock to send water downstream more quickly, though he acknowledges that that might cost more than heaping up a big

earthen levee. Even with the project, Dale says, there will still be
flooding over about 500,000 acres in the affected area if there is a
repeat of the 1973 flood, according to the Corps's own projections.
"The truth is that there has always been and will continue to be
flooding in the Delta no matter how many projects are built. That
is the nature of the land on which we have chosen to live."

Pragmatics aside, Dale voices another sort of argument. "At what
point do we let Mother Nature take her course?" he asks. "The more
we protect, the more people there are who will build homes we will
then need to protect. The truth is that in the 1970s we cleared
hundreds of acres that we shouldn't have. The philosophy was plant
from fencerow to fencerow, feed the world." Now, he notes, the
government will pay you to reforest. The proposed levee, he thinks,
will destroy remaining wetlands and encourage farmers to put more
marginal land into production.

The larger question, then, is When do we say it is time to stop?
Perhaps those who raise crops in a flood plain should have to plant
what can survive a flood. Wouldn't the farmers of North Dakota like
a federal snow-removal project each year that would let them start
the tractors two months earlier? Is it a nationally significant loss if
a portion of Mississippi Delta farmland is forced out of production
for a couple of months every year or so?

It is his own little bit of wetland Dale is surveying when he talks
about rethinking our philosophy. Ducks, raccoon, and deer live
alongside the riverbank by his house. But he sees the big picture as
well. Moving more water out of the Yazoo and into the Mississippi
River puts that much more pressure on the levees and control
structures downstream. "When the people in Louisiana learn what
the Corps is doing up here, they will go crazy," he says, with a thin
smile.

The Upper Yazoo Project is, of course, but one part of a far larger
federal flood-control scheme. The original Mississippi River and
Tributaries design, conceived in 1928, has now cost $4.1 billion and
is considered only about 78 percent complete. It is designed to control a "project flood," which by definition carries a discharge of 3
million cubic feet of water per second, a hypothetical catastrophe
that might occur once every hundred years. In the Delta the Jadwin
plan has given us, in addition to major levees and four lakes, new

harbors in Vicksburg, Greenville, and Rosedale, channel improvements on the Big Sunflower, the Bogue Phalia, the Hushpuckeana River, the Quiver River, Steele Bayou, Lead Bayou, Porter Bayou, the Cold Water River, Yalobusha, the Yazoo River, the Tallahatchie River, Big Sand Creek, and Pelucia Creek, control structures on Muddy Bayou, Snake Creek, Wasp Lake, Chulia Lake, and Bee Lake, and the creation of the Will M. Whittington Auxiliary Channel and the Pompey Ditch. And this is just in the thirteen or so counties of the Mississippi Delta.

All of this illustrates once again an overriding fact of life in the Delta: there is very little that is not touched by the federal government. What to plant, when to plant it, where to plant, whom to hire, how to house farmworkers, how to finance the farm, not to mention public welfare, the schools, and local government itself, are all strongly influenced and generally financed by federal government. The Delta is sort of a substation of Washington. One effect is loss of the farmer's autonomy. Robert Neill, a former Delta planter, is a great-nephew of Sam Drake Neill, one of the few "leading men" of the Delta acknowledged by LeRoy Percy. The title of one of Neill's books, *How to Lose Your Farm in Ten Easy Lessons and Cope with It* (written with James R. Baugh), sums up Neill's career advice. His premise is that between the high cost of operating a farm and government bungling, the bank is going to take everything.

The typical case, he says, involves starting out with a heavy mortgage necessary to buy out the other heirs to a family farm. In his book he writes that "there are few fields which offer a young person the opportunity of becoming so deeply in debt so early in life as the family farm does." And this new farmer, unlike his father who never got his britches dirty, actually has to ride the tractor.

Government programs based on total crop acreage encourage land clearing. "Voluntary" federal programs in which the government tells you what to plant are truly mandatory in nature, because the mortgage holder requires participation since the bank wants an assignment of that government check. Try borrowing money from a bank or Production Credit Association for crop production if you cannot give as collateral an assignment of a government allotment program check. This coupled with the embargo of 1973, which Neill and others say ended the good years for farming, and sending U.S. experts abroad to teach the Asians to grow cotton, spelled doom for the Delta planter. Neill writes wistfully of the eradication of the sharecropper system by the "ignorant bureaucracy" and the passing of the old gentlemen tractor drivers, still plentiful in the 1960s, "who would roll their eyes and sigh remorsefully when having to correct the 'Little Boss.' "

I met Robert Neill at the Shoney's on U.S. 82 in Greenville on a Sunday morning. Shoney's at that time of the week is more than crowded. He arrived looking a little haggard and whiskered from a late night he had spent emceeing a charity ball in Leland, from which he told me he and his wife were the last to leave.

Neill says that the FHA sent out 48,000 foreclosure notices to farmers in Mississippi over the Christmas holidays (right after the presidential election), out of 90,000 nationwide. Neill got out of farming before then. His last crop was in 1985 when the bank asked him to put a mortgage on his house: that was where he called a halt. His farm was between Leland and Indianola, and he planted cotton, milo, wheat, and beans. "Just because you went under didn't mean that you were necessarily a bad farmer. Sometimes that was true, but in a lot of the cases not. You don't see the whole agricultural economy of the United States going under because of personal mismanagement. There's a bigger reason. And that's explained in the farm book. My tendency is to say that had the government stayed out of it, most of us would be all right. But I'm not one of those people who say that the government ought to get completely out of it now. I think they've screwed it up to the point to where if they got out, it would really be a mess." I think he struggles to find exactly what the big problem is or what the big solution might be. But he has certain ideas.

"You've got maybe $50 million in cotton being produced down there in South America now that, had it not been for government interference with the free market, wouldn't be down there for us to compete against. You've got China, which we've just put into the cotton business, and India. And it's my understanding that we're paying farmers in Pakistan and Turkey to plant cotton instead of growing poppies. That cotton is on the market in competition with United States cotton. You're shooting yourself in the foot."

I've heard Neill's speech on how personally devastating the failure of a family's farming enterprise can be, and it is touching indeed. The audiences he reaches understand the loneliness and self-criticism that must assail any farmer who has inherited acres from generations of ancestors and who finds himself facing crushing debt, unable to hold on to the land. He speaks to this subject not only as a writer and lecturer trying to make a point but also, now, as a trained "farm credit mediator," which is not unlike a ministry. This service was begun a year ago in Mississippi by a state "rural crisis task force" directed initially by the Episcopal Church. Neill himself is a Baptist, and the program is now secular. The state Department of Agriculture partially funds it today. Basically the mediators sit down with farmers who are facing tough financial situations and attempt to work out arrangements with the creditors to avoid foreclosures.

"One of the problems is so many times there are several creditors involved. For instance, you've got the bank that you've started with. That loan didn't get paid back. Then you've got the FHA guaranteed loan on behind it, and if you had two or three bad years back-to-back, like so many folks did then, you're behind with the FHA. Your land is financed with the Federal Land Bank, perhaps, and maybe even with a second mortgage with another bank somewhere. So you've got four or five lenders involved. And when a man's trying to work it out by himself, so much of the time you're running back and forth between them; and there seems to be always somebody who wants all of their piece of pie, when there's not that much pie left.

"It's one of the reasons farmers don't get any sympathy from the public as such. It's hard for the average person to understand the huge amounts of money it takes to farm nowadays. For instance, the last year that we were farming all of our place, two thousand acres, it cost us around $350,000 for a production loan. And we were trying to farm close to the vest. I was driving an eight-year-old pickup. All our tractors were old, and we tried to keep them repaired ourselves. We drove the tractors, the combines, the trucks ourselves. We didn't have a lot of management money. We didn't take trips to Las Vegas.

Loading a finished cotton bale, Gunnison Gin, Gunnison

In other words, we were trying to do it right. We could have spent a half-million dollars on that kind of acreage, if you go by the agricultural service 'guesstimates.' And the production loan doesn't include what you owe on your equipment and your land and your personal debt. The average person in New York City or Winston-Salem, North Carolina, can't really relate to that. They say, 'Well good God, that man just really went out on a limb, didn't he?' But at one point you had the collateral for it. Now I'm seeing land that the Federal Land Bank had on their books by their own valuation as being worth $1,700 back during the late seventies selling for $400 today. And a lot of it had $800 or $900 borrowed against it." He notes that the Federal Land Bank in Louisiana, Arkansas, and Mississippi is now in receivership.

In Neill's speeches, along with the sad tales of individual farmers' troubles and his own encouraging words, he also adds a mixture of jokes and stories that might help out just as much. He talks about the day-to-day personal farm "disasters" such as the tractors that catch fire, shed their drivers, and head for the barn by themselves, and farmhands who put gasoline in radiators.

I mention the Delta's "war against nature," and Neill lays that at the government's doorstep, too. "The government does not encourage leaving the habitat behind. In our case, for instance, we made it a personal choice to try to leave the tree lines and ditch banks and fencerows that had been there for fifty years. We probably wasted twenty-five acres over the whole two thousand. We had doves and rabbit and squirrels and quail. People say there ain't no quail in the Delta because of the poisons. It's not the poisons, it's the people cleaning up their habitat. I've got maybe twenty coveys of quail, maybe twenty-five, on two thousand acres, simply because I left their habitat."

He pointed to the traditional south Delta duck habitat in and around Sharkey and Issaquena counties. It has been cleared, though it is marginal land, at the government's behest. Now the farmers on that land have gone broke. To take part in the cotton programs you have to put land in "set-asides." Why not plant the turn-rows in millet to attract rabbit and quail? he asks. The regulations say, however, that the set-asides must be disked. So, no habitat, plus there is runoff into the lakes. Now the rule is that you have to plant

Dallas Wills, Gunnison Gin, Gunnison

grass on the lake and creek banks. You would not have the runoff if you could plant on the set-asides.

"For my money," says Neill, "the Corps of Engineers is a wonderful organization, if you can keep them between the levees of the Mississippi River. Personally, I think they've done just as much harm as good with their projects. But it's like that with most government agencies. It's a bureaucracy and it survives on its work. If they go in and do a great job and say, 'We are through. We've done all the drainage that needs to be done in the United States of America,' hey, they're fired."

He says that since the 1960s the traditional lifestyles of both the planter and the sharecropper have disappeared. The planters, the "high-flying folks," were whipped by debt. "The aristocracy's gone. Twenty years ago, maybe a dozen formal dances were held between Thanksgiving and Valentine's Day, or Easter. I mean the good kind with ballrooms, bands, everybody wore tuxedos and evening gowns, and you saw folks from the whole Delta. There are maybe two or three left. And most of those are charity-type. The old-style ball, the planter's cotillion, that is just gone because the people are gone. Or else they can't afford it anymore."

As for the sharecroppers, "It was a good life. There may not have been a lot of money in some households, but there was not a lot of want or need either. We got along. We lived together, we enjoyed each other. Some folks were richer than others, same as anywhere. Some is and some ain'ts. But at the same time the people who lived out on the place, be they black or white, had a pretty good life and were happy with it. There was a work ethic. It may have been feudal, but it was a protective system, a big family if you want. These folks are mine, and I'm going to take care of them. It's not that way anymore. There's nobody there."

Neill thinks that we are now seeing the creation of a third lifestyle, and he likes it about as well as Will Percy liked the prospect of a society dominated by poor whites. Neill's bleak vision is of a Delta society consisting of part-time farmers or sharecroppers farming land owned by big corporations or absentees. It is also part of the new lifestyle that blacks will be running the local governments, not something that he anticipates with pleasure. "That's going to affect how a lot of people plan their lives," he says. "I'm no longer tied here.

My family's been on that place for eighty-something years. I've still got a house there. But my kids—I've got two in college and another that's coming up on being a junior in high school—I'm not making my living on the farm. And if something were to pop up, I'm not actively looking, but I'm not shutting my eyes either. If something pops up somewhere else and some dude walks up and says I want to pay you a certain amount of dollars for that house out there in the country, he'd probably be able to get him a house.

"I would miss the Delta, but a lot of it nostalgically. I don't know that I would miss what's coming. I think we've got some harder times coming than we've seen. It's going to get wussa before it gets better." I say that catfish are a bright spot, and he says, "Well, they'll probably teach the Mexicans how to farm them." He laughs.

Neill's "good years" were the late 1960s, the ones in which I was first introduced to the Delta, and the difficult conversion from share-cropper to modern farming then occurring was hastened by fairly high cotton and soybean prices. In that period bigger and costlier machines were developed that could plant, weed, and harvest six and eight rows, rather than four rows, at a time, and the investment required to farm began to go up. According to Matt Dale's memory, when his father quit farming in 1973 a tractor cost $6,000 and cotton sold for 60 cents a pound. In 1988 cotton was 58 cents, and a tractor ran to $50,000. The new tractor is better, of course: you cannot find a tractor today without air conditioning, heat, and an AM/FM radio and tape deck. As a camouflage-suited farmer told me at an equipment auction in Isola, there is nothing more expensive to run than a tractor with air conditioning in the noonday fields. (The same farmer pointed out to me with patriotic pride that there were no Russian "Beleruski" tractors on sale at Isola.) Along these same lines, a laborer in Louise, gazing at a new cotton gin, reported in awe that it takes "one thousand dollars wuth of electricity just to turn it on."

There are also the costs associated with chemical agriculture. Microbes, insects, and unpopular plants are attacked with products with names like Treflan, Baythroid (from Bayer), Roundup, Cotoran, Whip, Freedom, Bolero, Assure, Tri-Scept, Tackle, Agrosol, Storm, Scepter, Prowl, Ridomil ("Jump Start Your Cotton"), Canopy, Vita-vax-M, Karate, Gramoxone, Curacron, and Orthene. All of these and more are rained in abundance upon Delta fields from dashing yellow biplanes piloted by Mississippi cowboys, and still the bugs keep coming. One wonders if the insects are not better adapted than we are for living here. Is it possible that we and our lumbering John Deere pickers and noisy orange tractors are really too big for this planet? Even cotton has gotten smaller. Once it was high enough to hide a man on horseback. Now new seeds produce more fiber and less stalk and a dog couldn't lose itself in the field. Is smaller better? Is efficiency, and ultimately survival, with the microchip, the Walkman, and finally the insect? While the final outcome remains in doubt, Delta farmers will tell you that cutworms, wireworms, sugar-cane beetles, budworms, bollworms, army worms, thrips, stinkbugs, cotton fleahoppers, cabbage loopers, and saltmarsh caterpillars have proven themselves to be very tough opponents.

To finance all of the modern equipment and the ongoing war with small organisms, and to maximize involvement in government programs that may only be available to small-size producers, farmers now engage in complicated partnership and corporate structures. One farmer Matt Dale knows has nine corporations: nine corporations require nine sets of books. The effluent of that is a deluge of accountants and lawyers. For example, Sumner, Mississippi, which even its most patriotic resident will concede is not a very big town, has five lawyers. The Episcopal church there has tennis courts. Little Marks, Mississippi, seat of Quitman County, where the mule train that led King's Poor People's Campaign started its slow trek twenty-some years ago, boasts seven attorneys. Another result is that today's farmer spends a lot of time keeping books and staring out at a back-lit computer screen rather than at sunrise over a pasture. If Robert Neill's generation in the 1960s was the first of the plantation owners who actually had to drive a tractor, the farmers of the 1990s may be the first generation that does not have the time to ride a tractor because it is punching the keyboard.

The prestige that went with planting is now much diminished. The farmer's annual meeting at the bank, where he will humble himself for next year's "furnish"; where he will pick up the federal loan check which the government sends, not to him, but to the bank; where he will read in black and white the printouts of his current debt; and where he will learn if his house must be added to next year's mortgage, is reminiscent of the annual settling-up between the sharecropper and the landowner a generation ago. To say that the cotton, rice, and bean planters of the Delta are today's sharecroppers, and that Uncle Sam and the banker are the bossmen, would not be far off the mark.

twelve

VEIL OF
THE MISSISSIPPI

▲▲▲

The work is never completely interrupted. When one
group is at rest another is at labor. Axes swing through
their measured rhythm, logs dwindle into firewood, and
the music of song moves in and out of the ringing of
steel like figures weaving with faultless precision
through the steps of an intricate ballet. Sometimes the
voices are silent. For a little while there is no sound
save the loud bite of steel on wood as it is riven
asunder. Then unexpectedly and unaccountably a voice
far away is lifted in song, to be joined by another in a
distant group, and then another and another, until all
the voices merge and blend into one great and splendid
voice, and a tall column of song trembles on the air.
For crime in Mississippi is expiated to music, and these
Negro convicts on the state prison penal farm at
Parchman sing at their work until they are released
or die.
—David L. Cohn, *Where I Was Born and Raised*

I n conversation with a river planter I learned that Mike Espy
▽▽▽ had proposed a "wayport" for the Delta, a new concept in air
transportation that would create airline hubs remote from any pas-
senger's destination and useful solely for the purpose of changing
planes. We agreed that sounded a little far-out, but when I got home
I read that Charlie Capps had introduced a bill in the state legislature to create a wayport in Mississippi. Later I learned it had passed

and that the legislature had offered for this purpose some five square miles of what is probably the largest state-owned farm in America, Parchman prison.

The Mississippi State Penitentiary at Parchman is part of the soil, grit, and folklore of the Delta. "Parchman Farms" has been lamented by blues singers without number from Leadbelly to B. B. King. The "prison" is a 17,000-acre institution between Tutwiler and Drew, straddling Mississippi Route 3 with an adjunct 5,000-acre farm near Marks. Historically, what prisoners did here was pick cotton under the gun and lash, and the prison was intended to give a taste of slave times to farmhands who acted too free in the free world. The penitentiary board and the parole board were both traditionally controlled by Delta planters. It was just a big plantation.

Twenty years ago Parchman housed about 2,000 prisoners and was self-supporting. In fact, the sale of penitentiary products, mainly cotton, netted the state treasury $310,000 in excess of the money apportioned in 1967. About half of the 6,000 bales of cotton produced then were picked by hand under the supervision of only 40 armed civilian guards. Such a small paid force was possible because they were supported by four times as many armed prisoners, called "shooters."

Then came a wave of prison-reform lawsuits. The most sweeping of these, *Gates* v. *Collier* in 1972, presented a gruesome picture of insect-infested living quarters, lack of food, medical treatment, and clothing, and a lack of security in the living quarters to protect inmates from assaults and rape. The court ordered the prison to end mail censorship and to halt physical abuses such as administering milk of magnesia, using cattle prods, and turning fans on naked and wet inmates. It also prohibited Parchman officials from allowing armed prisoners to guard other convicts. In response, Parchman initiated a statewide recruiting campaign to try to locate civilian guards, but initially could only find twenty-four who qualified in terms of intelligence and willingness to work, and ten of those quickly resigned. At that time, civilian guards got free housing but were only paid about $5,000 per year. I visited Parchman in 1973 while this transition was in progress to write a report for *New South Magazine*.

The obvious problem at that time was that the guard shortage was forcing the prison to keep many inmates who had formerly been working outside confined in their barracks. It should be mentioned that until recent days Parchman bore almost no resemblance to the grim fortress most of us associate with a central state prison. The prisoners were spread out over the farm in seventeen isolated "camps": each one consisted of a brick or wooden barracks around which were tiny huts for the trusties and, outside the encircling fence, two or three small cottages for the civilian guard force. Only one building, the maximum-security unit, near the prison's main gate, actually had cell blocks and looked like a prison. The barracks appeared to be most unpleasant places to live, and with the limited guard force they were truly unsafe. Some of them encircled open sewage pits into which toilets were flushed, which certainly gave the appearance of an epidemic in the making.

The place, however, was full of contradictions. In 1973 I met with a convicted confidence man who had literary skills and helped to edit *The Inside World: Mississippi's Most Popular Penal Publication.* The print-shop inmates who published *Inside World* were also running off the first edition of a court-ordered document, official "Rules and Regulations" for the penitentiary. While the booklet provided rules for such anachronisms as the "plasma program," in which inmates gave plasma units to the Cutter Laboratories of Berkeley, California, in exchange for $4.00, which was the only legal money they could then earn, and provided punishments for major offenses which included "confinement for a period not to exceed twenty-four hours in the dark hole," the very notion of a rulebook was progress in those years.

But Parchman also had an almost wide-open visitation policy. Just about anybody who wanted to could come in on the first and third Sundays of each month and bring lunch to share with whatever relative or friend he might have there. This policy made visiting at Parchman a sort of family affair experienced by almost every black and lots of whites in the area and part of the routine of life, not just in the Delta, but across the whole state. In the old days the Yazoo and Mississippi Valley Railroad ran a special train from Jackson for visiting Sundays. It was called the "Midnight Special," since that was when it left the capital to reach Parchman by dawn. Most

surprising of all was that Parchman, alone among major state prisons, fostered the maintaining of somewhat normal relations between husbands and wives. In 1973 the trusties' cottages at each of
the camps were made available on visiting Sundays for "conjugal
visits," a virtually unique program in American penology. I wrote
then:

> The sense of inadequacy, inefficiency, and of mismanagement runs
> so deeply through Parchman, as it does through most of the public
> institutions in Mississippi, that it is hardly commented upon by
> those who witness it daily. Conditions at Parchman have been,
> and continue to be, intolerable and below the lowest standards of
> "criminal justice." There is, however, something of a healthy
> nature in the Mississippi air, that soothes humanity's wounds,
> so to speak, something that provides for conjugal visits in a
> building bordered by an open sewerage pit, that makes the state
> seem better for the miseries it endures than all the other places
> where the tragic and ugly parts of life are kept so neatly out of
> sight.

Parchman is a much bigger operation today. There are now
about 1,500 free civilian employees and nearly 5,000 prisoners.
The Department of Corrections operates on a $70 million budget.
There is a new 1,000-cell maximum-security unit in the works, and
a new gas chamber has been built. The "dark hole" is gone, but
there is now a supermodern "Unit 29," a cluster of gray concrete
pillboxes with windows that look like gun slits, surrounded by a
double fence and electronic sensors. It would fit in well as a moon
installation or on the campus of Brandeis University, prison architecture being the ultimate expression of "form follows function."
The warden is now a thirty-eight-year-old Delta State graduate,
Steve Puckett. He favors expansion of the prison's pilot Regi-
mented Inmate Discipline (RID) program, which subjects selected
inmates, usually first offenders, to a boot-camp regimen for four
months in hopes of teaching self-reliance and discipline and reduc-
ing repeat offenses. The carrot for the prisoner is a sentence reduction, if he successfully completes the program. Though there have

been allegations of physical abuse, and some "drill instructors" have been pulled from the program, it is still held up as a model by the prison and is the centerpiece of the tours offered to civic and school groups.

Many of the changes at Parchman continue to be forced by class-action litigants. *Gates* v. *Collier* is still an open case, and even in 1988 the current prisoners' lawyer, Ron Welch, was filing motions seeking to compel the state to hire about 200 new guards. The idea of paying inmates for their labor, at 10 cents per hour, was even floated by the corrections commissioner appointed by Governor Mabus. The prison still permits "conjugal visits," though the program is a little less informal today, and about 400 prisoners a year are allowed to go home on ten-day Christmas passes. "Our murderers and manslaughters are our best releases," says a Parchman employee, who serves on the Christmas Leave Committee. "Most of the time, you find that those are a one-time deal. The burglars, arsonists, and armed robbers are the worst, because they're repeaters."

Prisoner escapes, which have always been a rare occurrence at Parchman because of the vast open spaces that must be crossed before one gets to any woods or a town large enough to hide in, occasionally enliven the humdrum of farming life. When a prisoner gets loose, roadblocks go up on the highways in all directions and troopers take a second look into the trunk of every car and the cab of every cotton picker that waddles past. Prisoner ingenuity now takes more sophisticated forms. Since 1981 quite a few Parchman prisoners, with the help of several guards, have been caught altering the U.S. postal money orders they can buy and getting them cashed outside for the higher value. Using prison art supplies, inmates have turned about 9,000 money orders worth $12,000 into forgeries worth about $4.6 million, and despite some thirty-five convictions this practice seems hard to stamp out. That ongoing investigation uncovered a computer whiz at the penitentiary who, while working as a clerk for prison industries, reportedly got a shipment of prison cotton diverted to a private gin in Drew, presumably for his own profit.

One of the veteran guards, Marilyn Brumley, showed us around the Parchman complex. She is a good source of local information, and a former reporter for the *Sunflower County News*. Since most Parchman employees live on or near the prison grounds, social life is centered there, and there is a lot to report just in terms of the comings and goings of relatives and parties being held by employees. Readers might have wondered if Brumley were serious when she wrote that "we who attended really enjoyed the class on 'Personal Searches and Shake Downs,'" but it seems that she was. Two officers pretended to be inmates. "They were dressed in inmate attire for the class with contrabands hidden in their clothing and on their bodies. You wouldn't believe the amount of contrabands hidden on the two. They had knives, money orders, cash, and even a small gun. They had some of it hidden so that the class didn't find it at all. They really woke the class up showing the different places to conceal illegal items." Such are the challenges of a career in corrections.

She lives in a neat white cottage across the road from the fence line of Camp 12. She has raised two children at Parchman. The kids grew up playing with convicts at the prerelease camp, but now both have moved quite a distance away. The elder is married to a newscaster in Jackson; the younger is studying at Memphis State. Marilyn tends her ailing father, who was himself once a security officer in Arkansas.

She has held most of the available security jobs at the prison, from manning a gun tower to running the switchboard. Before the women's prison was moved to Rankin County, she traveled with the female members of the Parchman prison band. Now she sits in a room by herself at a medium security unit, operating communications equipment. The job pays the same as that of a correctional officer, but she does not have to wear a uniform. A lot of the employees are women, and the reasons for that, she thinks, are the low pay scales and that "women can be depended on more than men." She has a little garden behind her house, and one of the changes over the years is that she no longer gets the services of a convict gardener and housekeeper.

In June of 1984 a convict wielding a steak knife surprised her in her kitchen and bound her hands and mouth with clothes from the

Parchman Penitentiary guard Marilyn Brumley, at her cottage on the prison farm

laundry room. He demanded her car keys, and then had to untie her mouth so that she could tell him that the keys were on the seat of her car. He raced away and was gone for a month. Her screams alerted a convict planting peppers in her garden, and he ran to a nearby house to phone in the escape. "I never dreamed that old car would outrun some of those trucks like it did," she says. They did not find her car until a week later, wrecked in a gully behind the prison. It was only luck that her daughter was not home at the time of the escape. The child was in fact in Paris, traveling with her French class. When she flew into Memphis Airport the next evening, her mother had to borrow a car to pick her up. Brumley relates this incident, which must have been terrifying, as if she were reporting the weather. Just a day in the life of a Parchman professional, I guess, but it bespeaks an inner toughness you wouldn't think she had.

Brumley is loyal to the prison and points with pride to its virtues—the family visitation program and the RID program. She was incensed at the British Broadcasting Corporation, which, after being allowed to set up shop at Parchman for a month, broadcast a documentary on capital punishment that she perceived as a put-down to Parchman. But she is a little bitter that after her scrape with the escaping prisoner the administration did not even offer to fix her car.

She drives us around to show us the sights. There are the cabins where families can visit with prisoners for three days at a time. They must carry in enough food for that entire period, and they do bring big feasts. No guards are present in that compound, but the men are called out three times a day for a count, just like every other prisoner at Parchman. We passed a "million-dollar hospital," housewives in their yards pulling up turnip greens, a new Spiritual Life Center, a firehouse with two engines, the John Bell Williams Arena for the annual prison rodeo, a restaurant for employees called "The Place," the building housing the gas chamber, and old, abandoned Camp 5, a deteriorating brick asylum that suggests how Parchman used to be.

Brumley used to give Tupperware and Avon parties and take part in the organized social life of the prison, but with her children gone she has gotten tired of it. Even after spending twelve years in this generally male environment she sadly reports that "there are no prospects whatsoever in this place." Rural life is relaxing, and the new administration portends positive changes, but, "I am ready to go somewhere and see some action, hon."

MISSISSIPPI ANDANTE

▲▲▲

You got to take sick and die one of these days.
You got to take sick and die one of these days.
All the medicine you can buy,
All the doctors you can hire.
You got to take sick and die one of these days.

Yes I know the Lord will answer prayers.
Yes I know the Lord will answer prayers.
Take you sick and can't get well.
Surely the Lord will be right there,
You got to take sick and die one of these days.
—Boyd Rivers

T hink of Parchman, and you think of the blues. It is impossible
▽▽▽ to capture, or even suggest, the great blues tradition in the
Delta in prose, though quite a few writers have tried. The railroad,
the prison, stoop labor, mistreatment, poverty, and a great sense of
style have given us Albert King, B. B. King, Ike Turner, John Lee
Hooker; dead stars like Muddy Waters, Robert Johnson, Big Bill
Broonzy, Howlin Wolf, "Big Boy" Crudup, and Charlie Patton; and
today's little-recognized players, Son Thomas, Wade Walton, Big
Jack Johnson, Ernest Roy, Jr., Lonnie Shields, and many more.

The blues is an old-fashioned type of music in that it does not
require a big band or much formal training. It is spontaneous, and
it is still alive and well in the Delta. Not only can you hear blues

performers in small clubs like Nell's Club in Farrell, Club Ebony in Indianola, or Booby Barnes Playboy Club in Greenville, but so well does the blues format present the enduring themes of sex and human misery that contemporary popular gospel groups and electric bands frequently shift into blues numbers during their performances.

There is a resurgence of interest in Delta blues today among those who see it as a cultural treasure that must be preserved and as a potential source of revenue. Not long before my visit James O'Neal, one of the founding editors of *Living Blues Magazine,* and Patricia Johnson, a California chiropractor and blues booking agent, moved to Clarksdale and opened a small recording studio and record store in the Stack House, formerly an ice cream store called the Cream Bar, in a downtown section undergoing a modest renovation. Somewhat to their surprise, they found themselves becoming a rallying point for white and black community leaders who, it seems, were waiting for something they could work together on enthusiastically. Says Mrs. Johnson, whose chiropractic clinic is next door to Rooster Records, "the city of Clarksdale and the county are alive with spirit and want to protect their heritage and also to promote the merchants downtown. Our recording studio became symbolic and it got people excited. We didn't plan this. We just wanted to do what we do, but both white and black communities think that it is bringing people together. I think that it is important that our cultural differences be preserved. Blacks have preserved their heritage much more than they have their culture. That is a gift that needs to be preserved.

"There is new life in the downtown merchants' association. The black merchants on Issaquena Street are on fire and have started a group called New World Association. We're on the border, on Sunflower Avenue, and we are also on a border culturally. This area used to be called New World. It was a lively section of black-owned stores. W. C. Handy lived here and started out here. W. C. Handy 'discovered' the blues on our streets here. This place is alive with incredible storytellers. It is rich in oral tradition. A lot of what we are hoping to record will be archival, and we will preserve it. But we hope that on some of this we and the musicians will make some money."

Johnson finds Clarksdale to her liking. "It is," she says, "like a California dream. Good people, absolutely beautiful ease of living, Southern hospitality. A warm and active community."

Clarksdale has also opened a blues museum on the second floor of the Carnegie library, and at this early stage of its development it has a certain bluesy aura to it. It is a little dark and dusty upstairs, and while you can listen to music on the stereo or watch a video documentary, you cannot do both at once, because there are not enough electrical outlets. The kindly librarian who unlocks the room and escorts you in could not be friendlier, but if you are struck with the urge to burst into song she will tell you to be quiet. There is great stuff here, though. In addition to the stack of rare records, you will find Wade Walton's harmonica and Son Thomas's pale clay sculptures of roosters and fish. And there are plenty of excellent photographs and old U.S. 61 road signs. Here are photographs of the Joe Rice Dockery plantation near Cleveland where B. B. King says the blues all began, because Willie Brown, Son House, and Charlie Patton all worked and played there.

The museum got a boost when the rock group Z. Z. Top announced its participation in a $1 million fund-raising drive to create a Muddy Waters exhibit at the museum, and when the group's singer, Billy Gibbons, came to town in April 1988 to take part in a catfish dinner and music festival. Gibbons contributed his shiny jacket with his group's name on the back. Most of the entertainment came from Wade Walton and James "Son" Thomas.

Wade Walton runs a barber shop with a little coffee bar in the back on Fourth Street in Clarksdale. The shop is easy to find because Walton's 1953 Chevrolet pickup truck with a cigar-smoking stuffed monkey named Flukie behind the wheel is parked outside. Walton was born on the LeMaise plantation south of Clarksdale in 1923, the sixteenth of seventeen children, and he learned how to play the guitar by swiping his brother Horace's instrument. Walton has not recorded an album since 1958 when Bluesville Records put out _The Blues of Wade Walton, Shake 'em on Down._ "I am a barber, not a singer," he says, but a corner of his one-room shop is decorated with photos of musicians and album covers, and there is a guitar hanging like a trophy behind the barber chair. His description of his occupa-

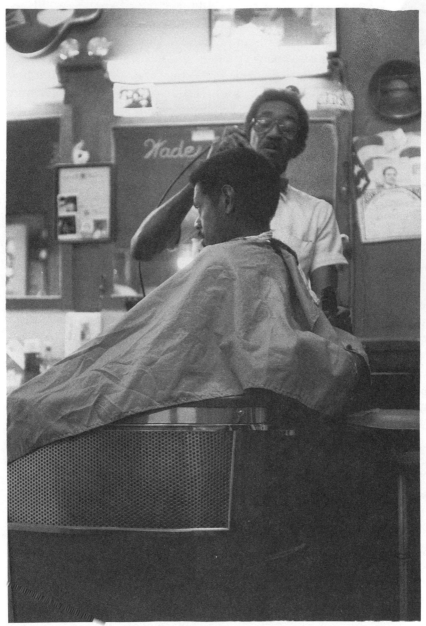

Blues guitarist Wade Walton in his barber shop, Clarksdale

tion may be rooted in frustration. Like many blues artists, Walton
has made very few dollars playing music. He has been on TV in
France, so he has been heard, but he has never been invited to tour.
He was asked to perform at the New Orleans World's Fair, but he
said no, because they did not offer to pay for his meals or his motel
room. Yet, wearing his neat bow tie, he will sit in with Big Jack, the
"Oil Man," who drives an oil truck, at the Club Casanova next door,
and occasionally he pulls out his guitar for the Japanese tour groups
that are beginning to find the Delta. He says that he is "a little out
of practice" since he made his record albums (thirty years ago), and
except when people come by who are willing to pay this dapper little
piper, that is the story that most blues enthusiasts are going to hear.
But on a good night you can catch him at the Casanova.

Son Thomas has fared a little better, but not much. He has just
released an album entitled *Gateway to the Delta* with his Swiss-
born harmonica-player partner, Walter Liniger. Thomas still lives
in a little wooden house that he rents in the Black Dog neighborhood of Leland. He sculpts from local clay life-size skulls with
human teeth contributed by a dentist, which were suggested, he
supposes, by the years he spent working as a gravedigger. They are
as frightening a work of art as you will see anywhere. He also
sculpts near-life-size heads with gold-painted pebbles for teeth. He
spraypaints the faces black or brown, gives them wigs and Mardi
Gras beads, and attaches black hair for eyebrows. Some he adorns
with sunglasses. The heads are mostly similar in shape, flat on top
(like Thomas's), and he builds each the same: when you face the
lump of clay and put your hands around it so that your fingertips
touch at the back, your thumbs are in the right spot to make the
eyes. That is his technique.

In general, I hate to hear musicians, especially British rockers,
talk, but that dislike does not extend to bluesmen. I could listen to
Son Thomas talk all day, and I did just about that. I did not record
it, and there is little I feel right about repeating here, because he is
"under contract," as he explained to me. He apologized again and
again that he could not talk for my book, but apparently he wants
to save his stories for his own venture. To be sure, he deserves it.
Blues artists are notoriously unappreciated by the public, even re-
gionally, and even when they do make a splash, the money seems to

slip right on past them. Thomas did perform at the New Orleans World's Fair, and he cannot understand how any of the concessionaires there lost money. "I ordered a Coke, and the lady said a dollar fifty. I said, I didn't order any whiskey in that." Followed by a throaty chuckle.

Blues festivals have begun to spring up around the Delta. The big one is the Delta Blues Festival, held annually on the third weekend in September in a field south of Greenville. It is one of the truly great open-air festivals. By "open" I mean that you can bring in anything that might make life on a crisp September afternoon more comfortable, such as beer coolers, grills for cooking, blankets, cameras, mixed drinks, tents, and lawn chairs. I've even seen bronzed young men carrying in a living-room sofa. And by "air" I mean vapors intoxicating to Southern olfactories, like the aroma of black, gummy mud (if it has rained, which it most often may do) and the fragrance of competing barbecues from a hundred smoky fires, with an occasional powerful hit of frying hushpuppies and catfish. The entertainment is not like anything you will hear anyplace else, at least not concentrated in one spot. Artists like Howling Mad and the Relaxations, KoKo Taylor and her Blues Machine, and The Nighthawks, featuring Toru Oki (introduced on stage as Toki-Oki), play in short sets, one after the other, well into the night.

The audience, a mixture of dashikis and cowboy boots, does a lot of gyrating. When Chick Willis, who has enjoyed success with his record "I Want a Big Fat Woman" ("with meat shakin' on her bones") asks all the big fat women to raise their hands, the hands soar. About the only person wearing a suit and tie at the blues festival is Son Thomas, dressed in sky-blue cotton and a yellow straw Panama, who spends his time when not performing hunched over a picnic table backstage, ignoring the brightly costumed young musicians who congregate there. He generally plays on the big stage at sundown, accompanied by Walter Liniger on harmonica, picking his acoustic guitar with authority.

Sugar Mama, Sugar Mama,
Wonder where you got your sugar from,
You got it way down in Louisiana,
Out in your daddy's sugar farm.

I like my coffee sweet in the morning,
You know I'm crazy 'bout my tea at night.
You know I like my coffee sweet in the morning,
You know I'm crazy 'bout my tea at night.
If I don't get my sugar three times a day,
You know I ain't feelin' just right.

The "Catfish Blues" is what Thomas sings:

Well I wish I was a catfish,
Swimming in the deep blue sea.
Well I'd have some of the women
Setting on hooks for me,
On hooks for me.

Every year about fifteen thousand people come to the Delta Blues Festival. At least ten times that many now attend the seven-day Jazz and Heritage Festival in New Orleans, and a few columnists always reminisce about the easy spirit the New Orleans festival had when it was young. Those old veterans would feel right at home, feet propped on an ice chest, in Greenville. Not only does the after-dark experience at the Delta Blues Festival conjure up by smell alone all the nighttime fishing trips, campouts, and lake parties you have ever been on, but it is law-abiding. Usually, at about eight o'clock, Malcolm Walls or one of the disk jockeys who emcee the show will announce that once again there have been "zero incidents." They have everybody stand up to applaud themselves for being "real Mississippians."

The Delta Blues Festival is sponsored by a well-established civil rights organization, Mississippi Action for Community Education (MACE), and has its roots in smaller musical events once held to encourage blacks to register to vote. Now it gives an opportunity for bluesmen to "come home."

It seems that now almost every Delta town has somebody famous who "comes home" about once a year. It did not seem, twenty years ago, that so many celebrities could or would claim Mississippi. But now country music singer and songwriter Johnny Russell comes home to Moorhead every year, and the town has organized an annual Johnny Russell fair in his honor. In 1988 the festivities were kicked off by the Parchman Prison Band. Russell sang his hit, "Red Necks, White Socks, and Blue Ribbon Beer," and then awarded six scholarships in his name, totaling $1,000, to Mississippi Delta Junior College. Country humorist Jerry Clower has been coming home to Yazoo City for years, but recently shocked his neighbors by announcing that he was moving a bit farther south to East Fork. The Ephram and Nola Smith Gazebo was dedicated this past year in Drew at the former site of the Yazoo and Mississippi Valley Railroad depot, immortalized in "The Yellow Dog Blues" by W. C. Handy; the guest speaker who came home for the event was native son Archie Manning, gentleman quarterback of the New Orleans Saints and now sports announcer.

When Oprah Winfrey came home to Kosciusko, the county named the gravel road that ran past her home place Oprah Winfrey Road. Charlie Pride, country music's great black singer, comes home to Sledge, and Conway Twitty comes home to Friars Point. Otis Rush, joined by the Ladies' Choice Band, came to Clarksdale for his first major appearance in Mississippi after leaving the state as a child. Jazz-great Mose Allison comes home to Tippo. B. B. King comes back every year for free concerts in his hometown of Indianola. After one of his last performances, he said, "When we were growing up, we wouldn't have been allowed out here while a concert was going on, let alone allowed to do a concert ourselves." After Mayor Tommy McWilliams came up to shake his hand, King said, "When I was growing up I swear I never even knew who the mayor was. Indianola has progressed and so much has happened since I left here in 1946."

The Delta has its blues shrines, though not necessarily signposts to them. In Tutwiler we went in search of the grave of Aleck Miller, the second of the legendary harmonica players to perform under the name "Sonny Boy" Williamson. We inquired at the Tutwiler grocery, and while the white proprietor couldn't put her finger on it, the black lady behind the counter grasped what we wanted and went to a nearby house to get us a guide. He was J. D. Irving, a deacon at the Whitfield Baptist Church, where Sonny Boy is buried. It is a plantation church, about four miles from town on a narrow blacktop, and is beginning to look a little neglected.

Irving was born on this place in 1928. While an evening breeze cooled us off, he looked out over the flat bean field spreading out from the church in every direction and recalled that in 1939, when he began working, there were 150 houses on the place. Now there are seven. "The colored man is last," he murmurs, a general statement. Only about ten people still come to church every Sunday, and the Reverend P. H. Taylor of Ruleville preaches. "Some of them died," he says sadly, "but even those here don't go to country church anymore. They don't go to town either. There are empty seats there just as there are here." Sonny Boy's headstone is in a little glade beside the church. It is the only one that has harmonicas glued to it, with cement and even chewing gum. Irving explains that people come by and take them, others come by and stick them there. Thinking back he remembers that Sonny Boy was "not too much of a worker." "Of course," he says, "you can't blame him for that if you can make some money easier."

The Delta and its music are the focus of considerable study at the Center for Study of Southern Culture at the University of Mississippi in Oxford. Its director, William Ferris, has written books about both Delta blues and folk art, and the Center publishes and underwrites two slick magazines, *Living Blues* and *Rejoice: The Gospel Music Magazine.* The Center's activities are diverse and range from providing headquarters space to the Jimmie Rodgers Memorial Association to organizing a scholarship fund at Ole Miss in honor of D. J. Early, a legendary black disk jockey on WROX in Clarksdale, who has logged more than 41,000 hours on the air and is heard all over the Delta. The Center has become one of the authoritative sources on the South for the foreign press; the *New York Times* quotes Ferris on the history of Southern barbecue, and the *Los Angeles Times* cites the Center's *Encyclopedia of Southern Culture* for the proposition that "in the South, 33 percent of tractors have air conditioning."

Ferris, now forty-something, grew up south of Vicksburg and learned much of what he knows now by conducting field interviews in 1967 while writing *Blues from the Delta.* His first discovery sums up the premise that guided my own research in the Delta at about that same time. "It was impossible to maintain rapport with both blacks and whites in the same community, for the confidence and

Gravestone of Aleck Miller, better known as "Sonny Boy" Williamson, ornamented with harmonicas, Tutwiler

cooperation of each was based on their feeling that I was 'with them' in my convictions about racial taboos of Delta society."

Now he says, "The Delta is one of the most distinctive cultural regions of our nation. In the South several areas are producing rich folk culture: Harlan County, Gulla off of the Sea Islands, the Cajuns, the Mississippi Delta. This area is distinct geographically and extraordinarily rich musically. It continues to be distinct as a region. With the Delta you sense, as soon as you drive into it, that you are in a different world. Whether these plantations are owned by white planters, the Queen of England, Arabs, or insurance companies, they are still a different place."

It is obvious that he sees the growing awareness of the blues, and the culture generally, as a marketable item, like cotton and soybeans. "Culture is becoming more of an industry. We are beginning to see the emergence of its industrial base, entertainment. The region continues to produce outstanding musical and literary talents, as it has done throughout the century." He is speaking of Barry Hannah, Walker Percy, Richard Ford, Jim Henson (creator of "The Muppets" and "Sesame Street"), Hodding Carter, Shelby Foote, and Charles Bell of Greenville. I observe that few of these actually live in the Delta, but Ferris offers the odd thought that "leaving doesn't necessarily reduce your ability to participate in a place." I am still chewing on that one.

"The Delta is always going to be an enigmatic, fascinating world. The Wal-Marts and Holiday Inns will never dominate that world. If they attempt it, a flood or something will wash them back. The land gives a character and the Delta has its own spirit. White and black, Chinese, Jewish, Lebanese are entrenched in the Delta. It is a cultural zone that will always be fascinating."

This is a big idea with which I agree. I note, driving to Greenville and looking at the crop-duster planes in the sky, that visually this area inevitably has a molding effect on its people. It is also a gambler culture, what a Cleveland friend calls a "rattle-and-snap lifestyle," like playing craps. People can win or lose their fortunes in a card game or in a season of farming. And always present is the myth of an elite that may never have existed. Rattle the dice and snap them one more time and maybe you can sit on that porch rocker, sipping that julep, talking about old dogs with your broker.

Another Center scholar, James C. Cobb, on a video tape shown there, says that "the Mississippi Delta probably qualifies as the most Southern place on earth." He refers to his book, then in progress, as a "last look" at the "last developing regional society in the United States." He thinks that an observation of the Delta may be helpful in understanding foreign developing societies. Cobb is another who will "participate" in the Delta from afar, since he is now at the University of Tennessee. When, despite faculty complaints about their below-average salaries, the state college board awarded $56,000 in bonuses to the Ole Miss football coaches after a bowl victory over Texas Tech, Cobb moved on.

I wonder, however, if the Delta can be usefully compared to anything. Where else in America do so many Old South ghosts hang about? Where else in the world can an impoverished rural region be found in the midst of such national plenty? Where else in America does such cultural wealth keep generating from remote farmland? The most useful lesson found in the Delta's development that might benefit other countries is that one of the world's most segregated societies has, after some spilling of blood and venting of hatred, converted itself into a relatively peaceful integrated society. It remains a society fully aware of race distinctions, still attached to the preservation of separate cultural identities, populated by races somewhat wary of each other, but peace has descended with shocking speed. This miracle happened; there are many witnesses.

PASTIMES

▲▲▲

The social life of the school, among the sons and
daughters of the town people, was elaborate and highly
organized, and on weekends there would be two or
three parties and dances to go to, often in tuxedos and
evening dresses. All the middle-sized towns of the delta
were linked up in a ritualized social routine: the
weekend dances in the delta country clubs or school
gymnasiums, with a perambulating Negro band called
the "Red-Tops" playing the music for the Memphis
Shuffle, were suitable training for the feverish social
life that would come later at Old Miss or Mississippi
State.

—Willie Morris, *North Toward Home*

W hat is it that makes people cling to the Delta? One man who
▽▽▽ had left told me over a bottle of bourbon, "I sure do miss the
sunups and the sundowns."

It is just so spacious. Maybe "broad" is the word; so broad that near
sunset even lumps of dirt in the fields cast shadows. At night the sky
is full of stars and the roads are straight and long. You can have the
kind of fun on gravel roads at forty miles per hour that would be
absolutely lethal on a highway. You can drive with abandon, and
with nothing surrounding you but wildflowers and croprows flipping
by, and watch the flyboys soaring high in their crop dusters, going
faster than you in air so clear it tastes good.

As you zip through, it seems as if all the girls are cute and raunchy
and all the boys have pickup trucks and well-oiled guns. It is a world

of secret sinful pleasures and a not-so-secret racist culture. Race relations, as they are now, and as they were in the collective memory, are so out of sync with the rest of America that you know on first encounter that the situation is crazy though, as long as bigotry stays peaceful, not without humor. Believing that the mass of black people are stupid, or at least indecipherable, is like an ethnic joke among many Delta white folks which they cannot share when they venture out into polite society. It is always privately tickling their funny bone, but they cannot laugh until they get back home. Along with that secret, there are also a host of other charms and legends hidden in each white Deltan's heart, which together amount to a regional identity. Some of these secrets the reader would find too outrageous to believe, and I will not endanger my own credibility by reporting them. Among the ones that can be told are these: the federal government is in the hands of those who would reduce everybody and everything great in America down to common clay; there is probably no illegal substance that cannot be tried once, either by ingesting it or by spraying it on the beans; infidelity with someone no one in the family knows is a sin; anything you do not want or like can be disposed of by throwing it into the Mississippi River, and once in the river you will never get it back; the point of working in a bank is so that you can afford to hunt and fish; God created two races so that people would have something to laugh at; there is no true story that cannot but be improved by exaggeration and vulgarity; the Cotton Council's catfish supper at Delta State is one of the most important social gatherings in the hemisphere. And why do black people wear plastic bags on their heads anyway?

It is astonishing that certain ideas will survive even heavy doses of reality and indoctrination to the contrary in the great world outside. Exposure to higher education at Ole Miss or Yale may make you feel uncomfortable with "nigger" jokes for the first week you are back home, but after that the old sense of humor will generally return.

Any of us might muse, of course, how much simpler our lives might be if all those around us were of the same race as we. We would generally have a much better idea of what our neighbors were thinking and what sort of home life they had. Such is the comfort experienced by most of the world's people—the Danes, the Chinese, the Bolivians, the Iranians, and the Libyans, for example—but it is not something most of us get in the United States, certainly not in Mississippi, certainly not in the Delta. Tiny once remarked to me, "White people would be all right if you could put them up like a light cord and turn them on when you want to and turn them off when you wanted." In this spot, dominating the other group in the absence of segregation statutes is as difficult and intriguing as playing championship chess and avoiding them is just about impossible. What does this bizarre community do to those who grow up here?

I guess you always wondered where Larry Speakes came from. The press secretary who admitted making up presidential quotes is from Cleveland, Mississippi, and he spent his formative years rambling around with Charlie Capps, being an aide for Big Jim Eastland, and publishing the *Leland Progress* and the *Sunflower News,* until he saw how unprofitable the news business could be. Then he went to Washington and bared his behind in print. He was also Andy Griffin's Explorer Scout leader.

Andy, now a west Tennessee businessman, is "from" the Delta and has spent a good part of his life bobbing and weaving around and in general dealing with that fact, moving away to Boulder, to Asheville, to Nashville, but always returning to the flatlands. The Delta is the scene of his crime, the crime of growing up wild in the South, which is just a little harder not to do in the Delta than in most places. Andy was a young boy and man in Scott and in Cleveland, and a college student at Mississippi State in Starkville in the 1960s.

The Delta used to boast, and may still, the world's largest cotton plantation. It was the Delta Pine and Land Company plantation headquartered in Scott, Mississippi. The company was originally created by the Watson family of Chicago, who might qualify as real-estate robber barons, to hold some 450,000 acres acquired from the state, which had in turn acquired it from landowners who could not pay their taxes during and after the Civil War. After numerous boom-and-bust transactions, the charter passed to a group of British textile-mill people who bought approximately 40,000 acres to give themselves a sure supply of cotton. More recently it was owned by the Prudential Life Insurance Company, and it is said that the old

Delta Pine hunting club at Catfish Point has international enter-
tainers among its members and $150,000 clubhouses. Griffin's family
moved to the plantation's headquarters in Scott when he was a small
boy in 1954. Scott was then strictly a company town, and Andy's
father was the town pharmacist. "When we moved to Scott it was
still pretty much operating just a little removed from the sharecropper system. We were about ten years into mechanization at Delta
Pine. In the 1930s they had 25,000 acres and 2,500 black families
living on the place and 5,000 mules. Each family had 100 acres and
two mules. There was a company store there, a company doctor, a
company post office, a company phone system. The people were paid
off in silver dollars to prevent them from carrying the money to
Greenville to spend, and also because when they did have a payoff,
which was once a year, they always had a big crap game and the
silver dollars wouldn't get twisted and wadded up in the crap games.

"There were still remnants of that system by the time we got
there. There were an awful lot of black families living on the place.
Saturday night was the biggest night in town. Daddy had the drugstore. He was the pharmacist and ran the drugstore and a sundry-
type commissary that was next to the general store. A doctor had his
clinic there and free medical treatment was provided as part of the
system. They had broken it down by then into ten or twelve 2,500-
acre farms, and each one had a farm manager. They were still chopping cotton in those days, in 1954, and they were still picking cotton,
so they had to have an enormous amount of labor. There was a
village of probably 250 people, and the rest of the population lived
on the 25,000 acres around that.

"After that we moved to Cleveland. We had a corner drugstore
with a soda fountain, and in those days it was an interesting experience. We had blues singers come in to buy a guitar string and tune
up their guitar in the waiting area. The drugstore was connected to
a doctors' office, a clinic that had about four doctors working in it.
There was still a colored entrance and a colored waiting room. It was
still very much the Old South. Separate school systems, of course,
marked drinking fountains in the courthouse. That is what I was
raised in, and didn't really question it or think too much about it.
That was just the way it was. The big change came in '62, '63, and

'64 when the civil rights workers began coming in. By 1965 there was constant voter registration activity going on. There was a fair amount of civil rights activity in Cleveland because Mound Bayou, being only twelve or thirteen miles away, was used as a base of operations. It was safer for them there. Of course, we also had Amzie Moore at the post office. He was a janitor, but he became a very active person in the movement that was going on in Bolivar County.

"The thing that struck me in the face more than anything else was that we had a soda fountain in the drugstore which I had worked in from the time I was about eleven years old. Every Saturday night the store would stay open till about seven-thirty or eight o'clock because that was our busy night. In 1964 I went to the National Junior Leader Instructor Training Camp for Boy Scouts in Mendham, New Jersey, and was gone for about three weeks, and when I came back my mother had had the soda fountain taken out of the store. Daddy had had a stroke and couldn't run the store and she was having to, and it was just much easier for her to take the soda fountain out than it was to have to deal with the tension. It was one of those classic old marble soda fountains, and it was a real surprise to me." One small bit of fallout from the war to integrate the South's lunch counters.

Those days were peculiar. "I was active in the Boy Scouts and later in the Explorer Scouts. We were sponsored by the Civil Defense. Larry Speakes was our coordinator, and one of the things that I remember was we also stored the stuff for the sheriff's auxiliary in the Civil Defense building that we used for our meetings. There were about thirty-five pump shotguns and several cases of tear-gas grenades. As part of our Boy Scout Explorer training we were trained in crowd control to prepare ourselves for the insurrection. Throughout those summers there were voter registration drives and constant demonstrations in front of the courthouse, all peaceful, but we were ready for the rebellion.

"My attitudes at that time were probably very racist. There was nothing I'd ever been exposed to in any way from the church, from the educational system, or anything around me that made me question anything that was going on. It was described to me as a group of outside troublemakers disrupting our economy and our way of life. I guess a lot of that started to change with the murders in

Philadelphia. In church it was not something we talked about. Except there were discussions. You'd overhear the older folks talking about, 'They'd better not come here. They'll be turned away.' And that gave me some problems because the Catholic Church in Cleveland had always admitted blacks."

I asked him if he knew any blacks growing up, and he answered, "Sure, I knew Bertha, our maid. I knew the string of delivery boys at the drugstore. We had a bicycle, then a motorcycle, then a delivery car. So I knew that bunch of people. I knew black people who would come into the drugstore. They were regular customers. They were still 'uncle' and 'reverend' and that sort of thing, but they were our customers. Daddy may have been 'hard-core' but he would go out at three o'clock in the morning and fill a prescription for a black family just as easy as he would for a white family. Those were professionalism-type things.

"But there was that change going on and nobody knew what was happening. It caused a rapid sea-change in me. I went to Valley State and Delta State when the kids went out on strike and were arrested at machine-gun point and were loaded onto buses. At Delta State, when the blacks went out on strike, they were arrested at machine-gun point and put on buses and taken to Parchman. Suddenly the Delta seemed to me very repressive. All of a sudden this place that I had grown up in, I was on the outside instead of on the inside.

"The fact that it all happened as peacefully as it did is a miracle, because the white people were armed to the teeth and the black people were getting that way, and it could've been real dirty. It could've been real nasty, I believe. It was a nonviolent revolution for all practical purposes. When you've got such a change taking place, for no more people to die than died and no more property damage to take place than took place was truly amazing. I had a Sunday-school teacher that told me he rode on a mule to school in the twenties and came upon a tree and there were nine black men swinging on that tree. On his way to Sunday school. *That's* over with. But it could've been that nasty."

What good values are bred into the young of the Delta? "In Cleveland, Mississippi, growing up, as a child, the most honored men in my estimation, the highest level of people in town, were members of the Cleveland Volunteer Fire Department. Firemen were the great role models in the community, and I wanted to be like them. 'Nap' Cassibry [Napoleon Lapointe Cassibry, on whose family's lands Aretha Franklin's evangelist father once labored], the president of the bank, was on the volunteer fire department, and when the whistle blew, it didn't matter who he was talking to, be it the bank examiner, be it making the biggest loan of the year, he would excuse himself and run to the fire station, put on his turn-outs, get in the truck, and drive to the fire. In Cleveland, Mississippi, it was a very high honor to be on the Cleveland Volunteer Fire Department, and they were real firemen. There was no prejudice. Joe Denton, Jr., gave artificial respiration to a black man's dog one time, and the dog revived. It was a very unique situation. The tears on their eyes were just as big and just as real when they had to carry a burned black kid out of the house as when the whole leading family in Cleveland burned up. It was human life, and grown men cried."

Among volunteer firemen, the test is whether you "answer the bell." As one explained it to me, "Nobody wants to be the only son of a bitch who shows up at the fire." In recent years the Cleveland and Bolivar County fire departments have taken on black members, particularly several employees of Cleveland's largest industry, Baxter Travenol. They were trained as part of the company's fire brigade, and they were later recruited for the communitywide departments because they are competent, and especially because they "answer the bell."

I also spoke with John Miller, a New Orleans photographer, about his upbringing as the son of a Delta Methodist preacher. "I went to church every time the door was open till I was fourteen," he says. The upbringing was not what one thinks of as typical in Mississippi—a father who could not stand to see injustice, who forbade the word "nigger," who was frequently engaged in dark "conspiracies" with black pastors bent on uniting the black and white Methodist conferees, and a mother who taught Mississippi history at Delta State and at Mississippi Valley Junior College, but it was not so atypical as some might think. Every town and county had a few such people, or else the South would have long since perished in fratricide. They blended in. This young man hung out at the Varsity and Bob's Drive-In in Cleveland, bought beer from the carhops, and committed various acts of vandalism, including the ultimate sacrilege of doing wheelies on the golf greens. He pledged Kappa Alpha at Delta State. The days of serious hazing, of kissing a goat's behind, were past, though on one fellow's initiation night they put a rubber on his hand and lit it. "I don't think my fraternity brothers were particularly racist," he says. "I think they were more scared that their parents would cut off their funds."

What mental images does one who grew up there, and then left, carry around with him? "I loved the Delta growing up. It was a safe environment for us. What held it together more than anything else were the plantations, but that's going, going, gone. When I was growing up, people like Dixon Dosset and Big Daddy Warren and all those people were the kings, and the towns were their fiefs. You either worked for them or you depended on their cotton for your economy. And now it's big corporations, and they make their profits and suck them straight out of the Delta. Those people plowed them right back in."

Miller worked for the TV station in Greenwood, and his claim to fame came in 1973 when Martha Mitchell, who had endeared herself to the media with insider stories about the spreading Watergate scandal, simply disappeared from New York. In fact, she had traveled secretly to Bolivar County to visit a college friend and gather her second wind. John, who knew the family, helped stand off reporters when they learned her whereabouts, and for that he earned an exclusive interview about the attorney general's responsibility for the cover-up, and from that an appearance on Dick Cavett and much short-term notoriety.

"It's a unique place. It's a wonderful place to grow up, in spite of the fact that my bones are probably 90 percent DDT. Everybody knew everybody. We ranged forty or fifty miles. The people traveled incessantly from town to town. We used to go to dances in Ruleville and Drew. In fact, Archie Manning kept me from getting my ass kicked one night in Drew. I was typically intoxicated and I stumbled into some football player who was going to wipe the floor with me.

We'd go to parties, and we knew people in Beulah, and Rosedale, and Greenville, and Greenwood, and all over. But I don't know if the Delta will ever again be what it was when I was growing up. Times have changed. For one thing they've got television now, so everybody's from the Midwest, even the people from the Delta. They all watch Geraldo and Oprah. I imagine everybody in Greenwood, Mississippi, could tell you who the skinheads are."

Race relations were weird then, in the sixties and seventies. "A friend of mine and I were riding in a car one time through a town. We'd had a few drinks. And I can remember him leaning out the window as we passed this old black gentleman and spitting right on the side of his face. I just thought that was about the worst thing I ever saw, but he thought it was funny. And I can remember someone putting a half a watermelon on a black man's head, one of those eaten-out rinds, at a red light 'cause the guy couldn't tell him where Beale Street was in Memphis, and we were on Beale Street. He felt the guy was being smart. He just put it on his head like a hat. And when we drove off the man was just standing there, looking at us, with a watermelon on his head. Most of our racism was just what we'd been taught, basically. A lot of my friends just didn't know any better. I did. I didn't have any excuse."

He loves to tell stories about the eccentric royalty of the past. Like the judge's wife who would pull up at a grocery store and hand the first black she saw her keys and tell him to park her car. Or another judge's wife who drove all the way into Cleveland with a highway patrolman behind her with his lights flashing. She toddled into the house of her friend, a state representative, and said, "That young man has followed me all the way from Rosedale." She was just "above it all." And, "I can remember when I worked in a grocery store, sacking groceries, when I was in high school. And there was one lady in particular, a wealthy planter's wife, who would shop when the store was closed. And we would push baskets along and let her fill them up. She'd spend four or five hundred a week on groceries. She'd go past the Raid insect spray and I remember that one day she got one of everything they had on display, eighteen cans of insecticide." And a wealthy lady in town, his early patron, who put a car telephone in her maid's car because the maid lived out in the country and they were afraid she might have a breakdown. "In those days a car telephone was an extravagance. And nobody in town had one except her maid." There were the people with a home in Itta Bena and an apartment on Fifth Avenue in New York City.

"Those people are just about gone now," he says. "The whole Delta's changed. The little towns have eroded to nothing. The big farms are whittled down and all are owned by corporations. It's the same old story. The federal government and the banks got people to borrow and get in over their heads, and they took the land away when they couldn't pay their notes. Times is hard. I don't know what it would take to rejuvenate the Delta. It's beyond my imagination." That same expression was used by Representative Capps with respect to salvaging the boarded-up towns. I wonder if any readers share some sadness that these overproud, overconsuming people are passing, that their towns are eroding. If so, welcome to the club, but please try explaining why.

"I'm not saying the Delta has not been an evil place, not unlike South Africa," Miller says. "Every time I see things on South Africa I think how much it must be like where I grew up. But I think the Delta's changed a lot from that point. I don't think that kind of oppression can ever exist again in this country. Because I don't think people are stupid enough to think they have to put up with it."

I have met others in New Orleans who have emigrated from the Delta who do not share that view. One, a young professional who left in 1974, told me, "Black people in the Delta will never change. How those people can make a living in any of those towns is just amazing. But I don't think they will ever stop worrying about their day-to-day existence long enough to unify and get anywhere. The blacks in the Delta will always be 'sirring' to the white aristocracy because it's just ingrained in them. They don't care if the whites have any money or not anymore. The big difference is the blacks in New Orleans have pulled themselves up to some point of equality and the blacks in the Delta never have. They've never tried to. They don't believe in themselves like people here do." I think the significance of that statement is that it points out the magnitude of the change that has taken place in the Delta since 1974 when this man was last there. While there has been no unifying black messiah in the Delta, there can be little doubt that a long-oppressed people has come to grips with political power and taken capable charge of the institutions of government and education. The noteworthy thing is, not that this New Orleans exile would hold such a view, but that events have proved him wrong in so short a time.

fifteen

HOUSE DIVIDED

▲▲▲

The day will inevitably come when a handful of
colored children, with a court order for admission in
their hands, will walk into a grammar school
somewhere in Mississippi. With every legal subterfuge
out of the way, Mississippi will be faced with the
alternative of complying with the will of the court
or of closing the school.
—James W. Silver, *Mississippi: The Closed Society*

W hat school desegregation in the 1960s and 1970s meant
▽▽▽ throughout virtually all of the Delta was that the white children were pulled out of the public system and enrolled in hastily
organized private academies. The public schools became virtually all
black overnight. That picture has changed gradually in some communities, but not much at all in others.

Many of the academies are still going strong. Since 1964, for example, Bayou Academy has occupied the old public school building in
Boyle, a little town south of Cleveland on U.S. 61. The school has
prospered and now offers a full elementary, junior high, and senior
high school program. In 1988 it broke ground for a new facility two
miles west of Cleveland. This attracts students from all over Bolivar

County, and under the direction of headmaster Arty Nute, it enrolled about 300 students, up from 260 a year before.

In other communities the bloom seems to be off the private-school rose. In Indianola, the busy little Sunflower County seat at the intersection of two major federal highways, the private academy founded in 1965 reported a 20 percent loss of students between 1986 and 1987, and a 17 percent drop from 1987 to 1988. According to Indianola Academy president Jimmy Clayton, "I think costs are one major reason, and also some parents are wanting an alternative education opportunity for their children through the public schools and in some cases other private schools." It is the convoluted reasoning of the Delta that public schools are the "educational alternative." Even planters in America's poorest region may be hard pressed to pay private school bills. The tuition at Indianola Academy is on a par with that at other similar institutions throughout the Delta: $1,700 per child in high school; $1,500 per child in elementary school. In an area where big families are still the norm, this can get costly.

The Indianola public schools, by contrast, are "literally bursting at the seams," according to Superintendent Robert Merritt. The greatest enrollment increase in 1988 was at Lockard Elementary, which is now 66 percent white. The junior high and high schools remain 87 percent to 99 percent black, indicating that, as in many racially divided areas, parents and students do not seem to object to race-mixing among little children, but only among teenagers. Whether that is because of the white parents' concern for academic excellence as college approaches, the high school student's desire never to be in the minority, or simply the fear of black and white adolescent socializing, is better territory for conjecture than for scientific analysis. There are signs that once some racial parity is achieved at the elementary level, however, it will gradually flow up the ladder into high school. Both white and black parents in Indianola joined together in 1987 to win approval for the addition of grades six and seven to Lockard, their most integrated school. The statistics quoted above, incidentally, are those reported in the *Indianola Enterprise-Tocsin,* which prints the racial breakdown of the student body at each school as part of the standard fare of September back-to-school news. Any Chinese or Hispanic youngsters are counted among the whites.

Are the public schools much different today? Rims Barber, of the Children's Defense Fund, says, "The new superintendents have been able to break the plantation mentality. The schools had been places to keep the black kids off the street until it was time to pick cotton. That was their only purpose—not to educate anybody. Schools were part of the control mechanism for plantation society. Black leadership has broken that syndrome and begun doing a few basic things that one would associate with the schools, like everybody will have a book and we're going to open them every period. That doesn't lead immediately to terrific gains so that we can now compare them with Harvard and Yale. But we have broken cycles that needed to be broken." Much remains to be done. In Humphreys County, for example, almost 70 percent of the students who enter the ninth grade drop out before graduation.

The battle for control of the schools continues to be fought throughout the Delta. In the past two years there have been black boycotts of white businesses in Indianola, Tunica, Drew, Vicksburg, and Greenville protesting various school policies, not to mention boycotts in Rosedale and Isola in reaction to various perceived harassments of black youths. In 1986, a boycott of Indianola schools began when the school board appointed a white school superintendent. The schools were effectively closed and most businesses suffered until the business leadership bought out the white superintendent's contract and replaced him with a black. In Greenville, the boycott in 1988 was also aimed at ousting the white school superintendent.

Leaf through any Delta newspaper from September through May and you will find pictures of school clubs, teams, and graduating classes that, more than any statistics, illustrate the diverse nature of race relations in Mississippi's public schools. The award-winning Yazoo High School cheerleaders are evenly divided between white and black, and all have dazzling smiles. The all-girl Yazoo High Future Business Leaders of America in 1987–88 had five blacks among its thirty-one members. It also included two Traceys, three Tammys, and a Shondra, a Rondra, and a Shondell. In contrast, the

Humphreys Academy "Rebels" in Belzoni, whose symbol looks like Colonel Sanders after a few of Will Percy's mint juleps, fielded all-white teams to compete with those from the other private schools. Except for Daisy Woo, Debbie Jue, and class salutatorian Kermit Kwan, all of the 1988 senior scholarship winners at Indianola Academy were unmistakably Occidental.

It is sad that the Central Delta Academy Lady Tigers and the Inverness Hawkettes women's basketball teams never compete head-on, though both represent the same little cotton-gin town and seem equally endowed with grace and height. Surely the roughly ten white students among the seventy or so 1988 graduates of Rolling Fork High School must have felt like pioneers (or abandoned dregs), just as the first blacks in all-white public schools felt twenty years ago. At three Holmes County public high schools, both the valedictorian and salutatorian were black; at the fourth, the private Central Holmes Academy, both were white. Just about everybody who graduates from Sharkey-Issaquena Academy, the elite Washington School, and Greenville Christian is white, but in some towns, like Cleveland and Drew, people seem to be making a real effort to make the public schools work for everybody.

What makes the difference? One town where the dream is still alive is Leland, and the consensus there is that it starts with teachers and administrators remaining dedicated to the public school. One who has watched it from the inside is Dot Turk, librarian and yearbook sponsor at Leland High School. We met her by chance at Jeremy's, a restaurant she and her husband, Jere, run in Indianola. It is quite a nice spot, serving dishes like catfish in beer batter with pecan butter. "All we've got is excellence," she told us. "Nobody is going to just pass by and drop in." Impressed by her restaurant, I dropped in on her school, which is now about 70 percent black. This is a figure considered good by those who believe in integration, and it is approximately in line with the community's racial mix. Turk was one of the majority of white teachers who decided to stay with the Leland schools when they desegregated. The operative plan then sent half of the white teachers to the formerly black schools and vice versa. Most of the veterans of that period are still in the system and are proud of what they accomplished. One small accomplishment: the private academy eventually closed. Turk, who has written a book about Leland, talks with evident satisfaction about the black student editors of her yearbook who are now in college, of the school Christmas parties and plays starring black Santa Clauses, and of the lovely black class queen and her prim white maid of honor. Three whites and two blacks sit on the school board. In the past, whites have replaced blacks on the board and vice versa. "We have such a wonderful relationship here," Turk says, "so much better than any I have seen."

The principal of Leland High is a young man with a beard and occasionally in jeans, Harry Dickman. He is no slouch; he runs a tight ship. Any kid caught with drugs or a weapon, even a pocket knife, is out of school for the year. He can suspend students for up to nine days without review by the superintendent, a power he uses but which many school principals lack. Drug abuse at the school, Dickman says, in contrast to some in nearby Greenville, is not a big problem. He was formerly an assistant principal in Greenville, and he was there through integration in 1970. For two years, he says, the "atmosphere was unnatural." There was not even a fistfight during that period; in short, it was not an ordinary teenage time. Then the academies opened, and the program never really recovered from the white flight. Few of the whites ever returned, and the system now is about 95 percent black. Leland, however, is "an entirely different story. The attitudes of the teachers have superseded any administrative follies. The teachers have held things together."

How have they done that? Here Dickman and other teachers I talked to at Leland seem to retire into intangibles. Leland teachers, they say, are willing to work with kids. They are unwilling to lower their standards. That attitude comes from the top man, the superintendent, and reaches all the way down. Leland has always thought of itself as "a little special." Its annual "Christmas on Deer Creek," at which community clubs and schools build floats on boats and barges and drift them in the moonlight through town, is nationally known. The existence of the Stoneville Agricultural Laboratory adds a measure of Ph.D.'s to the town. In general, Leland is a strange mix of the very conservative and the progressive, much like the rest of the Delta, only here an above-average number of whites are in the progressive category.

In contrast to Greenville, where often the "beliefs in the community are contrary to the beliefs among students," in Leland "we're past the point of saying there is a black and white issue." Dickman is proud to report that seventy-eight of his graduating students last year accepted $400,000 in scholarships. Sixty percent of the graduates went on to college. He explains the school's high dropout rate on the grounds that a lot of kids cannot hack it. They require a 75 average to pass, the highest in the state. The commitment to excellence makes Leland public schools attractive to parents over a wide area. Quite a few white parents in Indianola, for example, send their children to Leland rather than to the Indianola public or private schools. All that is required for enrollment in Leland is that a student's parent or "guardian" live there. The social fabric of the Delta is such that few students cannot claim a "guardian" in just about any town they want to.

Dickman says race is no longer an issue in Leland. "We haven't had a problem here for years," he says. But there might be a debate on that. Down the street from the school, I struck up a conversation with a woman in an office-supply store who, it turned out, was Atlanta-educated just like me and who regaled me with her theories on the differences between the distinguished blacks of Atlanta and the "registered blue-gums" of the Delta. She feared what would happen when the city next held elections and blacks took over, as they had in Hollandale and Rolling Fork. Her husband walked in near the end of this exchange, got the drift of his wife's comments, and said, "Honey, that's bullshit." Many in Atlanta would agree.

When the kids leave high school in the Delta today, most of them follow familiar trails into the service or to Valley State, Delta State, or Ole Miss. College life for many of them is a lot like it was supposed to be in the 1950s and what a fair number of deans think it should be like in the 1990s. That is, peaceful, with heavy emphasis on sports and fashion. And on "old-fashioned." It is not that long ago that a young gentleman from Mayersville attended Ole Miss in Oxford and brought along his black servant, who was quartered in the basement of the fraternity house, to attend to the young master's needs during his four years of higher education.

Ole Miss is still the school of choice for the children of the gentry. The Kappa Alphas are a big force there and continue to celebrate "Old South Week" in Confederate uniforms, escorting beautiful ladies in antebellum dresses to the ball. The secretary and parliamentarian of the KAs at Ole Miss in 1988 were both from Belzoni, and the historian was from Cleveland, indicating how the power of tradition still emanates from the plantation. The KAs are less all-white than they used to be and will pledge black students who can live up to the ideals of the order; "if," as one white student said to me, "you can imagine a black Confederate soldier." As a historical fact, there were quite a few. In fairness, Ole Miss has made great strides since the riot against the federal marshals that accompanied James Meredith's enrollment on September 30, 1962. In the midst of that calamity, virtually instigated by Governor Ross Barnett and the *Jackson Clarion Ledger*, Ole Miss students sang the "Never, No Never" song at the Ole Miss–Kentucky football game:

> *Never, never, never, never, no-o-o never, never, never.*
> *We will not yield an inch of any field.*
> *Fix us another toddy, ain't yielding to nobody.*
> *Ross's standing like Gibraltar, he shall never falter.*
> *Ask us what we say, it's to hell with Bobby K.*
> *Never shall our emblem go from Colonel Reb to old black Joe.*

Before the violence in this little town ended, 160 United States marshals were hurt and President Kennedy sent in 20,000 federal troops. James W. Silver, who chronicled that period in his best-selling *Mississippi: The Closed Society*, ended his own witness to a dramatic era in 1988. In the prefatory note to the 1963 book he wrote: "Some day Mississippians are going to have to grow up, to accept the judgments of civilization, else we are doomed to many September 30ths to come." Perhaps that day has finally just about come in Mississippi. Ole Miss elected a black student-body president in 1988, and the first black fraternity house opened on formerly lily-white fraternity row that same year. To the university's great embarrassment, the house was burned down by arsonists, but state funds and contributions of labor have got the place rebuilt. To continue the irony of time passing, James Meredith, first a teacher in Cincinnati and now an aide to Jesse Helms of North Carolina, writes angry letters to the Greenwood paper, saying, "I support Republican candidates because the greatest enemy facing the black race in 1988 is the white liberal. . . . The only thing worse than a Democratic liberal is a Republican liberal. Thank God, there are only a few of those left."

The major institution for higher learning actually in the Delta is Cleveland's Delta State University. Its mascot is the Fighting Okra. The school has about 3,700 students, roughly 300 of whom are black. I visited on January 18, 1988, to see how Martin Luther King's birthday, a new national holiday, was being observed. Except for exhibits in libraries and community centers scattered about the area, a one-man play by Robert Haynes in Clarksdale, and a pretty big celebration held at the Carver Middle School in Indianola, Delta State's was one of the major observances in the Delta. Though the public schools were all closed, Delta State was open for classes. What was happening there was that the Black Student Union and Alpha Phi Alpha fraternity (Martin Luther King's fraternity) were showing a series of videotapes of King's speeches and civil rights documentaries on a large television in the lobby of the student union, which a dozen or so black students were watching, quietly and respectfully.

Outside a newsman from a Greenville TV station was calling the students out for interviews in groups of two or three. He was a newcomer to the area, from Orlando, Florida. Bolivar County was his beat, and he was clearly hoping that an opportunity to move along to a bigger "market" would soon come his way. In reply to my comment that there was no shortage of stories to report in the Delta, he retorted, "But they're all about the same things . . . four hundred thousand Mississippians above the age of sixteen can't read. The black-white issue, poverty, the legislature with their inability to fund the state university system. Those were some big stories. Heavy taxation, corrupt supervisors, the unit system. Am I repeating myself?" He seemed a little startled by life in general in the Delta. "You come in from the outside, from a state or area where there isn't any prejudice at all. You come in here and you see all this and it just floors you. It's the 1960s all over again here. This area is twenty to thirty years behind the times. Every single aspect of interracial activity is that far behind."

Most of the students inside had been crawlers when King was alive, but they felt the observance as an important show of black solidarity. Several nodded in agreement with one who expressed satisfaction that Delta State had remained open. "We wanted the holiday, but I did not want the day off from school. My instructor was white, and she didn't understand what I was saying. I told her if we get off school the majority of the people are just going to sit home and drink beer. They're not going to go out to the park and remind their kids of what happened. If the blacks are not going to do that, definitely the whites aren't. It's about like Saint Patrick's Day. We should keep the schools open to keep everybody informed and to keep that communication going." One remarked that had they not been at the school, the newsmen outside would not have been able to find a story.

I asked about the relatively small turnout and was told, "Well, it's lunchtime. What we go by is that most of the blacks are dressed up. That's our silent way of saying, 'Hey, we remember you.' That's what we go by. Sitting out here, this is for the white people." The students were proud that they had just elected a black homecoming queen. They accomplished this because the blacks voted in a block while the white vote split, a dress rehearsal for real life. The president and dean seemed to be "pretty tickled about it," but the students thought some of the white kids had been "trained the wrong way and didn't appreciate it."

One of the black students was from Arkansas and told us, "I went through a culture shock when I got here, so to speak. I'm not saying that the Delta is any worse, but I was never exposed to the relations problem back home. Every high school I've seen here is either totally black or totally white. Where I come from the closest private school is thirty miles away. I couldn't believe that there were three high schools in this one little area. It's not so much a racial problem. I think it is an economic problem. With three high schools in this general area, one private and two public, that's a lot of money going out. I think that's going to hold Mississippi down for a long time."

Tryphonia Cleveland was the head of the BSU and of Alpha Phi Alpha fraternity. He told me that this was the third year that King's birthday had been commemorated at State. Tryphonia, in fact, looks a little like a young Dr. King. He lives with his grandmother in Glendora, close to the home of Matt and Pie Dale. He is a finance major and hopes to go into banking or real estate. Does he plan to stay in Mississippi? That question was one he could quickly answer: "Oh, no. Oh, no. I am leaving as soon as I graduate. I don't think there's too many jobs here for finance majors. The only jobs here really seem to be for teachers in the school system." His only complaint about Delta State was that the program seemed geared to white, not black, students. While both get along pretty well, "a lot of the whites are from the academies and have never been around any blacks. A lot of the blacks are from public high schools and have never been around any whites. I think the guys adjust better than the girls do. The average guy says a guy is a guy. They can go out together. The white girls seem to be more to themselves." The dormitories at Delta State are integrated, he says, but not the rooms. A black will be assigned a black roommate unless he specifically requests otherwise, and, of course, few do.

I asked why there are so few blacks at State since it is the major school in an overwhelmingly black area and costs relatively little to attend. Cleveland offers two answers. First, he says, "The black students are not motivated in high school. A lot of high schools don't have counselors and those that do don't have good counselors. That's a stage when you need some help deciding what to do. I'm here because I had some teachers to encourage me. They talked to me every day and pushed me to come." These teachers, by the way, were white, and as always it is the teacher who put his or her hand on your shoulder, not the one with the most technical knowledge, who gets remembered. His other answer speaks to racial identity: "The majority of blacks who are going to go to college prefer to go to a black university, because it is easier for them to fit in, to socialize. The

MACE's Malcolm Walls, organizer of the Delta Blues Festival, with acquaintance in Glen Allan

programs there are geared toward blacks. Here the programs aren't, and blacks spend a lot of time trying to find themselves. A lot of them try to be white."

When pressed, he expands on this idea: "Blacks need to come up with some way to encourage schools to set up more black programs—interracial programs. If we did this right, I really think that white students and black students would enjoy this too. They wonder what we are like, what we enjoy, what we do for fun. If we were able to express these things then everything would be all right. One of my instructors asked me the question, 'Why do blacks do such a poor job in school here?' We were trying to figure out why, because Delta State gets some of the cream-of-the-crop black students here. Some are honor students in high school, valedictorians of their classes. It's that blacks have a hard time finding themselves here. A lot try to be white. There is a difference between black and white, you know. Although we both are human there are still cultural differences, certain values, certain ways you were brought up to think and do. We have some who'll say blacks and whites dress differently. If I go to a black university they can tell because of the way I dress and act that I go to a white school. There is something wrong if you prefer whites over blacks just because they are white or black. There are blacks here who are doing that. They will not associate with blacks at all. The kids who go to black schools are missing something, too. You need to try to interrelate with whites as well."

While at Delta State I also visited the Science Museum. This is an attraction that is not only mentioned in most of the state tourist publications today, but was even noticed in the WPA *Mississippi: A Guide to the Magnolia State,* published in 1938. I expected something impressive and kind of dull, but this museum is one of a kind. To gain access, you must track down a professor with a key, but then you have the room to yourself. In it is a two-headed calf, donated in 1936; a headless goat in pickling and another with two heads; a three-legged bullfrog; huge alligator snapping turtles with heads the size of footballs; the lower jaw of a mastodon found in 1953 on Choctaw Bar in the Mississippi River, believed to be 20,000 years old; a bison bone identified, obviously without benefit of carbon dating, as "probably 2,000 to 200,000 years old"; the skeleton of a female Indian found near Leflore, still with most of her teeth; and several cardboard boxes full of outdated adding machines and laboratory equipment. In addition, there are lots of fossils, stuffed squirrels, and birds. It is the kind of collection you would keep in a very special attic, and it is well worth a visit.

Outside of school, hunting and fishing are still prime activities. Walk into the Western Auto in Indianola, situated next to 94 FM (black radio), and you will be confronted with two racks of knives, all blades open, and easily one hundred rifles and shotguns on the wall. This is still one of the macho capitals of America. Getting that first deer is a rite of passage for almost all young men.

The ultimate symbol of being a part of this place is membership in the Merigold Hunting Club. Of the scores of hunting clubs in the Delta—those open or sometimes fenced-off preserves along both banks of the river or on the fringes of the hills ringing the Delta—some are larger, some are fancier, but none is more prestigious. You are born into the Merigold Hunting Club; you may acquire a membership by inheritance, or by a wise marriage, but you cannot join. Membership is drawn from the townsfolk and politicians of Merigold and the farmers of the surrounding vicinity. To a resident of Bolivar County, membership in the club carries the sort of significance that having keys to the firehouse might have to a citizen of North Hadley, Massachusetts. A local who is *not* a member of the club sniped that a friend of his, a Jew, married a girl whose father belonged to Merigold. "And I'll always believe he married her to hunt in that club."

The preserve itself is a 20,000-acre stretch of forest, swamp, and jungle between the river and the levee, which at some points are better than seven miles apart, near Beulah. To gain entry you must take a narrow gravel road that certainly looks private across several miles of uninterrupted cotton fields, crossing cattle guards along the way, until the levee looms ahead, giving no hint of what might be on the other side. Cows graze on this hill and look down on all who approach. Crossing over the top, the road becomes narrower still and twists out of sight into a dark forest. You know the river is somewhere beyond the woods, but it cannot be seen. A little plank No Trespassing sign announces that this is private land for members only, and this warning is almost universally respected. Those who do venture back into the woods eventually will find the "camps," cottages built on the old levee and raised on pilings fifteen feet in the air to withstand floods, often with spacious screened-in porches and all the comforts and amenities needed for a weekend retreat: beds, baths, bars, and well-stocked kitchens.

The club has a "blue hole" where the river once hit soft land and went deep, maybe because of a whirlpool, and when the river moved away it left a pool of clear water, cold blue because of its depth. It is fed indirectly by the Mississippi through a shoot from an oxbow lake, which is itself fed by the river when it floods.

The land is leased from Anderson-Tulley, a timber company based locally in Vicksburg, and it is stocked with deer, turkey, ducks, squirrels, and wild pigs. Actually, the land is not so much stocked with game as it is preserved as a habitat. Deer, especially, thrive here. One awed visitor told me, "You can't even shoot a buck less than eight points. You don't have to. If you want a deer you can get one. It's the most amazing hunting place I've ever seen. It's unbelievably well maintained. Invitations to hunt there are as rare as hen's teeth."

Almost as rare as an invitation to hunt is an invitation to _watch_ a hunt. That means you can join in the camaraderie of eating and drinking for the weekend, but you cannot actually shoot at anything. I managed an invitation to an even lesser event, a party, but an important party nevertheless, a Fourth of July barbecue. For that occasion the older generation pretty much stays at home and abandons the camp to the sons and daughters. It is a day of beer drinking and merriment, bumpy pickup truck rides on barely visible trails out to the river to drink and tell stories and watch the occasional passing barge, all culminating in a flotilla of ski-boats and Boston Whalers skimming across the mile-wide Mississippi to the great treeless sandbars found at the mouth of the White for campfires and a picnic. It is wild country there where the two rivers meet. The west bank is also carved up into hunting preserves, and the whole region is as uninhabited as it was when Huckleberry Finn sailed through. The only obstacles to uninhibited navigation and frolic over the huge Mississippi is the passage every half-hour or so of line boats moving toward New Orleans, pushing thirty-five or more barges of grain or coal. These massive loads, some of them looking to be more than a quarter of a mile long, cannot readily stop or change direction, and woe to the fisherman whose pleasure boat's motor conks out midstream.

This freedom of wide-open spaces, of easy access to the great natural wonder of the river, ever-dangerous, ever-changing playground, the ruggedness of hunting, and the ease of living in a place where a certain amount of laziness is a well-guarded social virtue, is what a lot of people think makes the Delta worth living in. All are equally available to poor and rich alike. Not membership in the hunting club, to be sure, but even at the lowest rung on the ladder there is hardly a young man who has not marched with a friend over great estates of cotton-field stubble, casting a long shadow, gun resting in the crack of his elbow, hunting rabbits at dawn; or a girl who has not sat under a bridge, quietly fishing with her mother.

As the woodland vanishes from the Delta, some of the charm of life departs. Over parts of this clear-cut region, the major intrusion of the wild these days is the wintertime arrival from Canada of huge flocks of blackbirds like those that trouble Greenwood and Greenville every year. Undeterred by shotguns, barrages of loud noises, and foul chemical bombs that strip away their protective body oils, they nest in any available thicket or park and are thoroughly odious to people. I saw one of these herds pass over U.S. 82 in Greenville one day, and the organization and number of the flock was truly amazing. They passed ninety feet overhead in a whiplike column, five or ten birds wide at any given point. They flew very fast, maybe full-out, and by my estimate a hundred of them passed my spot every three or four seconds. I watched this phenomenon for more than fifteen minutes until a curve in the whip carried the line too far back into the mist for me to follow. Once there may have been ducks in something like this profusion passing here every year. The Mississippi flyway is the wintering habitat for several duck species, but each year their number dwindles as the requisite marsh and swamp habitat is lost in the South and the North. The blackbirds are more adaptable.

But for now, growing up with the wild remains a vital part of the experience of living in the Mississippi Delta, and as hunters and wildlife lovers become better acquainted it may continue to be so. It says something that rugged hunting land in the Delta sells for more per acre today than well-cultivated farms and fields. All of man's works in the Delta have a certain temporary quality about them. The Mississippi River flows nearby, often at a level with the treetops. Eventually it must flood. Despite its levees, it is the wildest thing of all.

sixteen

THE TRAIN DOESN'T RUN THERE ANYMORE

▲▲▲

NO SHOOTING FROGS FROM BRIDGE
—Sign on the road between Merigold and Drew

WHITNEY, 29.1 m. (26 pop.), is headquarters for the
Gritman-Barksdale plantation, owned and operated by a
large Northern life insurance company. Divided into
small tracts, the acreage of the plantation is worked by
tenants on the sharecropper system. Cotton fields
stretching out interminably for miles on both sides of
the highway are dotted with the tenants' cabins, each
with its small front porch, a cistern, and a garden for
growing vegetables, and each shaded by a chinaberry
tree or two. The furnishings are few, usually consisting
only of beds and chairs. When the families are large,
the children often sleep on pallets on the floor.
DREW, 31.7 m. (136 alt., 1373 pop.), is a pleasant town
typical of the new Delta in its lack of provincialism.
Drawing a wealthy planter trade, the shops cater to
expensive tastes for smart frocks, shoes, hats, and the
latest novelties. Restaurants offer a good cuisine.

WPA, *Mississippi: A Guide to the Magnolia State*

$\mathbf{E}$very little town is interesting. No doubt a book could be written
▽▽▽ about most of them; Dot Turk's volume about Leland, *From*

Hellhole to Garden Spot, proves the point. And take Onward, a little
village crossroads on U.S. 61 halfway between Rolling Fork and
Vicksburg. Here President Theodore Roosevelt, accompanied by
Stuyvesant Fish, president of the Illinois Central Railroad, came to
hunt bear in the swamps and canebrakes in 1907. Their guide was
Holt Collier, a black Confederate veteran who had killed Yankees
and defied Reconstruction and who himself lassoed a wild bear so
that the president would have the opportunity of making the first
kill. Legend has it that Roosevelt was too sporting to shoot a captured animal, thereby, I am told, inspiring the teddy bear.

In Gunnison, a town near the levee in Bolivar County, natural
gas in the ground water has blown the tops off the town's hydrants.
Grave markers in the cemetery read "Killed in Concordia," the
early name of the town, dating from when this was one of the
rougher spots on the river. The county history tells us that Concordia was noted for "saloons, gambling houses, and wild Western
ways." Now it is known mainly for having one of the area's last
cotton gins. Dennis and Delores Wills run it, along with all of their
children and many of their in-laws. While Dennis minds the equipment, Delores rocks babies in the office, keeps the books, and hands
out gin tickets. All of her kids, she says, were "born between the
bales." Her oldest, Dallas, shows us around the deafening machine
with perfect confidence. The hardest job, she says, is working the
pipe that sucks the cotton out of the trailers. Indeed, the hard-
looking T-shirted young men performing this task are sweating
hard, not enjoying themselves. A thunderstorm rumbles through,
blowing bean plants flat to the ground, and the gin shuts down till
tomorrow.

In Benoit, between Rosedale and Greenville, is the Burrus House,
which is not only antebellum but has a war record as the headquarters of Confederate general John Early. It is one of the few mansions
still standing in the Delta, but barely. Mrs. Pearson says that the
Bolivar County Historical Society tried to fix it up but ran out of
funds. Now a house trailer stands guard in the yard where officers
once camped.

Near Glen Allan are the ruins of the first Episcopal church in the
Delta, from which all others were spawned. The building was begun
in 1852 and was built by slaves, who were given an upstairs gallery

Dennis Wills, manager of the Gunnison Gin, Gunnison

in which to pray. The altar was carved by the black sexton, Jesse Crowell. It is said that he was buried in an adjacent cemetery, but we could not find his grave.

In Yazoo City is a man who has trained his pigs to come up to the trough and all eat at once. They will stop together and eat together, at his command. People come from all around to see.

A woman in Inverness ran to her front porch to rescue her beef-steak begonia from a tornado sweeping through the town. She was blown clear through the long central hall and into her back yard, still clutching her beefsteak begonia.

Rena Lara is a thriving but tiny spot on U.S. 1 by the river that is now home to about five hundred people. It was once among the homes of Edmund Richardson, the "richest cotton man in the world," who was reputed to own thirty-seven plantations. His son John, who lived there, owned but seven plantations. During the Depression, Rena Lara was the location of one of President Franklin Roosevelt's resettlement projects, to provide homes and gardens to starving sharecroppers. Rena Lara is nearby Sunflower Landing, no longer much of anything, which according to the most widely ac-cepted theory is where De Soto's malaria-ridden conquistadors "dis-covered" the Mississippi in 1541. Memphis and Tunica also claim that honor, but their claims are discredited by almost all Coahoma County historians.

One of the southernmost towns of the Delta is Egremont on U.S. 61. There is not much to do there, but even the attention of the high-speed traveler will be grabbed by the towering reptilian road-side sculptures—a green tyrannosaurus, a blue triceratops, and a yellow giraffe, fashioned of sheet metal—at BoBo's Ceramics and Plaster. The eyes of the dinosaurs are bicycle reflectors.

On his way to shoot bear at Onward, Teddy Roosevelt had the train stop at Mound Bayou so that he could greet the people of the Delta's unique all-black town. He had his picture taken shaking hands with blacks, and in doing so confirmed all white Mississippi-ans' suspicions about Republicans.

Mound Bayou is a part of the Mississippi heritage that has not disappeared, but that has certainly suffered from neglect. Situated a few miles north of Cleveland, it has its origins in Brierfield and Hurricane, the plantations of the Jefferson Davis family at Davis

Wrought-iron fence around ruins of the Delta's first Episcopal church, Glen Allan

Bend, south of Vicksburg. Jefferson's older brother, Joseph, a Natchez lawyer and soldier, had been taken with the idea of "harmoni-
ous cooperation" for profit espoused by Robert Owens. Joseph was
one of only a handful of people in Mississippi before the Civil War
who owned more than three hundred slaves, and the only one of
them who provided incentives for production and "courts of justice"
which heard each slave's case before an overseer could administer
punishment.

The star of Davis's "slave-utopia" was Benjamin Thornton Montgomery, a slave who ran the commissary and ultimately became the
buying and selling agent for all of the plantation crops. Montgomery
was permitted to retain a share of his profits, and with them, he paid
Davis the value of his wife's services, so that she could stay home and
raise Montgomery's five children. During the Civil War the Davises
abandoned their plantations when Admiral Porter's gunboats came
up the river. General Grant made Davis Bend a sanctuary for "contrabands," slaves who trailed the Union army for freedom, and had
the land divided among teams of blacks to farm. In 1865 nearly 2,000
blacks, divided into ten-person companies, farmed nearly 5,000
acres, and they showed a profit. In the following year, however, the
original landowners regained their title and the great experiment
ended. Partly to avoid claims for reparations, Joseph Davis sold his
plantation to Montgomery. Unfortunately for the buyer, the Mississippi River changed course the next year and greatly reduced river
access to, and the local importance of, the Davis Bend plantations.
Montgomery, nevertheless, moved his twenty-seven-person house-
hold into Jefferson Davis's Brierfield "mansion," on whose grounds
his daughter Virginia developed extensive flower gardens. Without
a doubt Benjamin Montgomery was the foremost black businessman
of slave and Reconstruction times.

Jeff Davis, never satisfied with his older brother's sale of Brierfield
and Hurricane, sued, and in 1881 the Mississippi Supreme Court recognized him and the other heirs of Joseph Davis as owners of Davis
Bend. Ben Montgomery died before the ruling. His son, Isaiah, opened
a little store in Vicksburg. In 1887, the Louisville, New Orleans, and
Texas Railroad, building a roadbed through the Delta, offered cheap
land to settlers along its right-of-way. Isaiah and his cousin Ben
Green sold all of their possessions and with the proceeds bought 840

acres of railroad land in Bolivar County near an Indian mound and called it Mound Bayou. They recruited a small band, primarily former Davis slaves, to settle there, to multiply, and to buy more land.

Much of their success was due to the high regard the white community had for Isaiah Montgomery. He was the only black delegate to the 1890 constitutional convention, where he rose to speak in favor of black disenfranchisement as a means to racial peace.

By 1907, 800 families possessed close to 30,000 acres and had cleared about 6,000 of them from the wild. They organized a bank, a town-meeting form of government based on the Davis Bend experiment, and a committee to rid the community of any "loose family relationships." Isaiah was a friend of Booker T. Washington, and with his help and that of Sears, Roebuck president Julius Rosenwald, the townsfolk organized a cottonseed-oil mill and a farmers' cooperative. White visitors who passed through were accommodated at the twenty-one-room Montgomery home. It was the collapse of cotton prices after World War I that killed the town, or at least its usefulness as a model for black economic development. The bank, the mill, and the cooperative all failed, and the townspeople yielded to the greater culture and went off to sharecrop.

The town produced early civil rights leadership, like Dr. Theodore Roosevelt Mason Howard, who opened the first meeting of the Mississippi Regional Council of Negro Leadership in 1952 and led resistance to Governor Hugh White's bid for black support of "separate but equal" schools in 1954. Isaiah's daughter Mary Booze was a Republican national committeewoman from 1924 to 1948. During the movement of the 1960s, Mound Bayou was a haven and meeting place for civil rights workers, white and black.

The town was noted in the 1960s as the home of two black-owned hospitals. Both were created by black fraternal associations, the Knights of Tabor and the International Order of Friendship, and they were financed with the nickels and dimes of sharecroppers. They were basically the only medical facilities for blacks between Jackson and Memphis. In 1967 Tufts University opened a health clinic in Mound Bayou; the sprinkling of whites among its professional staff lived in the town for safety and became its first white residents. It spawned another short-lived cooperative farming experiment, which distributed the bounty of its harvest to the poor and shipped a line of "soul food" north for profit.

The black fraternal hospitals closed in the 1980s after the more modern medical facilities in nearby Cleveland desegregated, but the Tufts project, now the federally funded Delta Health Center, has survived. Its director is L. C. Dorsey, a diminutive fifty-year-old social worker whose soft eyes and constant good humor conceal an energetic and combative spirit. She is one of those who have "come home" to the Delta and stayed. She was born to sharecropping parents near Shelby and picked cotton herself until the last of her six children was born. Then the civil rights movement touched her, and by 1968 she was director of the 400-acre cooperative farm in Mound Bayou. In 1971 she took a chance and left Mississippi to pursue a social-work degree at the State University of New York, though she had only a GED and no college degree. She fought against the death penalty in Mississippi, and then earned her master's and a doctorate at Howard before joining the faculty at the University of Mississippi in its Rural Health Research program.

In 1988 she returned to the Delta to run the health clinic and says, "I love being back." True, there are things she misses in her little town, like a daily newspaper, a restaurant, and a place where adults can go for drinks and conversation, but there are compensations, like neighbors who check on you when the porch light is lit and stop in when you are sick, a "caring, sharing thing," she calls it. Plus the challenge of grabbing federal dollars that are increasingly scarce and delivering quality health care in one of America's poorest counties. "I was so bored in academia," she says, "that I was thinking about joining the Peace Corps. The faculty thought I had a character defect because I wanted to be in service to people. Now, every day, I see things I want to accomplish."

Her first year on the job, the clinic sponsored a back-to-school party for the town's teenagers around the theme of "Say No to Pregnancy," and Dr. Dorsey says, "We would like to see our program expanded into Sunflower County. And I would like to get the Mississippi Symphony to come and do a performance for the town and staff." And the ideas keep coming.

The town could use more with energy like hers. While there are several new public buildings in Mound Bayou today, vestiges of the federal gravy train during the War on Poverty, the town suffers from much the same miasma that affects most little towns in the Delta. It is clean, but storefronts are boarded up and the most notable activity is around the beer store and the video rental outlet. The Montgomery house still stands, and the gardens are tended, but a few of the window panes have been knocked out. Though it has more than the average number of black landowners and professionals, Mound Bayou is basically poor, and if its experience stands for anything, it is that it is difficult in America, and especially difficult for blacks in a segregated society, to create a successful enterprise zone without drawing upon resources from beyond the zone's boundaries. Mound Bayou's future success, like that of most Delta towns, will depend on its ability to attract outside investment. It may have a special advantage in that its citizens can boast a long history of resourcefulness and self-reliance. Some of that may play a part in the surprising fact that Mound Bayou eleventh-graders did much better than the state average, and vastly better than the state average for black children, in Mississippi's 1987 functional literacy exam. Because the people of Mound Bayou own much of the surrounding land, they are in a better position than most Delta blacks to reap the benefits of any development the town may enjoy. The sign as you leave town reads, "Remember the Past as We Venture into the Future," courtesy of the Mound Bayou Business League, and if the town can continue to persuade its brightest and best émigrés to come back home, it may indeed have a future.

It is of historical interest that Mound Bayou was not the only model community attempted in the Delta. In 1935, when sharecroppers in Arkansas were evicted from the plantations for taking part in a cotton pickers' strike called by the Southern Tenant Farmers' Union, Sherwood Eddy, an international evangelist for the YMCA, and Reinhold Niebuhr, a political theorist and theologian, bought a 2,100-acre plantation to serve as a refuge at Hillhouse, near the river in Coahoma County. Thirty families of white and black sharecroppers moved in to farm the acreage cooperatively. In its early days, Hillhouse was financially aided by Northern socialists, and it even had a little Socialist Party local. It was further supported by John and Mack Rust, whose mechanical cotton picker, the prototype of the machine that revolutionized Southern agriculture, was used at the farm following its introduction in 1936. Labor was divided into cooperatives: a producers' cooperative to supervise planting and building, and a consumers' cooperative to sell the crops and distribute supplies. Housing was segregated, in keeping with Mississippi law, but in defiance of local custom courtesy titles were used in addressing blacks as well as whites.

The soil at Hillhouse was mostly "buckshot," however, and in the late 1930s the cooperative moved to a new farm located in Holmes County, under the direction first of a Presbyterian missionary from Tennessee, Sam Franklin, and later a Texas bookkeeper, Eugene Cox. They renamed their enterprise Providence Farms. A medical clinic was opened on the grounds by David R. Minter, a doctor, and Lindsey Hail, a nurse from Boston General who married Cox. The operation continued quietly until 1955, when a rumor was spread in the vicinity that "interracial swimming" was occurring at Providence. The White Citizens Council had been formed the year before in Indianola, and its Holmes County chapter, the second to organize, began an "investigation" into this swimming incident in an emotional public hearing at the high school in Tchula and a decision to expel the "outsiders," who had lived there about twenty years. A state police barricade went up around Providence, and after threats and a siege of several weeks, the Minters moved to Arizona and the Coxes moved to the Memphis suburb of Whitehaven. Thus ended this modest experiment in interracial cooperation in Mississippi. The old clinic building still stands today in a field where the Delta gives way to the hills, and is used as a barn.

Down the road, Greenville hosts the annual Delta Blues Festival each September, sponsored by Mississippi Action for Community Education (MACE). This is one of the few remaining institutions of the civil rights movement. The festival's chief organizer, Malcolm Walls, told us, "You'd love it, you'd absolutely love it." He is possessed of a gentle and persuasive voice, so we accepted his invitation to come. He says that over the past ten years the target for financing the festival has been away from community philanthropy and toward "special marketing." "Now, instead of a proposal talking about how you're doing something for the poor Delta community, your proposal talks about advertising ratios and how you can increase the consumption of beer or chicken wings. We're getting money from Miller Beer instead of from the National Endowment for the Arts."

With Walls, we also toured several communities that illustrate the progress and lack of it in the lives of ordinary people here. We went to the town of Metcalf and on the way passed an unfinished MACE housing project, utilizing barracks from the old Greenville air base. This is the same base that striking sharecroppers took over in 1966, the same base that the city later leased to Boeing in a celebrated example of Delta industrialization, and the same base that Boeing vacated in 1988 when its defense contracts failed to materialize (because Senator Stennis retired, some said). Funds to renovate the barracks were cut shortly before Reagan's reelection, and the barracks are empty.

Metcalf was incorporated in 1978. With MACE's help it has obtained $20 million in development money for sewer, water, and gas systems, and for fire and police protection. It is all paying for itself. The initial money came from revenue sharing and from the Farmers' Home Administration and other government sources. Half the town is still ten years behind the other half; but the idea is not to have a substandard house in town in five years.

We passed Metcalf Gardens, a senior citizens' complex, which is government-subsidized. The streets have curbs. They are trying to get an elementary school, a grocery, and a branch of a bank. Thirteen hundred people live in Metcalf, mostly old and young. There's a park and recreation center and a business owned by Heinz called something like Chico-San, a manufacturer of rice cakes. Sixty percent of its employees must be residents. The police force is Jim King, a forty-four-year-old former military policeman and truck driver. He is paid about $13,000 a year but he doesn't plan to leave because "you don't have many problems when you are the department." Walls says, "It's beginning to take on the flavor of a little community where I would like to live."

We stopped at the home of a man named Roosevelt who refused to let us take photos or record his conversation. Roosevelt is bitter. He says that it used to be that a black man once could not wear a white shirt to town. Blacks are "still treated like dogs." he says.

Roosevelt's house is listing and seems to be propped against a tree. Inside, a light hangs by a cord from a ceiling covered in cardboard, acoustical tile, and linoleum mixed together. He is opposed to the town's efforts to impose garbage, gas, and sewer fees. He believes he can help himself with the aid of the good Lord. "If you need help, who else is going to give it to you, huh?" He and his wife are caring for five boys and two girls. In the fall he hauls cotton choppers to the field, but in general he is a "master of all trades." He says he can put any machine together without instructions in thirty minutes, and he shows off the coffee table and end tables he built. The house is very neat and full of plastic flowers. On a shelf are several bottles of fancy wine and brandy, unopened, as if they were presents.

We went to Leland, of which Walls says, "This little community's been like this for years. The only thing that's really changed is the style of the cars." We visited Black Dog, a neighborhood named, we were told, for a train that used to pass there. It is a sleepy spot. We met Jacqueline Jackson on her front porch. She works for the Washington County Union for Progress, and her comment on neighborhood conditions is that she doesn't like the sewers being stopped up. Down the street drives Bill Wallace, and the lady remarks that "he's with the blues." Malcolm says Wallace plays in the B. B. King style. Son Thomas lives about two blocks away.

I asked about gang activities, and the group of neighbors that had assembled agreed there are no gangs in Black Dog, but "they smoke the dope." One lady said, "They be up by that store smoking the mess." Another neighbor, Ruth Cortright, arrived. When asked about her general assessment of community affairs, she said, "No jobs." But from the sixties up until now, everybody who wants to vote can do so without a problem. "You don't have to pay no poll tax anymore." There are now two black aldermen. The town paved the streets the year before last and built a sidewalk, and "it's not muddy out here anymore." She thinks the streets in the white community are not much better. Now more kids go to college, to Valley State (alma mater of football great Jerry Rice), Delta State, Mississippi State, Jackson State, or Alcorn. Not many go to Ole Miss. But the kids have to leave Mississippi to get jobs. Her son went to Chicago, then to Iowa, and now to Kentucky to keep a paycheck coming in. He has a degree in business administration.

Remains of a tractor at South Central Tractor Parts, Leland

Leland has a drug problem. "It's the hard, hard stuff, the bad stuff," says Cortright. "We caught it from Chicago. The hard stuff is here. They don't have the money; they're breaking in and stealing it. The people don't publicize it, but it's going on. They can sell the TVs, VCRs, microwaves, and stereos. You can't get too many of the younger ones out of here for civil rights anymore. This dope is what's got it. That has taken the place of the movement."

Cortright blames the Mafia and says the Mafia is in Leland. Walls says Holmes County flatlands, near the Interstate, provide a major airplane drop-off for drugs and that a Greenville dealer can make $30,000 a week selling crack. Cortright says she keeps a hammer in the bed. It is the same type of conversation one hears almost anywhere in America nowadays.

After Leland, we took a drive south through Glen Allan, a little town on Lake Washington. This is a scenic spot, on an oxbow lake created by the Mississippi's relentless process of "tearing down on the bend and depositing on the point." We cruised its narrow streets abutting cotton fields, and Walls pointed out how the sewage runs into the ditches and out into the lake. The houses are mostly dilapidated and their porches are full of people. Walls campaigned here in an unsuccessful 1984 race for chancery court clerk, and he remarked that if he said anything interesting on one side of town, he wouldn't need to repeat it on the other if it took him more than ten minutes to get there. We bought a beer after dark at the town's main grocery, under the sheriff's watchful eye. Outside, Walls slipped an elderly lady a dollar and then, embarrassed when caught, said, "If I can make a difference in her life for a dollar, then I'm satisfied." Then we headed back to Greenville, he to the Flowing Fountain, a blues bar he favors, and we to the Levee Inn, where the water in the bathtub is the color of premium gas. Better to take a shower. The band in the lounge was the Red Hots, and they were hot as firecrackers that night.

seventeen

WHAT IS IT ABOUT GREENVILLE?

▲▲▲

I suppose the trait that distinguished it from
neighboring towns was a certain laxity in church
matters. We didn't regard drunkenness and lechery,
Sabbath-breaking and gambling as more than poor
judgment or poor taste. What we were slow to forgive
was hardness of heart and all unkindness.

—William Alexander Percy, *Lanterns on the Levee*

What is it about Greenville? As home to the Percys and other
▽▽▽ well-respected planters it long symbolized to those in Mississippi and abroad an enlightened Bourbonism. The city had turned
away the Klan, and it stood in defiant opposition to Vardamanism
and Bilboism. The city had a free press. For that it is also indebted
to Will Percy, who was partly responsible for bringing Hodding
Carter to town to run the *Delta Democrat-Times*. Under Carter's
direction and that of his wife and son the paper struck a moderate
tone in civil rights; better than that, it was downright outspoken in
its calls for an end to racial violence and for compliance with federal
desegregation orders. The paper provided a rallying point for the
scattered Mississippi democrats and freethinkers in the 1960s. It

brought the city a reputation for reasonableness and liberalism, perhaps better than it deserved.

Now, in certain respects, Greenville is the most segregated city (and with 45,000 souls it can fairly be called a city) in Mississippi. There has been a withering process. In 1979 the Carter family sold the *Delta Democrat-Times* to a chain of papers, owned by Libertarians, called the Freedom Press.

A lot of white parents in Greenville kept their children in the public schools for the first couple of years after integration, maintaining about a 65–35 ratio between blacks and whites. But that eroded away until now the city's public schools are virtually all black. It doesn't have to be that way: Leland, twelve miles to the east, has successfully maintained a racially balanced system and so, to a fair extent, has Rosedale, thirty miles to the north.

To try to understand the transformation I interviewed Billy Percy, sitting in his father's office, at his father's desk, at the family's cotton compress in Greenville. A little Percy genealogy might help. Billy's dad, Roy, is one of three brothers: Walker, Roy, and Billups. Billups, an esteemed Tulane law professor during my sojourn there as a student, loves to write letters to the papers, and now is retired so, to the benefit of the city's populace, he has more time to write them. Roy wheels and deals and is a director of Mississippi Power and Light Company. Walker, the oldest, is a distinguished novelist and counselor to the Vatican on arts and culture. Roy walked in during my talk with his son and mentioned that the day before he had been in New Orleans and had seen a picture of Walker on the cover of *New Orleans* magazine. "Walker never sends us that stuff," he complained. All three brothers were born and raised in Birmingham, but when they were youngsters, their mother and father died. Greenville's Will Percy, the Senator's son and author, was a bachelor and their father's cousin; he adopted the three boys.

Today, Billy farms Trail Lake, the "basic part" of the family's present farming enterprise. Trail Lake was "full of people" when he was growing up, but now employs about fifteen to eighteen men. The compress where we met is a cotton warehouse where bales are pressed from gin size to smaller transportable size and stored until they are sold. It is public; anybody can bring cotton in.

I visited Billy Percy because I thought if anyone had a vision of the Delta's future, it would be he. He is the farming member of an important Delta family; he is a member of the Atlanta-based Southern Regional Council for "people of good will," and he was active in school integration. When I ask him what he sees coming, he says, "That's always fun to do, to try to guess what would be going on here forty or fifty years from now," as if the undertaking, though fun, might not be too useful. He does see some bright spots as far as the economy is concerned. The catfish industry, obviously. "We're growing 95 percent of the catfish that are produced in the United States right here in the Delta, and that's increasing at a pretty good clip. Catfish is going to continue to grow. It can't do anything but get better. It's got growing problems just like any other industry, but the basic economics that it's founded on are real, real sound."

He says that only 80,000 acres of the Delta are now being used for catfish ponds, and 2 million more are available. This is somewhat of an exaggeration, he acknowledges, because much of the best land has been so heavily treated with chemicals for farming that it is really unsuited for raising a fish that someone might eat. So far, we do not know how to clean up the land that has been poisoned, but we can still grow crops on it. It is the marginal land, which has not been cotton-farmed and thus not chemically treated, that is being put into pond production. It is actually better suited for ponds because it has a clay soil that holds water.

Percy also thinks the Delta has a big rice advantage that will last at least ten years. For example, he says that in Stuttgart, Arkansas, the rice capital of the world, it costs $85,000 to drill a well for a hundred-acre rice farm. It only costs $10,000 to drill the same well in the Delta today. But he does not expect much from gimmicks.

The bridge in Rosedale? "I think it is absolutely ridiculous. To spend a hundred million dollars to build a bridge in Rosedale just doesn't make sense to me." He compares it to the Sunshine Bridge in Louisiana, largely regarded as a boondoggle that went nowhere but, because of its very existence, required ultimately the development of major highway approaches on either side. "I suspect if I lived up there in Rosedale I'd be a supporter," Percy says. "It's not gonna cost them a quarter."

Speaking of imaginative ideas, he says that at a recent Delta Council meeting a new guy from Mississippi State, a "black Ph.D.," said, "I know what the answer for the Mississippi Delta is: a theme park." Said Percy, "Before he explained it I was trying to figure out what a theme park was; that shows you how far out of tune I was. He said, 'You know, like Disneyland or Six Flags over Texas.' And I couldn't even respond to that. We could service it with that highway off the bridge in Rosedale, I guess, and even the wayport. My only problem with it is, who would come to it? That may be a minor problem, but how is a guy in Cincinnati, Ohio, going to make up his mind that he wants to go to Rosedale, Mississippi, to a theme park?" Percy wondered what the theme might be: the old plantation or the glorious Confederacy?

We laughed at the time, but later I thought that a park beside the Mississippi River, with the river for a theme, might not be such a bad idea, though it would surely eliminate more of the duck habitat.

With Percy, I discussed the liberal image Greenville once had in comparison to the segregated schools of today. First I asked him about the "new" editor and he drawled, "He's not from here. I don't think there's ever been a Libertarian from Greenville. I just don't think anybody here knew what a Libertarian was. And I'll have to say that after seven or eight years of the paper being here, we're still not sure what a Libertarian is." He says, "Greenville suffers the type of ills of any urban area, if you can call 50,000 people urban. It is the urban area of the Delta. In the last twenty-five years or thirty years, the black population has increased compared to the white. There are fewer whites now than twenty-five or thirty years ago. The town has always had a substantial black majority. Historically, it might have been 55 to 45 percent, but today it has shifted to about 60 to 40 percent." As always, I am struck with the frequency with which life in the Delta is translated into numerical ratios.

"What has happened here," Percy continues, "and I think this is most probably true everywhere, is when you get to a school system with a 60–40 black-to-white ratio you hardly ever stay there. You progress toward the heavier black ratio." This is part of a continuing saga. Greenville experienced court-ordered desegregation in 1970–1971 and went to a unitary school system, replacing the former "freedom of choice" schools. Initially the court order was to require busing and gerrymandering in an attempt to get each school to reflect the overall racial balance of the community. But within a year Greenville public schools lost over 2,000 white students to the academies. Now the system is over 90 percent black. Just about all the whites who can afford to have gone to the private schools.

"Frankly, I'm very pessimistic," Percy says, "because I've been involved in the school system for twenty years. My children went to the public schools in Greenville. I served on a court-appointed biracial committee which was set up to kind of oversee the implementation of the unitary school system. After that I served on the local school board for fifteen years and served as the chairman of that board for four or five years. So I've had some pretty hands-on experience with it." That is an understatement. "My main reason for pessimism is not that Greenville isn't doing all that they can to try to turn it around. It's just that I think that the numbers are so strong that it doesn't make any difference what Greenville does. They can't turn it around."

I offer the comparison of Cleveland, where I had seen plenty of students of both races milling around a high school early one morning, and he responds that Cleveland has a 90 percent black school and a 60 percent white school. "We may have had one chance, and that was right when the unitary school system was put into place, and by and large white Greenville fled. Had they not fled right then, and had we been able to maintain a 60–40 black-white ratio, no private schools, no segregation academies at all, it might have worked. But I don't think we could afford to lose 5 percent of the white students at that point. Once you got into the heavy black majority, then inevitably . . . I mean, you just don't see any 70 percent black schools *anywhere*.

"I think there might have been a slight chance that had the leadership in Greenville—whatever that is, that's always a vague thing—that if the two or three folks who decided to bail out and build private schools, if everybody else had said we ain't going, that may have made some difference."

It is obvious that while he is a little wistful at the missed opportunity, in retrospect he does not think it was ever a practical possibility. And he should know, for no one else is more certainly a part of the leadership. Greenville went back to court, and the original order was modified to return the city to an essentially neighborhood school system. Now the city has one elementary school that is 50–50. One out of eleven. When the white kids reach junior high age, lots of them leave the system. The city has the private schools, good and bad, Christian and college prep. I ask if these schools don't use up a lot of resources.

"No question about that. We are supporting two school systems. We could be educating the same kids in the public schools for less than half of what we're spending in the private schools." And the private-school teachers are not necessarily better. "Of course they don't import the teachers from Harvard or Princeton to teach those folks. They got them from the public schools. So they're the same teachers, but they pay them less than the public schools are paying them. Either they left because they didn't want to teach blacks or they were at the bottom; they were the guys that the public schools let go because they didn't need them since the kids were leaving. They haven't gone out and recruited a bunch of supereducators to come down here to run these private schools.

"It's been a tremendous drain on the economy of the town. There ain't no doubt about that. A lot of these middle-income families have just forgone everything, like new automobiles and houses. They've done everything to sacrifice in order to be able to send their children to the private schools. Often there will be three or four children in the private schools. And even though the tuition is less, they make them join a building program, sign on long-term notes, you know, all that kind of mess, and that money just isn't available for capital for businesses, or adding a room onto the house, or buying a new automobile."

I ask whether Greenville's reputation for liberalism was deserved twenty-five years ago. The city did, after all, have its civil rights confrontations. The winter of 1966 was very cold, and a large group of hungry and homeless sharecroppers took over a part of the Greenville Air Force base. The "takeover" was easy; they just rode up, waved at the guards, and moved into a barracks. After about a week, President Johnson sent in troops and threw everybody out. Some

moved a few miles south where the Delta Ministry organized Freedom Village, a self-help enterprise that is still around today.

"I'm not sure that Greenville isn't the same way now that it was,
a little bit more liberal than most other places," says Percy. "Greenville, in fact, just elected Mike Espy to his second term in the U.S.
Congress. Greenville is by far the largest metropolitan area in his
district, and he got over 40 percent of the white vote here." Percy
supported Espy in both races. "What I'm saying is that maybe
Greenville didn't deserve its reputation for being a liberal mecca
thirty years ago, but I don't think now that Greenville has changed
very much."

He shares one characteristic with his namesake: Percy is not exactly a booster of Greenville as a home for industry. "If you move to
Greenville you're going to be faced with a 90 percent black school
system, a population 60 to 65 percent black, and not near any urban
area. You are a hundred and twenty miles away from Jackson and
a hundred and fifty miles from Memphis. It's my feeling that in order
for economic development to take place in a region that for whatever
reason can't compete, the federal government is going to have to
take some kind of measure to prod economic development. I don't
care how much you spruce up these little rinky-dink things like
transportation and utility rates and tax advantages. Everybody is
doing that, too." In other words, the Feds must provide the muscle.
He has in mind apportioning a percentage of defense contracts and
other federal investments. Isn't this *affirmative action?*

Percy seems to tire of this talk, and we take a tour of the "sample
room" in the cotton compress. Every bale of cotton has a sample cut
out of it and put in a paper wrapping here, and it is taken to Greenwood to the government classifying office. The compress handled
almost 80,000 bales in 1988, almost all of it from Washington
County: a big year. Each bale weighs about 500 pounds. It uses an
enormous steam-operated press forty or more years old that runs off
a natural gas boiler.

Billy grabs a little cotton sample out of one bale; just by fingering
it and stretching it with a light touch he asserts that it is an inch
and one-sixteenth. Staple length is determined by the weather. The
wetter the season, the longer the staple. The longer it is, the finer
it can be spun, and the more it is worth. He allows that there is a

big difference in value between a one-sixteenth and a five-thirty-seconds staple. I am amazed that he can tell a thirty-second of an inch difference just by pulling apart the fluff. There are farmers' arts that can never be known to bankers or explained by writers.

For another perspective on Greenville I met with the director of MACE, Larry Farmer, a sixties activist now dealing with middle age and parenting a teenaged son. He is a burly, handsome man, favoring plaid shirts open at the collar. He joined the MACE staff as a student organizer in Panola County in 1970, but before that, in high school, he had helped start the Young Black Liberation League, an offshoot of the decade-old Panola County Voters League. Now his former friends from Liberation League days are school-board members, city councilmen and councilwomen, and county supervisors.

"We all got our start in those youth activities. The Young Black Liberation League, that's what we called ourselves. To pay for our early registration activities we set up a record shop. We had all listened to a lot of Temptations and Miracles and so someone said, 'What about records?' A guy who was working with MACE gave us the idea. That's how we got our start. That record shop supported our youth organization for about eight or nine years."

The MACE program has many fronts, including programs for teen parents in the schools and "leadership" development that provides stipends for community leaders and community groups in numerous communities in the Delta. The latter has been a consistent program throughout the twenty-one-year history of the organization. Many key figures in the state, such as Robert Clark, the first black congressman, were once upon a time MACE trainees. Now Ernest White and Pearl Carpenter in Belzoni are "trainees." The organization in past years was very active in promoting the equalization of municipal services required by *Hawkins* v. *Shaw*, which has resulted in some $17 million in municipal improvements coming to towns in the Delta. As an outgrowth of that, MACE has helped people in several small communities incorporate their towns. "I call it the quiet revolution," says Farmer. "The strategies and tactics now have changed somewhat, but the battles remain to be fought."

Foundation dollars for the sort of activities that MACE is involved with have largely dried up. "There's a perception that all is right," says Farmer. "It's like the magazine and TV commercials. The air is fresher, the water is clean. The food tastes better. The cost of living is low, life is easy, and that is the perception about life in rural America. If you don't see the horrors in magazines or on television, they don't exist."

I asked him what it means in the long run that blacks have taken over local offices in many of the towns. "You take pride in the fact that a lot has changed. Older blacks, especially, the blacks in general who have been excluded from the process for so long, felt that even when we gained access that we shouldn't or couldn't participate, or that there was something magical and mystical about running towns because white folks had done it for so long. But there's a sense of frustration in the realization that there's so much more that could have been done. You see these little towns are dying grapes on a vine. We have now gone to a global economy, and at the same time these little towns do not have a real tax base, or any commercial center, and housing in some of them is just deplorable. What has gone awry here?

"Black workers left en masse in the sixties and early seventies. You are now seeing the emergence of rural ghettos. Folks who live in Leland, or Shaw, or Belzoni even, they're not leaving here to go to Jackson or to Chicago anymore. They're going to Greenville, Yazoo City, Greenwood, and Indianola. Our communities don't have the infrastructure to absorb all these people. These are not the people with the college degrees. They are disadvantaged, functionally illiterate, teen parents, substance abusers. And the small communities now have crack and cocaine, something unheard of.

"When I live in one of these rural communities with no hope of advancement in life and I see America on television, I want some of it. Where am I going to get it? I try to imitate what I see. It frustrates me as a parent and as a black person to see blacks portrayed on television as profiting in drugs. It scares me. Remember, that stuff is not seen just in the cities, but in every little town.

"In many respects Mississippi, especially the Delta, is akin to an underdeveloped country. You've got a lot of Third World characteristics in this one little place. Where do we look for change? Twenty years ago if you were on one side of the table you pointed the finger at Whitey. Who do you point the finger at when you're the government? Yesterday I was the activist, today I'm the elected official.

Getting elected is obviously just a step in the process.

"Look at our schools, for example. I sarcastically say we have our all-black integrated schools now. We've got integration supposedly, but our schools are either 100 percent black or 95-percent-plus black. And you still have many public schools that are administered by whites who have children in the private schools. I have a great fear. It is that the New South is going to be a reincarnation of the Old North in that racism has gotten slick and subtle. You don't see the kind of overt racism that you saw twenty, twenty-five, or even ten years ago. We tout the progressive image that we have here. The elections of Mabus and Espy are great, but everything is not okay in Mississippi.

"We need an investment from outside. We can do for ourselves only what we are equipped to do. It's a human capital question. The greatest financial distress we have is really human. We continue to lose our best and brightest from the small rural communities. They go to Jackson and Memphis and areas where they see opportunity."

I ask him what can be done. "What local folks are starting to say is, if we don't begin to take an active role in what's going on within our communities, then we're going to lose them. The reign of old-fashioned downright racism is starting to crack. As those barriers start to fall you see—especially among enlightened white politicians, even if they were enlightened only by increased black voting power—folks who say, 'This is the right thing to do. This is our community, let's work with it.' Among the young folks, the old stereotypical attitudes, the biases, are no longer important." He points out that his son plays baseball in a neighborhood league on a team that is about half white. But during the week, the white kids go to the private academies. "I look at the camaraderie on that team and say maybe we old folks better get out of the way."

Out of his window he can see Delta Towers, the $6.2 million senior citizens' complex that MACE administers and in which about 40 percent of the residents are white. He comments that these senior citizens, just like the young people of different races, get along fine. It is just the people in the middle who keep their distance. He recalls the football game between Rosedale and Greenville High the year before. Greenville's team is completely black; Rosedale's is racially mixed. There was no racial strife or tension at the game or among the teammates. A pity that Rosedale is the exception and Greenville is the rule.

I asked Farmer if he is optimistic and he says yes. The basis for his "optimism," however, is that the safety net has begun tearing for whites as well as blacks, and they are beginning to find a common interest in the unions and in grass-roots associations. "For the first time whites in this area see themselves as potential victims."

I ask him about Greenville. "I must admit to you that I still to this day do not understand Greenville. We have social interaction around formal professional kinds of events, but in terms of the interaction of people you just don't see it.

"I would like my son to have the option if he wants to stay in Greenville. You know, if we can ever defeat this damn racism and see each other up close, I think we can start seriously addressing problems. In the long run we've got to come to a meeting of the minds."

STEPPING OUT

▲▲▲

The Mississippi Delta begins in the lobby of the
Peabody Hotel in Memphis and ends on Catfish Row in
Vicksburg. The Peabody is the Paris Ritz, the Cairo
Shepheard's, the London Savoy of this section. If you
stand near its fountain in the middle of the lobby,
where ducks waddle and turtles drowse, ultimately you
will see everybody who is anybody in the Delta and
many who are on the make.
—David L. Cohn, *Where I Was Born and Raised*

T he north and south boundaries of the Delta are marked by
▽▽▽ cities, Memphis and Vicksburg. Although Memphis brokers
bought and sold a lot of cotton, they gave their city more of a Tennessee, make-a-buck flavor than a Mississippi, rock-on-the-porch state
of mind. The city was conceived and built as an immense planned
subdivision by Andrew Jackson, and it has a history of big-city,
ward-style politics, the Crump regime, and more recently, urban
decay. Still, it has Beale Street and the Peabody Hotel. It used to be
said that the Mississippi Delta began in the lobby of the Peabody
Hotel, where planters dealt in cotton futures and drank bonded
whiskey. After being shuttered for years, along with much of downtown Memphis, the Peabody has been refurbished and is now back
in business. In fact, the whole city is back in business, helped along

by being headquarters to major international companies, like Holiday Inn and Federal Express, and by the big Mud Island cultural park on the river to bring people back downtown. Today's Beale Street is so upscale that it is hard to imagine it giving birth to any more blues, but the Peabody Hotel still feels like the past.

The hotel is famed for its lobby bar and the ducks that parade through once or twice a day. The birds live on the roof in a little duck penthouse. Historically, the Peabody was the social center of the Delta. Here the planters' women often stayed in the summer months to avoid the mosquitoes and yellow fever episodes of that long Mississippi summer. The lobby of the hotel is surrounded by sixteen great marble columns which support a ceiling covered in dancing, winged cherubs. Today, from a player piano come strains of the sort of forties swing music played at Rick's Café Américain. The drinks are honest and upright. It is an altogether pleasant place to collect one's thoughts at the end or the middle of the day. The clientele today seems to be heavier on elegant blacks and Asians than it is on Delta belles and cotton brokers, however, and I would say that the Mississippi Delta now begins somewhere else. Maybe in the lobby of the Memphis International Airport, the AgriCenter International near Germantown, or the Macy's on I-240. Or maybe in front of the bologna and tackle counter at Erwin's Grocery Store in Robinsonville on U.S. 61 headed south. Stay at the Peabody, though. It has the best bar south of the Algonquin in New York.

Two hundred miles down the road, the length of the Delta, U.S. 61 lifts off the fertile plain and climbs the hills to Vicksburg. The city's famous bluffs, which rise in Vicksburg above the confluence of the Mississippi and Yazoo rivers, made it the Gibraltar of the Confederacy in the War Between the States, and are the anchor for the semicircular chain of hills running north to Memphis that define the Delta. The hills were formed two or three million years ago by a great storm that blew the topsoil off the plains states and deposited it in Mississippi. The hills formed of this loess soil are solid enough to build a city on, but the soil has strange properties. Make a cut in it straight down and the excavation will last for a century, but leave the slightest incline and the next rain will wash away your work.

Vicksburg is full of beautiful places: cobblestoned streets, fine views of the rivers, the National Military Park, exquisite flower gardens, and grand old houses landscaped into the sides of the bluffs on streets running nearly vertical down to the riverbank. It is the only Delta city that qualifies as a major tourist attraction. It has neat "southern Italian" restaurants like Tuminello's, and charming little estates down by the railroad tracks like Flowerine, almost buried in honeysuckle, in the middle of a neighborhood of neatly painted shot-guns with bright tin roofs, arrayed around the cotton compress. Many of the fine homes have become "bed-and-breakfasts," very calming sorts of places. We spent a night as guests of Cliff and Bettye Whitney at their home, The Corners. Like most old houses, it has an interesting history. It was built in 1873 by John Alexander Klein, who also built the grander antebellum Cedar Grove across the street. The Kleins bestowed the house upon their daughter as a wedding present. The groom, Ike Bonham, had joined the Confederate Army at age eighteen and had been a courier for Stonewall Jackson. He had returned to Vicksburg, a city reduced nearly to rubble by war, to make his way in peacetime as a clerk for the Floweree Ice Company. At age thirty-seven he tried to intercede in a fight between drinking partners in a saloon, and he was mortally wounded, in error, by his closest friend. He was carried to The Corners, and he died there. In other words, like all of the better homes of Vicksburg, The Corners has a ghost.

One hundred years later the Whitneys stopped at Cedar Grove en route from Dallas to Washington, saw the For Sale sign, and bought The Corners. To the project they brought unlikely talents—he a civil engineer specializing in modular housing; she a schoolteacher, marriage counselor, and sex educator—and they have transformed the mansion into a serene spot divided into beautiful guest rooms. In the process, they have converted themselves, at least when not swinging hammers and repairing the roof, into nineteenth-century hostelers. The nicest thing they do is to serve you a beverage of your choice upon arrival. And, of course, they present a perfectly cooked breakfast of eggs, cheese grits, and light biscuits in the morning. In between, the atmosphere is contemplative and satisfying, conducive to

Cliff and Bettye Whitney, proprietors of The Corners bed-and-breakfast, Vicksburg

a game of chess between spouses in a room paneled in cypress and cooled by a river breeze. It is a relief from late nights with Letterman at the Quality Inn.

Civil War monuments and cannons painted black are all around Vicksburg, for it was in that period that control of the city was most important to America's destiny. In the hands of the Confederate Army under General Pemberton, the gun emplacements on the hills were the last barrier to Union control of the Mississippi River. Unlike lightly defended New Orleans, Memphis, and Nashville, where the civic leaders virtually raced to the approaching Yankees to surrender and avoid the destruction of their cities, Vicksburg with about fifty thousand troops to defend it was condemned to resist. But for the guns of Vicksburg, the Yankees could move ironclads full of soldiers and all of the produce of Illinois and Wisconsin at will along the entire length of the river. For more than a year, General Grant tried numerous plans to capture the city, which included cutting the levee upstream at Yazoo Pass to inundate the Delta and flood the bayous enough to try to float Yankee gunboats down the Coldwater to the Yazoo River and hit the city from behind. That plan failed when the gunships were halted and one was sunk by Confederate miners and snipers hidden in the dense woods along the narrow waterways, and the major effect of the effort was to put much Southern farmland under water.

Finally, Grant marched his troops south of the city on the west bank and ran Admiral Porter's fleet past the Vicksburg batteries to ferry his battalions across the river at Bruinsburg. After allowing his arm of vengeance, William Tecumseh Sherman, to burn the city of Jackson to the ground, Grant surrounded Vicksburg from the rear. Then for two months the city was besieged and shelled continuously from the gunboats in the river and from the Union positions on land. It was a time of great privation in the little city, when women and children took shelter in caves dug in the sides of the bluffs, tended the wounded, and scavenged for food. When Pemberton finally surrendered on the Fourth of July, 1863, the worn army that marched to prison and parole was larger in number than the city's entire population today.

After the war, Vicksburg was the scene of vicious race riots aimed at overthrowing martial law, Republicanism, and black rule. In one instance, in 1874, two whites and twenty-nine blacks were killed, and for days afterward riders swept the country, killing black farmers.

On April 12, 1988, one hundred and twenty-seven years to the day after General Pierre Gustave Toutant Beauregard commenced firing on Fort Sumter, Vicksburg elected its first black mayor. Robert Walker is now the mayor of the largest city in Mississippi that has a black mayor, a distinction slightly difficult to express but nonetheless meaningful. Walker is the former field secretary of the state NAACP, but now he sits, harried, behind a big desk at city hall with a peach and Nabs to eat for lunch, and says, "I have always believed that government could solve all the problems till one morning I woke up and I was it."

Vicksburg does not have a strong mayoral system, but this mayor is working with what he has, basically lots of energy, to make Vicksburg important again. It is obvious he would find it hard to think of anything bad to say about his pretty city. "Vicksburg is a place unlike any other place," he says. "Not to be trite, but it's unique. Vicksburg has more potential than any other place in the state in terms of human relations, people getting along, and in terms of economic development." He waves his hand over the Mississippi River in the distance and talks of future plans for developing a waterfront for business and recreation. "We have more than a million tourists per year here," he boasts. "We can be a model in this country for race relations."

In a city where blacks make up about 51 percent of the population and 40 percent of the registered voters, Walker got elected with 52 percent of the vote. He concedes that he lacked "visible knock-on-doors" white support, but he believes that perhaps as many as 20 percent of the whites voted for him. A significant majority of the students in city public schools are black, as a majority of those in the county schools are white, but a recent consolidation agreement provides that all schools will strive for a 52 percent white and 48 percent black enrollment. "We have very good schools here," Walker says.

His own background, like that of so many of the state's young black leaders, is a blend of Horatio Alger, Norman Rockwell, and the freedom movement. Like his grandparents and parents, he was born in Vicksburg. Now forty-four, he was the second oldest of twelve

Robert Walker, mayor of Vicksburg

children and describes his background as "regular, all of us were poor." His father served in the navy in World War II and operated a saw at a lumber mill for thirty years. Growing up, Robert went with his father out to the country to cut wood to sell after school and on weekends. He graduated from the Vicksburg High School and went to Jackson State in 1962. He hung out on the fringes of the civil rights movement, never deeply involved. But he went to Ole Miss in 1966 (the same time as Ray Mabus) and says, "It was civil rights just being there." At Ole Miss he was made a teaching assistant in history, one of the first blacks on the faculty. I asked how he was received by the students, and he said, "Just fine. I was the guy grading the papers."

He can remember times as a kid when a big excursion for the family was to buy some ice cream and drive across the U.S. 80 bridge to Louisiana. Now he has three girls aged eleven to twenty-three, and he expects more; he wants a city that they can return to and raise families. "I'd like for Vicksburg to be a place where everybody who is here wants to stay and everybody who's left wants to come back. I want to involve people to plan what we want to be twenty-five years down the road." A powerful-looking, dark black man with a direct stare, Walker talks quietly and undoubtedly has a reassuring effect on people. "Some were concerned that we would paint the city hall black," he says, "but I'm concerned with good government." So far he has maintained the status quo in city government and retained several white officials, such as the police commissioner and the planning officer.

When he drives us around town, he beeps and waves at literally everybody. He verifies the city's claim that the first Coca-Cola was bottled here by Joe Biedenharn. "We tell the truth here," he says. To make sure we had no doubts, he took us by the Coca-Cola museum to introduce us to Ira Nichols, the curator and the man who knows all about the history of Coke bottling in America.

He drives us up to the spacious Mississippi Welcome Center beside I-20 and inside gives a big hug to the white and the black receptionists behind the counter. "This is a very fine city. Vicksburg is it. When you go through the National Military Park you are going to love it. Race relations are much improved here. We pretty much realize that we have a common destiny."

On the way back to his office he imparts that, after he got elected, his preacher told him that "there is politics and politricks." "I am into politics," says Robert Walker. In my experience, he is honest. So lengthy was our tour that my car, left at city hall, collected a parking ticket. I showed it to the mayor, and he told me where to pay it. I guess if the Mississippi Delta ends anywhere, it is in the Vicksburg City Hall.

EPILOGUE

▲▲▲

M - I - Crooked Letter - Crooked Letter - I - Crooked
Letter - Crooked Letter - I - Humpback - Humpback - I.
—Children's saying

A friend of mine recommended that I talk with Patrick "Peter
▽▽▽ Rabbit" McGarrh in Merigold, whom he described as "the
epitome of the Mississippi Delta man," from which I gathered that
Peter Rabbit was upright, was adept at bourré, and had overcome
many travails. Indeed, he had endured twenty years of farming and
then an operation for throat cancer, which had deprived him of
speech. But he had learned to talk again in a rough gravelly voice,
surprisingly rich, with a Southern drawl from someplace deep in his
neck, covered by a paisley scarf. When he told us that doves were
gone from the Delta, the "gone" hit the floor like an iron pan and
communicated "the end."

Mrs. McGarrh greeted us at the front door of their ranch-style
home on a Merigold back street, a block down from the Baptist

church. As soon as we crossed the threshold she was offering a
screwdriver or a Bloody Mary and he was pecking Patty on the lips
in welcome. Like many in the Delta, the McGarrhs have a rich back
yard. For some, like the Glendora Dales, it is a pool and patio house
invisible from the road. For the McGarrhs it is wide-open spaces and
a tall satellite dish. The suggestion is leisure, the best that America
has to offer: despite daily anxieties, an awareness of the potentiality
of calamity, and an uncertain future, there is serenity. After settling
in, we talked about where the Delta was and where it was going from
their perspective.

"Used to be doves would be in the grain fields that had been
harvested on all the small places. You can't find them nowadays;
that's gone," said Peter Rabbit. "The trees are gone. Not as many as
there used to be. The farms have gotten larger and there's not any
livestock. That's the main thing. You can't grow a hundred-dollar
calf on a thousand-dollar hunk of land. That's what put the livestock
out of business. The price of land got so high that the return on your
investment was not enough that you could justify growing livestock.
Livestock had to have feed, and feed fed the doves. Now if you are
going dove hunting you have to plant dove feed: sunflower, milo, or
millet, or wheat."

The couple farmed until Peter Rabbit got sick, but "Miss Nan" is
still nominally a farmer. "I have my name on the paper," she says,
"but I don't have to do any work, just write my name for hundreds
of thousands of dollars. I think I signed a note the other day for six
hundred thousand dollars. If they ask me for any of it, I'll just totally
die."

He says, "It's unreal how in the last twenty years the production
costs of farming have escalated. Man, they have gone up so much you
cannot believe it. Ever since I got out of farming, which was seven
years ago—I lost my voice seven years ago yesterday—the price of
farming has really gone up. Even before I got out of it, it got to where
it wasn't any fun anymore. It used to be a lot of fun years ago when
I had fifteen tractors and fifteen drivers and two or three people that
were helpers. You'd get out in the morning, and you'd all get around
the barn out by the shop, and they were laughing and talking, and
everybody was having fun, you know. And then you went to bigger
tractors with more horsepower requiring less labor, costing more

money, and the pressure on the farmer was greater, and obviously the pressure on all of the labor was greater. So they didn't work hard enough, and we didn't pay high enough. Maybe if we had paid more they would have worked harder. Or if they had worked harder maybe we would have paid more. I don't know. But it got to where everybody didn't enjoy what they were doing. And it used to be fun. But it just got to be too big of a hassle."

I ask what caused the hassle, and got a reply that was becoming familiar.

"The price of equipment went up. The price of commodities went down. George Meany decided one time that labor was not going to load the ships that were shipping anything to Russia because it would run the price of bread up here. And, by God, they didn't load the ships, and it dropped the price of grain—rice, wheat, soybeans, corn—it went from a good price to bloowie, and it never recovered. Then about the time it recovered, several years later, Jimmy Carter decided to put an embargo on, and the price went down to nothing again. Right when we needed the money. Then the Arabs decided oil was too cheap and jacked the price of oil up, and from then on it was a downhill slide. And it has been for a while.

"The last twenty years in the Delta," he says, "all of the farm labor left and went up North. Then the economics got to where it was not feasible for a small farm to operate. They're getting bigger and bigger. What we used to call a large farm, a thousand or fifteen hundred acres, they can hardly make it now. So it's gone to corporate. Prudential and other insurance companies are coming in. Prudential bought Delta Pine. They bought King and Anderson in Clarksdale. They bought Stovall. They bought quite a bit. They came in to buy aggressively and, in fact, they are one of the reasons that land values went up.

"What is distinctive about the Delta is our independence, but it's not here like it used to be. It used to be the majority of the businesses were directly engaged in agriculture. If you drove a John Deere tractor and the John Deere dealer jerked you off, you'd say to hell with him, and you traded 'em all and you bought International or Case. You could deal with the people you wanted to deal with. Now, with mergers, there are only two kinds of tractors you can buy in Cleveland. Chemicals, it's three places. Used to be eight or ten. So you get cornered up. And the money's not here like it used to be. They say it's the land of opportunity, but it doesn't look like it's here now like it was. But maybe I'm old and don't see the forest for the trees."

She breaks in to insist that life is not really so bad. They have friends all over the Delta. "It's nothing for us to drive fifty miles to go out to dinner," she says. "We went to Memphis yesterday to go to a play at the Orpheum and drove home. You know, we left home with a Bloody Mary at ten-thirty yesterday morning and got to Memphis and had lunch and went to the theater and came back and stopped in Clarksdale and ate with friends last night, and got home before midnight. It was a nice day. It was a fun play, *Me and My Girl.*" She tells us also that Cleveland has an active arts council with an annual festival on the courthouse lawn. There is a cotillion club at the school and debutante clubs in Greenville and in Greenwood. Greenville's Southern Debutante Assembly was once the only one, and "after my time," she says, they organized the Delta Debutante Assembly in Greenwood. Indeed she was, and is, a Southern deb.

Will the next generation share the fun? He says, "They don't know. They think we're nuts. You see, we still like at Christmas time to have a party and wear a dressy dress and a tuxedo. To us it's fun." Their son still lives with them. He likes to hunt and fish and has plenty of opportunity for both.

Peter Rabbit says, "Merigold was a thriving town at one time. There were about five or six big plantations. This was a plantation town, and that's all they wanted it to be. They didn't want it to be anything else, and that's all it was. Then the owners died and their heirs split it up, and there were no more big plantations. Merigold was not very progressive. They didn't want any business, so none came. It all went to Cleveland."

She gives the positive side of local history. "Merigold had the largest hotel between Memphis and Vicksburg at one time." It was called the Midway Hotel, but it has been torn down within the last ten years. He says it was built by people who didn't build them to fall down and even when they knocked down one wall, the roof stood. They knocked down the back wall and the roof sagged. "The Delta as a whole, all of the small towns, they're gonna be going, going, gone, if the price of old brick will stay up," says Peter Rabbit. "If the price of brick were high enough they would tear down the whole town of Merigold." Indeed, with a population that numbered about 3,000 in the 1930s, Merigold now is down to about 600 citizens.

But there is a future, she says. "People are beginning to move in here. It could be a bedroom community. We have a well-known pottery, Lee and Pup McCarty. We have a winery now on the Sunflower River. The guy who's the mayor got a grant to grow crawfish. Now there's a successful restaurant called Crawdads." The winery she is referring to is the Rushings', who after years of gradual development have produced a very acceptable variety of wines from Mississippi grapes.

"We're not an industrial area," he says, "and I don't think we ever will be. Our economic stability lies in agriculture. I think that manufacturing can be an asset. I think they can complement each other, but I think the greatest natural resource we've got is land. People would be very foolish to cover up our land, which is productive farmland, with industry. It's always going to be agriculture in the Delta."

We say it's time to go, but Peter Rabbit insists we have another drink. "A bird can't fly on one wing," he proclaims. Then he gets settled in his armchair and begins again in a more reflective vein. "I'll tell you what, though. The pace is still slow, and it's still kind of laid-back. And it's still one big happy family. And there's still that camaraderie. It's in your blood, and no matter where you might go you're still from the Delta. Our way of life is still different from other places, and we still have a little of that independence I was talking about. It's kind of closed up but it's still there. You don't have as many avenues and choices as we had, but it's still there."

She says, "It's home. I can't imagine anywhere else."

I admit that I often like the old better than the new. I think it is generally more interesting. I am satisfied that old men with mules know more than young men with big tractors and Isuzus. I feel secret sadness that the old communities of tenant farmer cabins in the Delta have been torn down and plowed over. I resent Wal-Marts on the bypasses around country towns, and I resent the bypasses just as much. I try not to see shopping malls, new bank branches,

Domino's Pizza, chain stores, Ramada Inns, and limited-access highways. Yet I know what the teenage girl felt who told me that "what
Rolling Fork needs is a Burger King," because I grew up outside of
Atlanta when the boom was just starting, and I wanted a Burger
King, too. But all that gloss, I say, smooths over the variety and
makes us forget that there are people more interesting than those
generated by Universal Studios. I say that, despite the fact that I
have written a fair part of this book in Greenville and Clarksdale
motel rooms with color television, two double beds with a mint on
each pillow, and an ice machine close by.

The Mississippi Delta has resisted the gloss in some ways, though
it does not necessarily want to. Almost everybody who lives there
imagines that they want the Delta to be like the other places they
see on television, with four-lane highways, Big Macs, and nobody
doing much hard work, like farming. There is an enormous attraction, and probably an irresistible power, to "life on the four-lane."
No dirt road exists, I guess, that cannot be widened, straightened,
and paved. As an Atlantan, I know that a community can be bull-
dozed right off the map and replaced overnight with a twenty-four-
hour superstore. Will a tour guide in South Africa ever point at a
shopping mall and say that is where the Sharpeville massacre took
place? That could happen soon in Mississippi. Such power is present
in the Delta, and it is transforming at a fantastic pace the world of
plantations and tenant farms into something quite different. But
that power has not yet penetrated so far back on the dirt roads that
the older culture cannot be seen and felt. The two for the time being
are existing together in a strange mixture of tin-roofed shacks near
modern supermarkets and video rental outlets in what used to be
plantation commissaries.

Another question is, What improvement does the glitz and glitter
bring? Race conflict at least gives a moral purpose to life. Rims
Barber remarked that "high tech" has already come to the little
towns in the form of the laser that reads the prices on the groceries
in the store, so the clerk does not need to touch the register. The
result was that two stock boys lost their jobs because they do not
need to mark prices on cans anymore. The fast-food restaurants,
which put lots of young people to work on the bypass, do not teach
the kids much. All they have to do is push a button with a picture

Arvell Bullock, storekeeper and elected official, Louise

of a hamburger on it. The register rings up the price and tells you
how much change to give. All you have to be able to do is count
money and know the difference between a single whopper and a
double whopper.

If the Delta is a taproot of black culture, can it stand up to the
invasion of America? If not here, then noplace, it seems to me. Black
roots are in this country, and there is not much to look back on for
immediate sustenance beyond our shores. A black's search for roots
in Africa is much like my search for roots in Scotland. It helps me
fix my place in history to know that my ancestors lived where the
Firth of Forth meets the North Sea and that I am a member of Clan
Dunbar, but I must admit that the emotional and cultural ties are
not that strong. Where are the black cultural wellsprings in this
country? Indisputably, one is the Delta. But the cultural drive of the
Delta's people seems to be to enter the mainstream, the mainstream
that flows through the irresistible American marketplace. I spoke
with blacks in Belzoni, for example, who expressed pride that Kentucky Fried Chicken was opening a location there.

Yet having said that, I will posit the contrary. Perhaps there is
some resistance to blandness born in sharecropper cabins, just as the
same allergy to assimilation may be spawned in hillbilly homesteads
of West Virginia. Maybe in the Delta, where a spring begins, where
there is a useful folklife that has proven its dependability, a living
music, and a self-reliant people. Maybe there is a community that
will endure. Maybe there is a black group that will help its members
survive as a group, as do the Chinese and Jews. Maybe there is a
white group that wants to stay Southern. We know there is power
in this area. Just as the white escapees are destined always to be
"from" the Delta, so do blacks throughout America have their Mississippi stories to tell. Maybe they are in the diaspora, and the Delta
will remain as their homeland. Perhaps William Ferris is right and
the enigma and fascination of the Delta are indestructible. Like Billy
Percy says, it's "fun" to imagine.

So much of the history of Mississippi is sad: the great poverty, Gus
Courts, Rainey Poole, all the people who left. But there was much
that was and is good, too—the wealth of community still treasured
by those who have left and return again and again, the sounds of the
plantation, the visceral effect of crops coming up green as far as the

Old jail, Louise

eye can see, good clean air. Over the past two or three decades, the history of the place has been moving too fast to record. The speed of change in "race relations," the for-instance most relevant to this book, has been breathtaking. Perhaps only in the United States, with a Constitution requiring equality under the law and a judiciary for one glorious moment intent upon enforcing it, could it have occurred as peacefully as it did. So far, fortune has smiled, though the story is not over yet.

The Mississippi Delta is a majestic place, and who am I to write about it? In a culture where those born there are always "from" Mississippi no matter how they try to deny it, I am not from there. I do happen to know a few important people there, for Mississippi, like South Carolina, Arkansas, and West Virginia, is the sort of state where even average citizens may know remarkable people who hold public offices, run newspapers, and preside over universities. The most remarkable Mississippian I knew well was a German Jewish refugee named Ernst Borinski, and I mention him simply to establish my bona fides to the half of the state's college graduates who are in his debt. But basically I see the Delta from the vantage point of an outsider looking in, and maybe for that reason I find it an even more valuable spot than the local people do. To me the daily pageantry of the spreading sunrise, of farmers gathering for a bitter cup of coffee in bright 7-Eleven stores at the crossroads and grabbing a bacon-and-biscuit to eat in the tractor's cab, is beautiful. I think it is great that the Delta's rising black leadership seems to really care about working together, white and black. People like Sarita McGee are actually excited about local government. How extraordinary that is in America today. An optimism flows through the black communities of the Delta that is completely at odds with economic reality. A pity that so few of the whites share in that optimism or pat themselves on the back for the distance they themselves have traveled.

The whites of the Delta have the greater variety of choices. The blacks, it is now clear, are not going to leave. Even if they would leave, would the whites want them to? Tiny says, "If they don't have black folks to work for them, who they got to work? Charlie don't work. Chinaman don't work." That about sums it up. So the whites could leave, in which case the plantation culture would vanish from

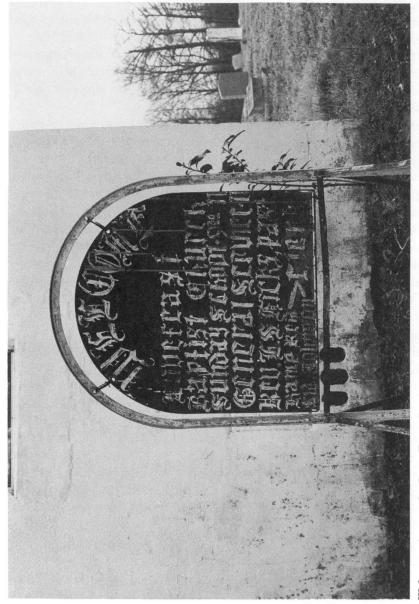

Welcome sign at the Love Feast Baptist Church, Love plantation, Humphreys County

the Delta and the South just as totally as that of the mound-builders. More likely those with land to farm will stay and watch their young drift away to Wyoming. Or they might decide to turn it around, get the economy moving again, build up those schools, and cast their lot with the black majority in a land too pretty to part with. The glory, of course, is in the third choice—a difficult undertaking, but to all who make it, a toast.

The potential is certainly there. The Delta has all the makings of a world-class agricultural and aquacultural laboratory. It may be inevitable, as Robert Neill believes, that the federal government will teach the entire Third World how to grow bountiful cotton, catfish, and beans, but why fight it? Why should the Delta not do the teaching? Is there no way to market this product, this know-how? Someday, perhaps, if the vision is there.

In any event, a land with such a gripping past should not be lightly abandoned. In truth, deserting such a valuable property should not be considered at all. It may be difficult to appreciate how rich and special life in the Delta is when reflecting on the size of the crop loan or the difficulty of upgrading public education. But when the sun comes up and starts burning the mist off the fields, green rows sparkling with dew, it can be seen that Delta time is slow, steady, and hot, but it heals old wounds and can bring new hopes alive.

BIBLIOGRAPHY

There is a wealth of written material about the Delta. Generally, it is apparent from the text of this book which works I personally found to be the most useful and interesting. The reader may wish to explore the context from which the selected quotations and references were drawn, and to encourage that examination I provide the following clues. The passage introducing Chapter One is from Hodding Carter's fine book *Lower Mississippi* (New York, 1942), page 21. The quotations from *Archaeological Investigations in Mississippi 1969–1977*, by John M. Connaway, Mississippi Department of Archives and History (Jackson, 1981), may be found in that publication on pages 8, 37, and 75.

The passage introducing Chapter Two is taken from David L. Cohn's lyric book *Where I Was Born and Raised* (Boston, 1948), page 42. Hodding Carter's discussion of the origins of the planter myth appears in his *Lower Mississippi,* page 205, and his comment about the unifying element of laughter is found on page 390. LeRoy Percy's description of the Klan as a "Negro fraternal order" is reported in Lewis Baker's *The Percys of Mississippi* (Baton Rouge, La., 1983), page 106. William Alexander Percy's classic *Lanterns on the Levee* (New York, 1941) is quoted at several spots. His compliments to Negro manners, and remarks on the importance of manners in general, appear on page 286, and his disparaging comment about Mississippi's Chinese is on page 18. The reference to "aristocrats gone to seed" appears on pages 23 and 24, and Percy's recipe for mint juleps may be found on pages 65 and 66. The background about Bolivar County, the Sillers family, and the history of the *Kate Adams* may all be found in *History of Bolivar County, Mississippi,* by Florence Warfield Sillers and Members of the Mississippi Delta Chapter of the Daughters of the American Revolution

(Jackson, 1948). In *Each Day a Bonus: Life on a Delta Plantation in Mississippi* (Tunica, 1966), page 38, Eva Tucker Denton also fondly recalls waltzes at the courthouse played by W. C. Handy. Walter White, early leader of the NAACP, wrote that Vardaman and his ilk "made as their sole platform hatred and vilification of the Negro," in *Rope and Faggot: A Biography of Judge Lynch* (New York, 1929), page 101.

The quotation beginning Chapter Three is from Lamar Fontaine's *A Plea for Peace, Preparedness and Good Roads Everywhere* (Lyon, 1917), page 5. This manuscript may be found in the Clarksdale Public Library in its special collection. Other Fontaine booklets found there include *The Cause and Effect of the Ku Klux Klan on the South,* published in 1910 in Clarksdale, and *My Life and Lectures,* on pages 80 and 81 of which appears "All Quiet Along the Potomac." This poem is believed to have been written by Ethel Lynn Eliot Beers (and to have been set to music by John Hill Hewitt). Authorship is credited to Ethel Lynn Beers by Edmund Clarence Stedman in *An American Anthology, 1787–1900* (New York, 1900), and to Ethel Lynn Elliott by H. M. Wharton in *War Songs and Poems of the Southern Confederacy, 1861–1865* (Philadelphia, 1904). The same poem, entitled "The Picket-Guard," was published in *Poetry, Lyrical, Narrative, and Satirical of the Civil War* (New York, 1866), edited by Richard Grant White, without any credit whatsoever. Beers's established claim to the poem was pointed out by Shelby Foote in a letter to the publisher.

Introducing Chapter Four is a passage from John Dollard's *Caste and Class in a Southern Town* (New York, 1937), page 120, a book generally assumed to be about Greenwood. William Alexander Percy, who defended sharecropping in *Lanterns on the Levee* as being "as humane, just, self-respecting, and cheerful a method of earning a living as human beings are likely to devise," also noted, "It has but one drawback—it must be administered by human beings to whom it offers an unusual opportunity to rob without detection or punishment" (pages 280 and 282).

The quotation at the beginning of Chapter Five is from Anne Moody's *Coming of Age in Mississippi* (New York, 1968), page 253. Arun Gandhi's statement to the *Los Angeles Times* was reported in the *Raleigh News and Observer,* "Gandhi's Grandson Defies Deep South Racism," by David Treadwell, May 29, 1988.

The verses introducing Chapter Six are by David Hall, radio newscaster in Laurel, and they appear on his album *I'm Mississippi,* volume 2. The statements of Bobby Moses about the union movement among catfish plant workers were reported in the *Delta Democrat-Times,* July 7, 1988, and the *Clarion-Ledger,* July 6, 1988, "Union Fishes for Members at Plants," by

Reed Branson. Kerry Hamilton's letter to his hometown paper was reported in the *Greenwood Commonwealth,* September 11, 1988.

The cheerful words introducing Chapter Seven are reprinted from the *Mississippi Travel Guide, Fall–Winter 1988,* published by the Mississippi Department of Economic Development, Division of Tourism. Sheriff Thompson's statement about the enthusiasm of his sons was reported in the *Clarksdale Press Register* by Sharon Braxton, January 4, 1988. A good history of the Chinese community in Mississippi is James Loewen's *The Mississippi Chinese* (Cambridge, Mass., 1971). Information about Jews in the Delta may be found in Eli Evans's *The Provincials* (New York, 1973), especially the appendices, and in *Jews in Early Mississippi,* by Rabbi Leo Turitz and Evelyn Turitz (Jackson, 1983). Rabbi Schultz is quoted by James W. Silver in *Mississippi: A Closed Society* (New York, 1963), page 131. Senator Sam Nunn's praise of Representative Mike Espy appeared in the *Greenwood Commonwealth* on October 26, 1988.

Chapter Eight begins with the words of Ethel Wright Mohamed as she was quoted in William Ferris's *Local Color: A Sense of Place in Folk Art* (New York, 1982), page 112. The statistics about Mississippi's dropout rate and poverty in general are derived from the *Legislative Bulletin* published by the Southern Regional Council, number 4, summer 1988, "Testimony of Rims Barber at the Select Committee on Hunger at Itta Bena on July 24, 1987," and the demographic data maintained by the U.S. Department of Commerce, Bureau of the Census. The photograph of public employees working on private property appeared in the *Indianola Enterprise-Tocsin* on December 31, 1987. The assault on the editor of the *Yazoo Herald* was reported in the *Greenwood Commonwealth* on December 30, 1987. The account (by Annie Laurie McRee) of the Greenville Junior Auxiliary charity ball in 1988 appeared in the *Delta Democrat-Times* on January 17, 1988. The quotation from Rita Halbrook about her artistic methods appeared in the *Belzoni Banner* on February 10, 1988. The statement by Paul Russell, and the name by which he is locally known, were reported (by Carol Leake) in the *Yazoo Herald,* April 9, 1988. Angelo Balducci's report on the artistic tastes in Clarksdale appeared in the *Clarksdale Press Register* on December 12, 1987, byline Panny Mayfield. The editorial concerning that city's anti-pornography campaign appeared in that paper on December 11, 1987, and Indianola's AIDS policy was reported in the *Greenwood Commonwealth* on December 13, 1987. The raid on Black Roy's Place was reported in the *Leland Progress* on September 22, 1988.

The passage beginning Chapter Nine is taken from the first pages of chapter 2 of William Faulkner's *Absalom, Absalom!* Ray Mabus's inaugural address was printed in, among other publications, *Southern Changes,* volume 10, number 2, March–April 1988 (Southern Regional Council, Atlanta). The governor's remarks at Delta State and to the 1988 graduates at Ole Miss are distributed by his office. Bill Minor's comments on the changes over forty years and a flattering appraisal of Mabus were made in his syndicated column, which appeared in the *Greenwood Commonwealth* on November 21, 1988.

The quotation beginning Chapter Ten appears in *Mississippi: A Guide to The Magnolia State,* compiled and written by the Federal Writers' Project of the Works Progress Administration (New York, 1938), page 30. The statement attributed to Lewis Baker in the text is a paraphrase of his observation on page 26 of *The Percys of Mississippi.*

Chapter Eleven begins with a description of Delta seasons by Ruby Sheppeard Hicks in *The Song of the Delta* (Jackson 1976), where it is found on page 23. The two reports cited for the depletion of the hardwood forests of the Delta are "Conversion of Forested Wetlands to Agricultural Uses," Environmental Defense Fund, Robert Stavins (New York, 1987) and "Documentation, Chronology, and Future Projections of Bottomland Hardwood Habitat Loss in the Lower Mississippi Alluvial Plain, volume 1," Fish and Wildlife Service, 1979. Will Percy's questions about the Yazoo levee plan are posed in *Lanterns on the Levee,* pages 244 and 322–23. The Corps's analysis of the Yazoo project is contained in "Project Status Report, Mississippi," U.S. Army Corps of Engineers, Vicksburg District, February 1988, and "Information Paper Upper Yazoo Projects." The farm book is *How to Lose Your Farm in Ten Easy Lessons and Cope with It,* by Robert Hitt Neill and James R. Baugh, published by Neill's Mississippi River Publishing Company. Neill's particular comments about gentlemen tractor drivers are on page 43.

Chapter Twelve begins with a quotation from David Cohn's *Where I Was Born and Raised,* page 103. The information on Parchman in 1967 is derived from "The Delta Prisons: Punishment for Profit," Southern Regional Council (Atlanta, 1968). My report in *New South* magazine appeared in volume 28, number 3, summer 1973.

Chapter Thirteen begins with a song by Boyd Rivers that appears in an album entitled, *Delta Blues Festival '79,* recorded at the Blues Festival and distributed by Mississippi Action for Community Education (MACE). The statements by B. B. King about growing up in Indianola were reported by Steve Alderman in the *Enterprise-Tocsin,* June 9, 1988. William Ferris's statement appeared in his *Blues from the Delta* (New York, 1979), page 11.

Chapter Fourteen begins with a quotation from Willie Morris's *North Toward Home* (Boston, 1967), page 127.

Chapter Fifteen begins with a quotation from James Silver's *Mississippi: A Closed Society,* where it appears on pages 63 and 64. The drop in attendance at Indianola's private schools was reported in the *Enterprise-Tocsin* on September 22, 1988. The pictures of 1988 graduates of Rolling Fork High School, the Holmes County schools, the Sharkey-Issaquena Academy, and the Greenville schools were printed in the *Deer Creek Pilot,* the *Holmes County Herald,* and the *Delta Democrat-Times,* among other papers. Dot Turk's book is *Leland, Mississippi: From Hellhole to Beauty Spot,* by Dorothy Love Turk (Leland Historical Foundation, 1986). The hometowns of the officers of the KAs at Ole Miss in 1988 were reported in the *Belzoni Banner,* December 23, 1987.

Chapter Sixteen begins with a quotation from the WPA *Guide to the Magnolia State:* it is a part of "Tour 7, Clarksdale to Jackson," page 408. Some of the historical notes in the chapter about Delta towns also come from that fascinating work. Much of the history of Mound Bayou included in this book, especially the history of Davis Bend Plantation, is dependent on Janet Sharp Hermann's *The Pursuit of a Dream* (New York, 1981). More about the origins of Providence Farm can be found in my own *Against the Grain* (Charlottesville, Va., 1981).

The quotation beginning Chapter Seventeen is from Percy's *Lanterns on the Levee,* page 231.

The concluding chapter starts with David Cohn's famous travel guide in a nutshell. It originally appeared in *Where I Was Born and Raised,* page 12. The history of The Corners is derived from various articles and scrapbooks maintained by its present owners, Cliff and Bettye Whitney.

About the Author

Tony Dunbar grew up in Atlanta, Georgia, and Aiken, South Carolina. He received his undergraduate degree from Brandeis University and a degree in law from Tulane University. He lives in New Orleans with his wife and daughters.